A GRAMMAR OF THE HINDUSTANI LANGUAGE

A

GRAMMAR

OF THE

HINDUSTANI LANGUAGE

IN THE

ORIENTAL AND ROMAN CHARACTER

WITH

NUMEROUS COPPER-PLATE ILLUSTRATIONS OF THE PERSIAN AND DEVANÁGARÍ SYSTEMS OF ALPHABETIC WRITING

TO WHICH IS ADDED

A COPIOUS SELECTION OF EASY EXTRACTS FOR READING,

IN THE

PERSI-ARABIC AND DEVANAGARÍ CHARACTERS

FORMING A COMPLETE INTRODUCTION TO THE TOTÁ-KAHÁNÍ AND BÁGH-O-BAHÁR

TOGETHER WITH

A VOCABULARY OF ALL THE WORDS

AND VARIOUS EXPLANATORY NOTES

DUNCAN FORBES

GYAN

Published by

GYAN

Gyan Publishing House
5, Ansari Road
Daryaganj, New Delhi-110002
Phone: 011-47034999, 9811692060
E-mail: books@gyanbooks.com

Distribution Network
gyanbooks.com
India, USA, Canada, UK, Australia

ISBN: 978-93-6920-043-6 (PB)

First Published, 1855

2nd Impression 2025

Printed at: Gyan Press, Delhi.

A GRAMMAR OF THE HINDUSTANI LANGUAGE
Author: DUNCAN FORBES

THE ELEMENTS OF THE DEVANĀGARI CHARACTER.

Pl. I.

NUMERICAL FIGURES.

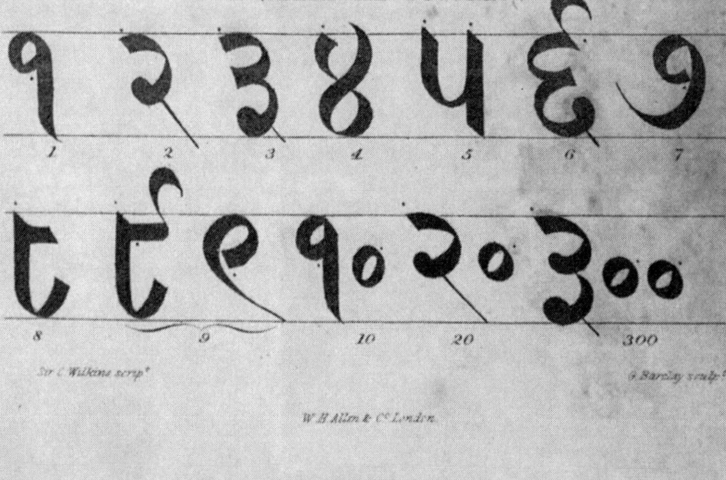

Sir C. Wilkins scrip.t G. Barclay sculp.t

W. H. Allen & C.o London.

A GRAMMAR OF THE HINDÚSTÁNÍ LANGUAGE,

IN THE

ORIENTAL AND ROMAN CHARACTER,

WITH

NUMEROUS COPPER-PLATE ILLUSTRATIONS OF THE PERSIAN AND DEVANÁGARÍ SYSTEMS OF ALPHABETIC WRITING:

TO WHICH IS ADDED,

A COPIOUS SELECTION OF EASY EXTRACTS FOR READING,

IN THE

PERSI-ARABIC AND DEVANÁGARÍ CHARACTERS,

FORMING A COMPLETE INTRODUCTION TO THE TOTÁ-KAHÁNÍ AND BÁGH-O-BAHÁR;

TOGETHER WITH

A VOCABULARY OF ALL THE WORDS,

AND VARIOUS EXPLANATORY NOTES.

A NEW EDITION.

By DUNCAN FORBES, LL.D.,

PROFESSOR OF ORIENTAL LANGUAGES AND LITERATURE IN KING'S COLLEGE, LONDON; MEMBER OF THE ROYAL ASIATIC SOCIETY OF GREAT BRITAIN AND IRELAND, ETC.

"HE THAT TRAVELLETH INTO A COUNTRY BEFORE HE HATH AN ENTRANCE INTO THE LANGUAGE, GOETH TO SCHOOL, AND NOT TO TRAVEL."—BACON.

LONDON:

WM. H. ALLEN & Co. 13, WATERLOO PLACE, S.W.

PUBLISHERS TO THE INDIA OFFICE.

1862.

TO

ELLIOT MACNAGHTEN, ESQ., CHAIRMAN,

COL. WILLIAM HENRY SYKES, DEPUTY-CHAIRMAN,

AND

THE DIRECTORS

OF

THE HONORABLE THE EAST-INDIA COMPANY,

THE FOLLOWING WORK,

INTENDED

TO FACILITATE THE ACQUISITION OF THE HINDÚSTÁNÍ LANGUAGE,

IS

RESPECTFULLY DEDICATED,

BY THEIR MOST OBEDIENT

AND FAITHFUL SERVANT,

DUNCAN FORBES.

London, 20th July, 1855.

PREFACE.

The following work has been compiled with a view to enable every one proceeding to India to acquire a fair knowledge of the most useful and most extensively spoken language of that country. Of late years, a new æra may be said to have commenced with regard to the study of the Hindústání language; it being now imperative on every junior officer in the Company's service to pass an examination in that language before he can be deemed qualified to command a troop, or to hold any staff appointment. Such being the case, it is desirable that every facility should be afforded to young men destined for India to acquire at least an elementary knowledge of Hindústání in this country, so as to be able to prosecute the study during the voyage.

A large impression of this work having been exhausted, I have availed myself of the opportunity, in this new Edition, of adopting such improvements as have been naturally suggested by several years' experience in teaching. The plan and arrangement of the work remain the same as before; and so do the numbers of the sections and the paragraphs. The first section treats very fully of the Persi-Arabic alphabet, and of the elementary sounds of the language. In this section I have been enabled to introduce several improvements, and, if I mistake not, the subject is now so simplified that a learner of ordinary capacity will have no difficulty in making some progress in this elementary part, even if he should not have the aid of a teacher. The next three sections treat of the parts of speech, to the defining and explaining of which I have strictly confined myself. I have carefully avoided mixing up the syntax of the language with that part of the work which is and ought to be purely etymological. The mode of confounding the syntax with the etymology, which prevails in most grammars, I have always looked upon as highly preposterous. It is utterly absurd to embarrass the student with a rule of syntax, at a stage of his progress where he probably does not know a dozen words of the language.

In the first four sections (up to p. 91), I have generally accompanied every Hindústání word and phrase with the pronunciation in Roman characters, in order that the learner might not be delayed too long in acquiring the essential rudiments of the grammar, and also to guard against his contracting a vicious mode of pronunciation. When he has made himself acquainted with what is technically called the accidence—that is, the declension of the nouns and pronouns, and the conjugation of the verbs—he may, after a few verbal instructions respecting the arrangement of words, proceed to read and translate a few pages of the Selections, by the aid of the Vocabulary. This done, he may read over the Grammar carefully from the beginning; for, in fact, the Grammar and Selections mutually assist each other.

Section V. (from p. 92 to 135) treats of the Syntax of the language. This is a portion of the work, in which, if I do not greatly mistake, I have made many improvements. I have been particularly careful in explaining those peculiarities of the language in the use of which I have observed learners most apt to err, when trying to translate English into Hindústání. I have also, in several instances, ventured to differ from all my predecessors on certain important points, which of course I have justified by an appeal to the language itself.

In the sixth and last section, I have given a concise account of the Devanágarí alphabet, together with the mode of transferring the same into the corresponding Persian character, and *vice versa*. To this I have added an explanation of the various plates accompanying the work, together with a brief account of the Musalmán and Hindú calendars. The perusal of the plates will initiate the student into the mysteries of the manuscript character, which is much used in India, both in lithographed and printed works, to say nothing of numerous productions which still remain in manuscript. When the learner is well grounded in the *Naskhi*, or printed character, he should, as an exercise, endeavour to write out the same in the *Ta'lik*, or written character. When he has attained some facility in writing the latter, he will find it a very profitable exercise to transcribe the various phrases, etc., in my *Hindústáni Manual*, from the Roman character into the *Ta'lik*, and at the same time commit them to memory, as directed in the preface to that small work.

An elementary grammar of a language is incomplete without a certain portion of easy extracts, accompanied by a suitable vocabulary, and occasional notes explanatory of any obscure or idiomatic phrases that may occur in the text. This is the more essential in a grammar of the Hindústání, or of any other Asiatic language, because the *characters* and *words*, being totally different from our own, it is necessary, though it may sound strange, *to learn the language* to a certain extent, before the grammar *can* be perused to any advantage. As to the use of translations and other fallacious aids, such as giving the English of each word as it occurs at the bottom of the page or elsewhere, it is a method deservedly scouted by all good teachers. On the other hand, to put a large dictionary in the hands of a beginner is equally useless; it is asking of him to perform a difficult work, with an instrument so unwieldy as to be beyond his strength. In order, therefore, to render this work as complete as possible, I have appended to the Grammar a selection of easy compositions for reading, commencing with short and simple sentences. All the words occurring in the extracts will be found in the Vocabulary, at the end of which I have added a few notes explanatory of difficult passages or peculiarities of the language, with references to the page and paragraph of the Grammar where further information may be obtained.

In the extracts from the 'Khirad Afroz,' a work which is considered to be the easiest and most graceful specimen of the Urdú dialect, I have left off the use of the *jazm* ـْـ, except in very rare instances, in order that the student may gradually learn to read without it. In like manner the *virâma* ् is omitted in the last five or six stories of the Hindí extracts. I have been careful, throughout, to give the essential short vowels, convinced that without them the most attentive learner will be apt to commit mistakes in pronunciation. I have also adopted a rigid system of punctuation, the same as I should have done in the editing of a Latin Classic. There may be a few individuals so thoroughly wedded to what is foolish or defective, merely because it is old, as to feel shocked at this innovation. They will complacently ask, What is the use of punctuation, when the natives have none in their manuscripts? I answer—The use is, simply to facilitate, for beginners, the acquisition of a knowledge of the language. When that is once attained, they will find no difficulty in reading native works, though utterly void, not only of punctuation but of vowel-points and other diacritical marks. The use of stops is merely a question of time; four hundred years ago we had no such things for our books in Europe, and the excellent monks who had the management of these matters went on comfortably enough without them. But, after all, it was found that stops were an improvement; and so they are admitted to be even in the East. Almost all the books printed in India since the beginning of the present century have punctuation; and those who would make beginners attempt to translate from a strange language, in a strange character, without the least clue to the beginning or end of the sentences, seem to have a marvellous love for the absurd. All Oriental as well as European books ought to have stops; the omission is a sure indication either of extreme idleness or culpable apathy on the part of the editor.

In conclusion, I may safely say that I have spared no pains to render this edition worthy of the extensive patronage which the work has hitherto attained.

D. FORBES.

58, Burton Crescent,
July, 1855.

HINDÚSTÁNÍ GRAMMAR.

SECTION I.

ON THE LETTERS AND SYMBOLS USED IN WRITING.

1. THE Hindústání language may be printed and written in two distinct alphabets, totally different from each other, viz., the Persi-Arabic, and the Devanágari. We shall at present confine ourselves to the former, and devote a section to the latter towards the end of the volume. The Persi-Arabic alphabet consists of thirty-two letters, to which three more are added to express sounds peculiar to the Hindústání. These letters, then, *thirty-five* in number, are written and read from right to left; and, consequently, Hindústání books and manuscripts begin at what we should call the *end* of the volume. Several of the letters assume different shapes, according to their position in the formation of a word, or of a combined group; as may be seen in the following table, column V. Thus, in a combination of three or more letters, the first of the group, on the right-hand side, will have the form marked *Initial;* the letter or letters between the first and last will have the form marked *Medial;* and the last, on the left, will have the *Final* form. Observe, also, that in this table, column I. contains the names of the letters in the Persian character;

II. the same in Roman characters; III. the detached form of the letters, which should be learned first; and IV. the corresponding English letters.

THE HINDÚSTÁNÍ ALPHABET.

I. Name.	II.	III. Detached Form.	IV. Power.	V. Combined Form. Final.	Medial.	Initial.	VI. Exemplifications. Final.	Medial.	Initial.
الِف	*alif*	ا	*a*, etc.	ا	ا	ا	تا	بار	اِب
بي	*be*	ب	*b*	ـب	ـبـ	بـ	شب	صِبر	بر
پي	*pe*	پ	*p*	ـپ	ـپـ	پـ	چُپ	سِپر	پُر
تي	*te*	ت	*t*	ـت	ـتـ	تـ	دسْت	ستر	تپ
ٹه	*ṭa*	ٹ	*ṭ*	ـٹ	ـٹـ	ٹـ	پیٹ	سٹا	ٹِپ
ثي	*s̤e*	ث	*s̤*	ـث	ـثـ	ثـ	خبث	بثر	ثُور
جِيم	*jím*	ج	*j*	ـج	ـجـ	جـ	کج	شجر	جبر
چي	*che*	چ	*ch*	ـچ	ـچـ	چـ	هیچ	بچه	چپ
حي	*ḥe*	ح	*ḥ*	ـح	ـحـ	حـ	صُبح	بحر	حر
خي	*khe*	خ	*kh*	ـخ	ـخـ	خـ	یخ	تُخْم	خر
دال	*dál*	د	*d*	ـد	ـد	د	صد	فِدا	دُر
ڈه	*ḍa*	ڈ	*ḍ*	ـڈ	ـڈ	ڈ	مُنْڈ	نڈر	ڈال
ذال	*z̤ál*	ذ	*z̤*	ـذ	ـذ	ذ	کاغذ	نذر	ذِمّ
ري	*re*	ر	*r*	ـر	ـر	ر	مر	مرْد	رم
ڑه	*ṛa*	ڑ	*ṛ*	ـڑ	ـڑ	ڑ	مُڑ	بڑا	ڑوڑا
زي	*ze*	ز	*z*	ـز	ـز	ز	گز	بزم	زر

I. Name.	II.	III. Detached Form.	IV. Power.	V. Combined Form. Final.	Medial.	Initial.	VI. Exemplifications. Final.	Medial.	Initial.
ژي	*zhe*	ژ	*zh*	ـژ	ـژ	ژ	پاپُژ	غژْب	ژرْف
سِين	*sín*	س	*s*	ـس	ـسـ	سـ	بس	فستق	سر
شِين	*shín*	ش	*sh*	ـش	ـشـ	شـ	پش	نشُد	شُد
صاد	*ṣád*	ص	*ṣ*	ـص	ـصـ	صـ	نِص	قصْد	صد
ضاد	*ẓád*	ض	*ẓ*	ـض	ـضـ	ضـ	بعض	خِضر	ضِدّ
طوي	*ṭoe*	ط	*ṭ*	ـط	ـطـ	طـ	خطّ	بطن	طي
ظوي	*z̤oe*	ظ	*z̤*	ـظ	ـظـ	ظـ	حِفْظ	نظر	ظفر
عَين	*aïn*	ع	*a*, etc.	ـع	ـعـ	عـ	صنع	بُعْد	عسل
غَين	*ghaïn*	غ	*gh*	ـغ	ـغـ	غـ	تيغ	بِغي	غُسل
في	*fe*	ف	*f*	ـف	ـفـ	فـ	كف	سفر	فِي
قاف	*ḳáf*	ق	*ḳ*	ـق	ـقـ	قـ	بق	سقر	قدّ
كاف	*káf*	ک	*k*	ـک	ـکـ	کـ	يک	بِکُن	کُن
گاف	*gáf*	گ	*g*	ـگ	ـگـ	گـ	رنْگ	جِگر	گز
لام	*lám*	ل	*l*	ـل	ـلـ	لـ	گُل	عِلْم	لب
مِيم	*mím*	م	*m*	ـم	ـمـ	مـ	سِتم	چمن	من
نُون	*nún*	ن	*n*	ـن	ـنـ	نـ	صحن	چنْد	نم
واو	*wáw*	و	*w*, etc.	ـو	ـو	و	بُو	پُور	وجد
هي	*he*	ه	*h*	ـه	ـهـ	هـ	نه	بہا	ہُنر
يي	*ye*	ي	*y*, etc.	ـي	ـيـ	يـ	بي	حِيد	يد

The alphabet here described is used, more or less modified, by all those nations who have adopted the religion of Muhammad; viz., along the north and east of Africa, in Turkey, Arabia, and Persia, and by the Musalmán portion of the people of India and Malacca.

In pronouncing the names of the letters (column II.) let it be remembered that the vowels are to be uniformly sounded as follows:—The unmarked *a* is always short, as *a* in *woman, adrift,* etc.; *á* is always long, as *a* in *war* or *art;* *i* is short, as in *pin;* *í* is long, as in *police;* *u* is short, as *u* in *bull, pull,* etc.; *ú* is the same sound lengthened, and pronounced as *u* in *rule,* etc.; *e* is sounded as *ea* in *bear;* *o* is always long, as in *no;* *ai* is pronounced as *ai* in *aisle;* and *au* is sounded as in German and Italian, or very nearly like our *ou* in *sound,* or *ow* in *cow.*

2. Perhaps the best mode of learning the alphabet is, First, to write out several times the detached or full forms of the letters in column III. Secondly, to observe what changes (if any) these undergo, when combined in the formation of words, as exhibited in column V. Lastly, to endeavour to transfer, into their corresponding English letters, the words given as exemplifications in column VI.

a. It may be here observed that the letters ا د ڈ ذ ر ڑ ز ژ and و do not alter in shape, whether initial, medial, or final. Another peculiarity which they have is, that they never unite with the letter following, to the left; hence, when the last letter of a word is preceded by any one of these, it must have the detached form, column III. The letters ط and ظ, in like manner, do not alter, though they always unite with the letter following on the left hand.

3. In the foregoing table, most of the characters are sufficiently represented by the corresponding English letters: it will therefore be necessary to notice only those whose sounds differ more or less from our own.

ت The sound of this letter is softer and more dental than that of the English *t*; it corresponds with the *t* of the Gaelic dialects, or that of the Italian in the word *sotto*. It represents the Sanskrit त.

ٹ This letter represents the Sanskrit ट; its sound is much nearer that of the English *t* than the preceding. In pronouncing it, the tongue should be well turned up towards the roof of the mouth, as in the words *tip*, *top*.

ث is sounded by the Arabs like our *th* hard, in the words *thick*, *thin*; but by the Persians and Indians it is pronounced like our *s* in the words *sick*, *sin*.

چ This letter has uniformly the sound of our *ch* in the word *church*.

ح is a very strong aspirate, somewhat like our *h* in the word *haul*, but uttered by compressing the lower muscles of the throat.

خ has a sound like the *ch* in the word *loch*, as pronounced by the Scotch and Irish, or the final *ch* in the German words *schach* and *buch*. This letter will be represented in Roman characters by *kh*, with a stroke underneath (*k͟h*).

د is much softer and more dental than the English *d*; it represents the Sanskrit द, and corresponds with the *d* of the Celtic dialects, and that of the Italian and Spanish.

ڈ This letter represents the Sanskrit ड, and is very nearly the same as our own *d*. The tongue, in pronouncing it, should be well turned up towards the roof of the mouth.

ذ is properly sounded (by the Arabs) like our *th* soft, in the words *thy* and *thine*; but in Persian and Hindústání it is generally pronounced like our *z* in *zeal*.

ر is always sounded very distinctly, as the French and Germans pronounce it.

ڑ This letter is sounded like the preceding, only the tip of the tongue must be turned up towards the roof of the mouth. It is very much akin to ڈ, with which it often interchanges; or, more strictly speaking, in the Devanágari the same letter serves for both; as will be seen in the section on the Devanágari alphabet.

ژ is pronounced like the *j* of the French, in the word *jour*, or our *z* in the word *azure*. It is of rare occurrence.

ص In Arabic this letter has a stronger or more hissing sound than our *s*. In Hindústání, however, there is little or no distinction between it and س, which is like our own *s*.

ض is pronounced by the Arabs like a hard *d* or *dh*; but in Hindústání it is sounded like *z*.

ط and ظ These letters are sounded in Hindústání like ت and ز, or very nearly so. The anomalous letter ع will be noticed hereafter.

غ has a sound somewhat like *g* in the German word *sagen*. About the banks of the Tweed, the natives sound what they fancy to be the letter *r*, very like the Eastern غ. This sound will be represented in English letters by *gh*, with a stroke underneath (g̲h̲).

ق bears some resemblance to our *c* hard, in the words *calm, cup;* with this difference, that the ق is uttered from the lower muscles of the throat.

گ is sounded like our *g* hard, in *give, go;* never like our *g* in *gem, gentle.*

ن at the beginning of a word or syllable is sounded like our *n* in the word *now;* at the end of a word, when preceded by a long vowel, it generally has a *nasal* sound, like the French *n*, in such words as *mon* and *son*, where the sound of the *n* is scarcely heard, its effect being to make the preceding vowel come through the nose. The same sound may also occur in the middle of a word, as in the French *sans*. In the Roman character, the nasal sound of ن will be indicated by *n*, with a dot over it (*ṅ*).

ه is an aspirate, like our *h* in *hand, heart;* but at the end of a word, if preceded by the short vowel *a* (Fatha § 4), the ه has no sensible sound, as in دانه *dána*, a grain; in which case it is called هاي مُختَفِي *háe-mukh̲tafí*, i.e., the 'obscure *or* imperceptible *h*.' As this final *h*, then, is not sounded in such cases, we shall omit it entirely in the Roman character whenever we have occasion to write such words as دانه *dána*, etc.

a. At the end of words derived from Arabic roots, the final ه is sometimes marked with two dots thus, ة; and, in such cases, sounded like the letter ت *t*. The Persians generally convert the ة into ت; but sometimes they leave it unaltered, and frequently they omit the two dots, in which case the letter is sounded according to the general rule. Lastly, the Hindústání usually receives such words in whatever form they may happen to be used in Persian.

b. The letter ه or ھ is frequently employed as a mere aspirate in combination with the letters ب پ ت ٹ ج چ د ڈ ڑ ک and گ; as in the words پھا, *pha*; تھا, *tha*, etc. In such cases the learner must be careful not to sound the *ph* and *th* as in English; the *h* is to be sounded separately, immediately after its preceding letter, as in the compound words *up-hill*, *hot-house*. In most printed books the rouud form of the *h* (ه and ھ) is employed to denote the aspirate of the preceding letter, otherwise the form ہ is used; but this rule does not apply to manuscripts, particularly those written before the days of Dr. Gilchrist, under whose auspices the distinction was first adopted.

c. Much might have been said in describing the sounds of several of the letters; but we question whether the learner would be greatly benefited by a more detailed description. It is difficult, if not impossible, to give in writing a correct idea of the mere sound of a letter, unless we have one that corresponds with it in our own language. When this is not the case, we can only have recourse to such languages as happen to possess the requisite sound. It is possible, however, that the student *may be* as ignorant of these languages as of Hindústání. It clearly follows, then, as a general rule, that the correct sounds of such letters as differ from our own must be learned *by the ear*—we may say, by a *good ear*; and, consequently, a long deseription is needless. This remark applies in particular to the letters ث ح خ د ص ض غ ق and the nasal ں.

OF THE PRIMITIVE VOWELS.

4. In Hindústání, as in many of the Oriental languages, the primitive vowels are three in number. They are represented by three small marks or symbols, two of which are placed above and one beneath the letter after which they are sounded, as in the following syllables, دَ *da*, دِ *di*, and دُ *du*; or سَر *sar*, سِر *sir*, and سُر *sur*.

a. The first is called فَتْحَه *fatha* (by the Persians زَبَر *zabar*), and is written thus, ـَ over the consonant to which it belongs. Its sound is that of a short *a*, such as we have it in the word *calamus*, which is of Eastern origin, and of which the first two syllables or root, *calam* or *kalam*, are thus written, قَلَم. In such Oriental words as we may have occasion to write in Roman characters, the *a*, unmarked, is understood always to represent the vowel *fatha*, and to have no other sound than that of *a* in *calamus* or *calendar*.

b. The second is called by the Arabs *kasra* كَسْرَه (by the Persians زير *zer*), and is thus ـِ written under the consonant to which it belongs. Its sound is that of our short *i* in the word *sip* and *fin*, which in Hindústání would be written سِپ and فِن. The unmarked *i*, therefore, in the course of this work, is understood to have the sound of *i* in *sip* and *fin*, in all Oriental words written in the Roman character.

c. The third is called by the Arabs *zamma* (or *dhamma*) ضَمَّه (by the Persians, پيش *pesh*,) which is thus ـُ written over its consonant. Its sound is like that of our short *u* in the words *pull* and *push*, which in Hindústání would be written پُل and پُش: we have also its true sound in the English words *foot* and *hood*, which would be written فُٹ and هُڈ. We shall accordingly, in the following passages, represent the *zamma* by the unmarked *u*, which in all Oriental words in the Roman character, is understood to have the sound of *u* in *pull* and *push*; but never that of our *u* in such words as *use* and *perfume*, or such as *u* in *sun* and *fun*.

OF THE LETTERS ا, و, ع, AND ي, VIEWED AS CONSONANTS.

5. At the beginning of a word or syllable, the letter ا, like any other consonant, depends for its sound on the accompanying vowel; of itself, it is a very weak aspirate, like our *h* in the words *herb*, *honour*, and *hour*. It is still more closely identified with the *spiritus lenis* of the Greek, in such words as ἀπὸ, ἐπὶ, ὀρθρός, where the mark [ʼ] represents the *alif*, and the α, ε, and ο

the accompanying vowel. In fact, when we utter the syllables *ab*, *ib*, and *ub*, there is a slight movement of the muscles of the throat at the commencement of utterance; and that movement the Oriental grammarians consider to be the مَخْرَج *makhraj*, or 'place of utterance' of the *consonant* ا, as in اَ *a*; اِ *i*; and اُ *u*; just the same as the lips form the *makhraj* of *b*, in the syllables بَ *ba*, بِ *bi*, and بُ *bu*. Finally, the ا may be considered as the *spiritus lenis*, or weak aspirate of the consonant ہ.

a. The consonant ع has the same relation to the strong aspirate ح that ا has to ہ; that is, the ع, like the ا, is a *spiritus lenis* or weak aspirate; but the *makhraj*, or 'place of utterance' of ع, is in the lower muscles of the throat. Hence the sound of the letter ع, like that of the letter ا, depends on the accompanying vowel; as عَب *'ab*, عِب *'ib*, عُب *'ub*, which in the mouth of an Arab, are very different sounds from أَب *ab*, اِب *ib*, and أُب *ub*. At the same time, it is impossible to explain in writing the true sound of this letter; as it is not to be found in any European language, so far as we know. The student who has not the advantage of a competent teacher may treat the ع as he does the ا until he has the opportunity of learning its true sound by the ear. In representing Oriental words in the Roman character, the place of the ع will be indicated by an apostrophe, thus, عَسَل *'asal*.

b. Of the consonants و and ي very little description is necessary. The letter و has generally the sound of our *w* in *we, went;* but occasionally in words from the Sanskrit it has the sound of our *v*, which must be determined by practice. The sound of the consonant ي is our own *y* in *you, yet*, or the German *j* in *jener*.

c. It appears, then, that the thirty-five letters constituting the Hindústání alphabet are all to be considered as *consonants*, each of which may be uttered with any of the three primitive vowels, as اَ *a*, اِ *i*, and اُ *u*; بَ, *ba*, بِ *bi*, and بُ, *bu*, etc.: hence the elementary sounds of the language amount to one hundred and five in number, each consonant forming three distinct syllables.

6. When a consonant is accompanied by one of the three primitive vowels, it is said to be مُتَحَرِّكْ *mutaharrik*, that is, 'moving *or* moveable,' by that vowel. Oriental grammarians consider a syllable as a *step* or *move* in the formation of a word or sentence. When, in the middle or at the end of a word, a consonant is not accompanied by a vowel, it is said to be ساكِن *sákin*, 'resting *or* inert,' and then it is marked with the symbol ـْ or ـْ called جَزْم *jazm*, which signifies 'amputation *or* cutting short.' Thus in the word مَرْدُمْ *mardum*, the *mím* is *moveable* by *fatha*; the *re* is *inert*,[1] having no vowel; the *dál* is *moveable* by *zamma*; and, finally, the *mím* is *inert*. As a general rule, the last letter of a word is *inert*, and in that case the mark *jazm* ـْ is unnecessary.

7. When a letter is doubled, the mark ـّ, called *tashdíd*, is placed over it. Thus, in the word شِدَّت *shid-dat*, where the first syllable ends with د (*d*) and the next begins with د (*d*), instead of the usual mode شِدْدَت the two *dáls* are thrown into one, and the mark *tashdíd* ـّ indicates this coalition. The student must be careful to utter each of the letters thus doubled, distinctly—the first letter ends the preceding syllable, and the second begins the following; they must not be slurred over as we do it, in such words as *mummy*, *summer*. The meaning of the term *tashdíd*, is, 'strengthening *or* corroboration.'

[1] The term *inert* is here employed for want of a better. In most Arabic, Persian, and Hindústání Grammars, a letter not followed by a vowel is called *quiescent*, which is objectionable, as it is apt to mislead the beginner, the term *quiescent* being already applied in the English Grammar in the sense of *not sounded*. For instance, the letter *g* is *quiescent* in the word *phlegm*; we cannot, however, say that *m* is *quiescent* in the same word, though we may say that it is *inert*. The student will be pleased to bear in mind, then, that a letter is said to be *inert* when it is not followed by a vowel.

OF THE LETTERS ا , و AND ي VIEWED AS VOWELS OR LETTERS OF PROLONGATION.

8. The letters ا , و and ي when *inert*, serve to prolong the preceding vowel, as follows. When ا *inert* is preceded by a letter moveable by *fatḥa*, the *fatḥa* and *alif* together form a long sound like our *a* in *war*, or *au* in *haul*, which in Hindústání might be written وَار, and حَال. Now it so happens that the ا *inert* is always preceded by *fatḥa:* hence, as a general and practical rule, *alif* not beginning a word or syllable forms a sound like our *a* in *war*, or *au* in *haul.* In the Roman character, the sound of long ا will be represented by *á*, whilst the unmarked *a* is always understood to represent the short primitive vowel *fatḥa.*

9. When the letter و *inert* is preceded by a consonant moveable by the vowel *ẓamma*, the *ẓamma* and و together form a sound like our *oo* in *tool;* which in Hindústání might be written ٹُول, or, which is the same thing, like our *u* in *rule*, which might be written رُول. The same combination forms also another sound, like our *o* in *mole*, which would in the same manner be written مُول, or, perhaps still nearer, like our *oa* in *coat*, which might be written کُوٹ. In the Arabic language, the latter sound of و, viz. that of *o* in *mole*, is unknown; hence Arabian grammarians call it *Majhúl*, or *'Ajamí, i.e.* the Unknown or Persian و; whereas the former sound, that of *u* in *rule*, is called *Ma'rúf*, the Known or Familiar و. If the

letter و be preceded by a consonant moveable by *fatḥa*, the *fatḥa* and و united will form a diphthong, nearly like our *ou* in *sound*, or *ow* in *town*, but more exactly like the *au* in the German word *kaum*, which in Hindústání might be written قَوْم. In the following pages the *Ma'rúf* sound will be represented by *ú*; the *Majhúl* by *o*, and the diphthong by *au*. If the و be preceded by the vowel *kasra*, no union takes place, and the و preserves its natural sound as a consonant, as in the word سِوا *siwá*.

b. When the letter و in words purely Persian is preceded by خ (moveable by *fatḥa*), and followed by ا; the sound of و is scarcely perceptible; as in the word خَواه pronounced *kháh*, not *khawáh*. When we have occasion to write any such words in the Roman character the *w* will be written with a dot under; thus, خواه *khwáh*.

10. When the letter ي *inert* is preceded by a consonant moveable by *kasra*, the *kasra* and the ي unite, and form a long vowel like our *ee* in *feel*, which in Hindústání might be written فِيْل; or, which is the same thing, like our *i* in *machine*, which might be written مَشِيْن. The same combination may also form a sound like our *ea* in *bear*, which would be written بِيْر or like the French *ê* in the words *prê*, *donnê*, but longer; or the German *e* followed by *h* in the words *sehr*, *gelehrt*. In the Arabic language, the latter sound of ي is unknown: hence, when the ي forms the sound of *ea* in *bear*, etc., it is called *Yáe Majhúl*, or *Yáe 'Ajamí*, that is, the Unknown or Persian ي; whilst the former sound—that of *ee* in *feel*, or *i* in machine—is called *Yáe Ma'rúf*, the Known or Familiar ي. When the letter ي *inert* is preceded by a consonant, moveable by *fatḥa*, the *fatḥa* and the ي unite, and form a diphthong, like *ai* in the

German word *Kaiser*, which in Arabic, Persian, and Hindústání, is written قَیصَر. This sound is really that of our own *i* in *wise*, *size*, which we are pleased to call a vowel, but which, in reality, is a genuine diphthong. When the letter ي is preceded by *ẓamma*, no union takes place, and the ي retains its usual sound as a consonant, as in the word مُیَسَّر *muyassar*. Lastly, if the letter ي be followed by a vowel, the above rules do not hold; and the ي is to be sounded as a consonant, as in the words بَیان *bayán*, and زِیان *ziyán*, not *bai-án* and *zí-án*, to represent which latter sounds the mark *hamza* (No. 15) would be requisite. A similar rule applies to the و.

a. It must be observed, that there are very few Hindústání works, printed or manuscript, in which all the vowels are marked as we have just described; the primitive short vowels being almost always omitted, as well as the marks ـْ *jazm* and ـّ *tashdíd*. This omission occasions no serious inconvenience to the natives, or to those who know the language. To the young beginner, however, in this country, it is essential to commence with books having the vowels carefully marked; otherwise he will contract a vicious mode of pronunciation, which he will find it difficult afterwards to unlearn. At the same time, it is no easy matter in printing to insert all the vowel-marks, etc. in a proper and accurate manner. In the present work, a medium will be observed, which, without over-crowding the text with symbols, will suffice to enable the learner to read without any error, provided he will attend to the following rules.

11. The short vowel *fatḥa* ـَ is of more frequent occurrence than the other two; hence it is omitted in the printing; and the learner is to supply it for every consonant except the last, provided he see no other vowel, nor the mark *jazm*, nor the ۂ (*butterfly*) form of the letter *he* (par. 3, *b*) accompanying any of the consonants aforesaid.

a. The letter و at the beginning of a word or syllable is a consonant, and generally sounded like our *w*, as in the words وس *wis*, وطن *waṭan*. When و follows a consonant, that has no vowel-mark or *jazm* accompanying it, the و has the sound of *o* long, as in the words سو *so*, کو *ko*. When the consonant preceding the و has the mark *zamma* ـُ over it, the و has the sound of *u* in *rule*, or *oo* in *fool*, as in the words سُو *sú* or *soo*, and کُو *kú* or *koo*; and if the preceding conson ant has the vowel mark *fatḥa* ـَ over it, the و forms the diphthong *au*, as سَو *sau* or *sow*, کَو *kau* or *cow*.

b. The letter ي at the beginning of a word or syllable is a consonant like our letter *y*, as in يہ *yih*, ياد *yád*. When the letter ي is medial or final, if the consonant preceding it has no vowel-mark or *jazm*, the ي is sounded like *ea* in *bear*, or *ai* in *fail*, as in the words بير *ber*, and سير *ser*. If the consonant preceding the ي has the mark *kasra* ـِ under it, the ي has the sound of *i* in *machine*, or *ee* in *feel*, as بِير *bír* or *beer*, and سِير *sír* or *seer*; and if the preceding consonant has the mark *fatḥa* ـَ over it, the ي forms the diphthong *ai* as بَير *bair* or *byre*, and سَير *sair* or *sire*.

c. There are a few instances in which the letters و and ي unite with the preceding consonant, as in the words سْوامِي *swámí*, and کْيا *kyá*; but such combinations being of comparatively rare occurrence, they may safely be left to the student's own practice. Lastly, in a few Arabic words the final ي occurs with an ا *alif* written over it, in which case the ا only is sounded, as in the words عُقْبيٰ *uḳbá*; تعاليٰ *ta'álá*.

12. We shall now at one view exhibit the practical application of the principles treated of in the preceding paragraphs. The vowels in Hindústání, as the student may have ere now perceived, are ten in number, the manner of representing which may be seen in the following ten words. The upper line (1) contains ten English words in common use, in each of which occurs the corresponding sound of the Hindústání word beneath. The lower line (3) shews the mode in which the Oriental

vowels will be uniformly represented in Roman characters in the course of this work.

1.	*fun*	*fin*	*foot*	*fall*	*foal*	*fool*	*fowl*	*fail*	*feel*	*file*
2	فن	فِن	فُت	فال	فول	فُول	فَول	فيل	فِيل	فَيل
3.	*fan*	*fin*	*fut*	*fál*	*fol*	*fúl*	*faul*	*fel*	*fíl*	*fail*

13. We have now, we trust, fully explained how the vowels are to be represented when they *follow* an audible consonant, such as the letter ف *f* in the foregoing list of words. In order to represent the vowels as initial or commencing a word, it will at once occur to the student that we have merely to annihilate or withdraw the letter ف from the above words, leaving everything else as it stands, and the object is effected. This is precisely what we do *in reality*, though not *in appearance*. The Arabian grammarians have taken into their heads a most subtle crotchet on this point, which is, *that no word or syllable can begin with a vowel.* Therefore, to represent what we call an initial vowel, that is, a vowel commencing a word or syllable, they employ the letter ا *alif* as a fulcrum for the vowel. We have already stated (No. 5) that they consider the ا as a very weak aspirate or *spiritus lenis;* hence its presence supports the theory, at least to the eye, if not to the ear. In order, then, to exhibit the vowels in the preceding paragraph as initial, we must, after taking away the letter ف substitute ا in its place, which ا being *nothing*, or *very nearly so*, the process amounts *in reality* to the withdrawal of the letter ف *f*, and the substitution of what may be considered as mere *nothing*, thus—

1.	*un*	*in*	*óót*	*all*	*ól*	*óól*	*owl*	*ail*	*eel*	*aisle*
2.	ان	اِن	اُت	اال	اول	اُول	اَول	ايل	اِيل	اَيل
3.	*an*	*in*	*ut*	*ál*	*ol*	*úl*	*aul*	*el*	*íl*	*ail*

Instead of writing two *alifs* at the beginning of a word, as in اال *ál*, it is usual (except in Dictionaries) to write one *alif* with the other curved over it; thus آل. This symbol ~ is called مدّه *madda*, 'extension,' and denotes that the *alif* is sounded long, like our *a* in *water*. M. de Sacy (v. *Grammaire Arabe*, p. 72) considers the mark *madda* ~ to be nothing else than a م *mím*, the initial of the word *madda;* but our business is simply with its practical use, and the reader if he pleases may view it as a contraction of our letter *m*, meaning 'Make it long.'

14. If, instead of ا in the above series, we substitute the letter ع, we shall have virtually the same sounds, only that they must be uttered from the lower muscles of the throat, thus—

عَن	عِن	عُت	عال	عول	عُول	عَول	عيل	عِيل	عَيل
'an	*'in*	*'ut*	*'ál*	*'ol*	*'úl*	*'aul*	*'el*	*'íl*	*'ail*

a. It appears, then, that when in Hindústání, a word or syllable begins with what we consider to be a vowel, such word or syllable must have the letter ا or ع to start with. Throughout this work, when we have occasion to write such words in the Roman character, the corresponding place of the ع will be indicated by an apostrophe or *spiritus lenis;* thus, عسل *'ásal*, عابد *'ábid*, بعْد *ba'd*, to distinguish the same from اسل *asal*, آبِد *ábid*, بد *bad*, or باد *bád*. In other respects the reader may view the ا and ع in any of the three following lights. 1st. He may consider them of the same value as the *spiritus lenis* (') in such Greek words as ἀν, ἐν, etc. 2ndly. He may consider them as equivalent to the letter *h* in the English words *hour, herb, honour*, etc. Lastly. He may consider them as mere blocks, whereupon to place the vowels requisite to the formation of the syllable. Practically speaking, then, ا and ع *when initial*, and the و and ي *when not initial*, require the beginner's strictest attention, as they all contribute in such cases to the formation of several sounds.

15. We have stated that, according to the notions of the Arabian grammarians, no syllable can begin with a vowel. In practice, however, nothing is more common, at least according to our ideas of such matters, than to meet with one syllable ending with a vowel, and the next beginning with one also. When this happens in Persian and Hindústání, the mark ـٔ called *hamza* is inserted between the two vowels a little above the body of the word, as in the words جاؤن *já,ún*, پائي *pá,e*; and sometimes there is a vacant space left for the *hamza*, like the initial or medial form of the *ye* without the dots below, thus [ئ] or [ـئـ] as in the words فائده *fá,ida*; کیجئي *kíji-e*. The *hamza*, then, is merely a substitute employed in the middle of words for the letter ا, to serve as a commencement (or as the Orientals will have it, consonant) to the latter of two consecutive vowels. Practically speaking, it may be considered as our hyphen which serves to separate two vowels, as in the words *co-ordinate*, *re-iterate*. It serves another practical purpose in Persian, in the formation of the genitive case, when the governing word ends with the imperceptible ه *h*, or with the letter ي as in the words ديدۀ دانش *dída-i-dánish*, 'the eye of intelligence,' where the *hamza* alone has the sound of the short *i* or *e*.

a. The sound of the mark *hamza*, according to the Arabian grammarians, differs in some degree from the letter ا, being somewhat akin to the letter ع, which its shape ء would seem to warrant; but in Hindústání this distinction is overlooked. We have here confined ourselves solely to the practical use of this symbol as applied in Persian and Hindústání; for further information on the subject, the reader may consult De Sacy's Arabic Grammar.

16. Before we conclude the discussion of the alphabet,

it may be proper to inform the student that the eight letters ث ح ص ض ط ظ ع and ق are peculiar to the Arabic; hence, as a general rule, a word containing any one of these letters may be considered as borrowed from the Arabic. Words containing any of the letters خ ذ ز or غ may be Persian or Arabic, but are not of Indian origin. The few words which contain the letter ژ are purely Persian. Words containing any of the letters پ چ or گ may be Persian or Indian, but not Arabic. Lastly, words containing any of the four-dotted letters ٹ ڈ ڑ are purely Indian. The rest of the letters are common to the Arabic, Persian, and Hindústání languages.

17. As words and phrases from the Arabic language enter very freely into the Hindústání, we cannot well omit the following remarks. Arabic nouns have frequently the definite article ال 'the' of the language prefixed to them; and if the noun happens to begin with any of the thirteen letters ت ث د ذ ر ز س ش ص ض ط ظ or ن, the ل of the article assumes the sound of the initial letter of the noun, which is then marked with *tashdíd;* thus النّور 'the light,' pronounced *an-núr*, not *al-núr*. But in these instances, though the ل has lost its sound, it must always be written in its own form. Of course, when the noun begins with the ل, the ل of the article coincides with it in like manner, as in the words اَللَّيْلَة *al-lailat*, 'the night;' and in this case the ل of the article is sometimes omitted, and the initial *lám* of the noun marked with *tashdíd*, thus, اَلَّيْلَة *al-lailat.*

a. The thirteen letters (ت etc.) above mentioned, together with the letter ل, are, by the Arabian grammarians, called *solar* or *sunny* letters, because the word شَمْس *shams*, 'the sun,' happens to begin with one of them. The other letters of the Arabic alphabet are called *lunar*, because, we presume, the word قمر *kamar*, 'the moon,' begins with one of the number, or simply because they are *not solar*. Of course, the captious critic might find a thousand equally valid reasons for calling them by any other term, such as *gold* and *silver*, *black* and *blue*, etc.; but we merely state the fact as we find it.

18. In general, the Arabic nouns of the above description, when introduced into the Persian and Hindústání languages, are in a state of construction with another substantive or preposition which precedes them; like the Latin terms *jus gentium*, *vis inertiæ*, *ex officio*, etc. In such cases, the last letter of the first or governing word, if a substantive, is moveable by the vowel *ẓamma*, which serves for the enunciation of the ا of the article prefixed to the second word; and, at the same time, the ا is marked with the symbol ـٙ, called وصْله, *waṣla*, which denotes 'union;' as in the words اميرُ آلْمُومنين *Amír-ul-múminín*, 'Commander of the Faithful;' اقبالِ آلدوله *Iḳbál-ud-daula*, 'The dignity of the state.'

a. Arabic nouns sometimes occur having their final letters marked with the symbol called *tanwín*, which signifies the using of the letter ن. The *tanwín*, which in Arabic grammars serves to mark the inflexions of a noun, is formed by doubling the vowel-point of the last letter, which indicates at once its presence and its sound; thus, بابٌ *bábun*, بابٍ *bábin*, باباً *bában*. The last form requires the letter ا, which does not, however, prolong the sound of the final syllable. The ا is not required when the noun ends with a *hamza*, or with the letter ة, as شيءً *shai-an*, حكمةً *hikmatan*; or when the word ends in ي *ye*, surmounted by ا [يً] (in which case the ا only is pronounced), هديً *hudan*. In Hindústání the occurrence of such words is not common, being limited to a few adverbial expressions, such as قصداً *kaṣdan̲*, 'purposely,' اتفاقاً *ittifáḳan̲*, 'by chance.' In the Roman character the letter *n*, with a stroke underneath [*n̲*], will be used for the 'núnation.'

19. We may here mention, that the twenty-eight

letters of the Arabic language are also used (chiefly in recording the *târîkh*, or date of historical events, etc.), for the purpose of numerical computation. The numerical order of the letters differs from that given in pages 2 and 3, being, in fact, the identical arrangement of the Hebrew alphabet, so far as the latter extends, viz., to the letter ت 400. The following is the order of the numerical alphabet with the corresponding number placed above each letter; the whole being grouped into eight unmeaning words, to serve as a 'Memoria technica.'

1000 900 800   700 600 500   400 300 200 100   90 80 70 60   50 40 30 20   10 9 8   7 6 5   4 3 2 1

ضظغ ثخذ قرشت سعفص كلمن حطي هوز ابجد

where ا denotes one, ب two, ج three, د four: etc.

a. In reckoning by the preceding system, the seven letters peculiarly Persian or Indian, viz. پ ٹ چ ڈ ڑ ژ, and گ, have the same value as their cognate Arabic letters of which they are modifications, that is, of ب ت ج د ر ز, and ک, respectively. The mode of recording any event is, to form a brief sentence, such that the numerical values of all the letters, when added together, amount to the year (of the Hijra) in which the event took place. Thus, the death of Ahlí of Shíráz, who may be considered as the last of the classic poets of Persia, happened in A.H. 942 (A.D. 1535). This date is recorded in the sentence بادشاه شعرا بود اهلي 'Ahlí was the king of poets;' where the sum of all the letters *be*, *alif*, *dál*, etc., when added together, will be found to amount to 942. The following date, on the death of the renowned Haidar 'Alí of Maisúr (A.H. 1196), is equally elegant, and much more appropriate: جانِ بالاگهات برفت 'The spirit of Bálághát is gone.'

b. Sometimes the title of a book is so cunningly contrived as to express the date of its completion. Thus, several letters written on various occasions by Abu-l-Fazl, surnamed 'Allámí, when secretary to the Emperor Akbar, were afterwards collected in one volume by 'Abdu-s-samad, the secretary's nephew, and the work was entitled

مكاتبات علامي *mukátabát-i 'allámí*, 'The letters of 'Allámí,' which at the same time gives the date of publication, A.H. 1015. We may also mention that the best prose work in Hindústání—the باغ و بهار 'Bágh o Bahár,' by Mír Amman, of Delhi, was so called merely because the name includes the date; the discovery of which we leave as an exercise to the student.

c. It is needless to add that the marks for the short vowels count as nothing; also a letter marked with *tashdíd*, though double, is to be reckoned but once only, as in the word *'allámí*, where the *lám* though double counts only 30. The Latin writers of the middle ages sometimes amused themselves by making verses of a similar kind, although they had only seven numerical letters to work with, viz., I, V, X, L, C, D, and M. This they called *carmen eteostichon* or *chronostichon*, out of which the following effusion on the Restoration of Charles II., 1660, will serve as a specimen:

Cedant arma oleæ, pax regna serenat et agros.

Here the numerical letters are C D M L X =1660.

d. In Arabia, Persia and India, the art of printing has been, till recently, very little used; hence their books, as was once the case in Europe, are written in a variety of different hands. Of these, the most common are, 1st, the *Naskhí* نسخي, of which the type employed in this work is a very good imitation. Most Arabic Manuscripts, and particularly those of the Ḳur'án, are in this hand; and from its compact form, it is generally used in Europe for printing books in the Arabic, Persian, Turkish, and Hindústání languages. 2ndly. The *Ta'líḳ* تعليق, a beautiful hand, used chiefly by the Persians and Indians in disseminating copies of their more-esteemed authors. In India, the Ta'líḳ has been extensively employed for printing, both Persian and Hindústání works; and within the last twenty years, a few Persian books, in the same hand, have issued from the Páshá of Egypt's press at Búláḳ. 3rdly. The *Shikasta* شكسته, or 'broken' hand, which is used in correspondence. It is quite irregular, and unadapted for printing; but not inelegant in appearance, when properly written.

SECTION II.

OF THE NAMES (اسما *asmá*) INCLUDING SUBSTANTIVES, ADJECTIVES, AND PRONOUNS.

20. Oriental grammarians, both Hindú and Musalmán, reckon only three parts of speech, viz. the noun or name (اِسْم *ism*), the verb (فِعْل *fi'l*), and the particle (حرْف *ḥarf*). Under the term noun, they include substantives, adjectives, pronouns, infinitives of verbs, and participles. This verb agrees with our part of speech so named; and under the general term of 'particle' are comprised adverbs, prepositions, conjunctions, and interjections. The student will find it necessary to bear this in mind when he comes to read or converse with native teachers; in the meanwhile we shall here treat of the parts of speech according to the classification observed in the best Latin and English grammars, with which the reader is supposed to be familiar.

OF THE ARTICLE.

21. The Hindústání—and all the other languages of India, so far as we know—have no word corresponding exactly with our articles *the*, *a*, or *an;* these being really inherent in the noun, as in Latin and Sanskrit. Hence, as a general rule, the context alone can determine whether, for example, the expression راجا کا بیٹا, *rájá ká beṭá*, 'regis filius,' signifies 'a son of a king,' 'the son of a king,' 'a son of the king,' or 'the son of the

king.' When, however, great precision is required, we often meet with the demonstrative pronouns یہ *yih*, 'this,' and وہ *wuh*, 'that,' together with their plurals, employed in the same sense as our definite article. Our indefinite article is expressed in many instances by the numeral ایک *ek*, 'one;' or by the indefinite pronoun کوئي *ko,í*, 'some,' 'a certain one'; as ایک مرد اور ایک سیر *ek mard aur ek sher*, 'a man and a tiger'; کوئي شخص *ko,í shakhs* 'some person'; but of this we shall treat more fully in the Syntax.

OF SUBSTANTIVES.

22. Substantives in Hindústání have two genders only, the masculine and the feminine; two numbers, the singular and plural; and eight cases (as in Sanskrit), viz. nominative, genitive, dative, accusative, ablative, locative, instrumental or agent, and vocative. The ablative, locative, and instrumental, correspond with the Latin ablative. It has been deemed proper here to retain the Sanskrit classification of the cases, in accordance with the grammars of the Maráṭhí, Bengálí, and other cognate Indian dialects.

23. *Gender.*—To the mere Hindústání reader, it is difficult, if not impossible, to lay down any rules by which the gender of a lifeless noun, or the name of a thing without sex, may be at once ascertained. With regard to substantives that have a sexual distinction, the matter is easy enough, and is pithily expressed in the two first lines of our old school acquaintance, Ruddiman.

1. Quæ maribus solùm tribuuntur, mascula sunto.
2. Esto femineum, quod femina sola reposcit.

This means, in plain English, that 'All animate beings of the male kind, and all names applicable to males only, are masculine. Females, and all names applicable to females only, are feminine.'

a. To the foregoing general rules, there is one (and perhaps but one) exception. The word قبيله *ḳabīla,* which literally means tribe or family, also denotes a wife, and is used, even in this last sense, as a masculine noun. Thus in the 'Bágh o Bahár,' p. 27, we have the expression قبيلي كو به سبب مُحبّت كي ساته ليا *ḳabīle ko ba sabab muḥabbat ke sáth liyá,* 'Out of affection I brought my wife with me,' where *ḳabīla* is inflected like a masculine noun. This, however, is merely an Oriental mode of expression, it being usual with the people to employ the terms 'house' or 'family,' when alluding to their wives. Our neighbours, the Germans, without any such excuse, have been pleased to decide that the word *weib,* 'wife,' should be of the neuter gender.

24. With regard to nouns denoting inanimate objects, the practical rule is, that those ending in ـِي *í*, ت *t*, and ش *sh*, are generally feminine. Those ending in any other letter; are, for the most part, masculine; but as the exceptions are numerous, the student must trust greatly to practice; and when, in speaking, he has any doubts respecting the gender of a word, it is preferable to use the masculine.

a. It is said that there is no general rule without an exception, and some have even gone so far as to assert that *the exception absolutely proves the rule.* If this latter maxim were sound, nothing could be better established than the general rule above stated respecting the gender of inanimate nouns. We have given it, in substance, as laid down by Dr. Gilchrist, succeeding grammarians having added nothing thereto, (if we except the Rev. Mr. Yates, who in his Grammar has appended, as an *amendment,* a list of some twelve or fifteen hundred exceptions.) This we have always looked upon as a mere waste of paper, believing as we do that no memory can possibly retain such a dry mass of unconnected words. The fact is, that the rule or rather the labyrinth, may be considerably restricted by the application of a few general principles which we shall here state.

Principle 1st.—Most words purely Sanskrit, which of course abound in Hindústání, and more particularly in Hindí works, such as the 'Prem Ságar,' etc., retain the gender which they may have had in the mother-tongue. Thus, words which in Sanskrit are masculine or neuter, are masculine in Hindí; and those which in Sanskrit are feminine, are feminine in Hindí. This rule absolutely does away with several exceptions which follow one of the favourite maxims of preceding grammarians, viz., 'that names of lifeless things ending in ىِ *í*, are feminine,' but *pání*, 'water,' *motí*, 'a pearl,' *ghí*, 'clarified butter' (and they might have added many more, such as *maní*, 'a gem,' etc.), are masculine: and why? because they are either masculine or neuter in Sanskrit. It is but fair to state, however, that this principle does not in every instance apply to such words of Sanskrit origin as have been greatly mutilated or corrupted in the vulgar tongue.

In the French and Italian languages which, like the Hindústání, have only two genders, it will be found that a similar principle prevails with regard to words from the Latin. The classical scholar will find this hint to be of great service in acquiring a knowledge of the genders of such French words as end in *e* mute, the most troublesome part of that troublesome subject.

Principle 2nd.—Arabic nouns derived from verbal roots by the addition of the servile ت *t*, are feminine, such as *khilkat*, 'creation, people,' etc., from *khalaka*, 'he created.' These in Hindústání are very numerous, and it is to such only that the general rule respecting nouns in ت *t*, rigidly applies. Arabic roots ending in ت *t*, are not necessarily feminine; neither are words ending in ت *t* derived from Persian and Sanskrit, those of the latter class being regulated by Principle 1st. Arabic nouns of the form تفعِيل are feminine, probably from the attraction of the *í* in the second syllable; the letter *í* being upon the whole the characteristic feminine termination of the Hindústání language. To this general principle the exceptions are very few, among which we must reckon شربت *sharbat*, 'sherbet,' and تعوِيذ *ta'wíz*, 'an amulet,' which are masculine.

Principle 3rd.—Persian nouns derived from verbal roots by the addition of the termination ـِش *ish*, are feminine. These are not few in Hindústání, and it is to such only that the rule strictly applies. Nouns from the Persian, or from the Arabic through the Persian, ending in the weak or imperceptible ه *h*, such as نامه *náma*, 'a letter,' قلعه *ḳil'a*, 'a fortress,' are generally masculine. This again may be accounted for by the affinity of the final *a* to the long *á*, which is a general masculine termination in Hindústání.

Principle 4th.—Pure Indian words, that is, such as are not traceable to the Arabic, Persian, or Sanskrit, are generally masculine if they terminate in ا *á*. Arabic roots ending in ا *á*, are for the most part feminine; nouns purely Sanskrit ending in ا *á*, are regulated by Principle 1st, but we may add, that the long *á* being a feminine termination in that language, such words are generally feminine in Hindústání. Words purely Persian when introduced into Hindústání, with the exception of those ending in ـِش *ish* and ه already mentioned, are not reducible to any rule; the Persian language having no gender of its own in the grammatical sense of the term.

Principle 5th.—Compound words, in which the first member merely qualifies or defines the last, follow the gender of the last member, as شکارگاه *shikár-gáh*, 'hunting-ground,' which is feminine; the word *gáh* being feminine, and the first word *shikár* qualifying it like an adjective.

b. It must be confessed, in conclusion, that, even after the application of the foregoing principles, there must still remain a considerable number of words reducible to no sort of rule. This is the inevitable fate of all such languages as have only two genders. Another natural consequence is, that many words occur sometimes masculine and sometimes feminine, depending on the caprice or indifference of the writer or speaker. We have also good grounds to believe that a word which is used in the masculine in one district may be feminine in another, as we know from experience to be the case in Gaelic, which, like the Hindústání, has only two genders.

25. *Number and Case.*—The mode in which the plural number is formed from the singular, will be best learned

by inspection from the examples which we here subjoin. The language has virtually but one declension, and the various oblique cases, singular and plural, are regularly formed by the addition of certain particles or *post-positions*, etc., to the nominative singular. All the substantives of the language may be very conveniently reduced to three classes, as follows :—

Class I.—Including all substantives of the feminine gender.

Singular.

	Nominative	رات	*rát,*	the night
Oblique cases.	Genitive	رات کا -کي -كِي	*rát-ká, -ke, -kí,*	of the night
	Dative	رات کو	*rát-ko,*	to the night
	Accusative	رات / رات کو	*rát,* / *rát-ko,*	the night
	Ablative	رات سي	*rát-se,*	from the night
	Locative	رات مين -پر	*rát-meṅ, -par,*	in, on, the night
	Agent	رات ني	*rát-ne,*	by the night
	Vocative	اَي رات	*ai rát,*	O night!

Plural.

	Nominative	راتين	*ráteṅ,*	the nights
Oblique cases.	Genitive	راتون کا -کي -كِي	*rátoṅ ká, -ke, -kí,*	of the nights
	Dative	راتون کو	*rátoṅ-ko,*	to the nights
	Accusative	راتين / راتون کو	*ráteṅ,* / *rátoṅ-ko,*	the nights
	Ablative	راتون سي	*rátoṅ-se,*	from the nights
	Locative	راتون مين -پر	*rátoṅ-meṅ, -par,*	in, on, the nights
	Agent	راتون ني	*rátoṅ-ne,*	by the nights
	Vocative	اَي راتو	*ai ráto,*	O nights!

Feminine nouns ending in ـِي *í*, add -ان *áṅ* in the nominative plural; thus روٹي *roṭí,* 'bread,' 'a loaf,' nom. plur. روٹِيان *roṭiyáṅ.* In the oblique cases plural, they add -ون *oṅ* as above.

In like manner a few words in ـُو *ú*, add ان *áṅ*, as جورُو *jorú,* 'a wife,' nom. plur. *joruwáṅ* or *jorú,áṅ.*

a. We may now take a brief view of the formation of the cases.

It will be seen that in the singular, the oblique cases are formed directly from the nominative, which remains unchanged, by the addition of the various post-positions. The genitive case has three forms of the post-position, all of them, however, having the same signification, the choice to be determined by a very simple rule which belongs to the Syntax. The accusative is either like the nominative or like the dative; the choice, in many instances, depending on circumstances which will be mentioned hereafter. The nominative plural adds *eṅ* to to the singular (*áṅ* if the singular be in *í*). The oblique cases plural in the first place add *oṅ* to the singular, and to that they affix the various post-positions; it will be observed that the accusative plural is either like the nominative or dative plural. The vocative plural is always formed by dropping the final *ṅ* of the oblique cases. Let it also be remembered that the final ن added in the formation of the cases of the plural number is always nasal. *Vide* letter ن page 6.

Class II.—Including all Masculine Nouns, with the exception of such as end in ا *á* (purely Indian), اں *áṅ*, and ه *h*.

Example, مرد *mard*, 'man.'

	Singular.	Plural.
N.	مرد *mard*, man.	مرد *mard*, men.
G.	مرد کا-کي-کي *mard-ká*, etc., of man.	مردوں کا-کي-کي *mardoṅ-ká*, etc., of men.
D.	مرد کو *mard-ko*, to man.	مردوں کو *mardoṅ-ko*, to men.
Ac.	{ مرد *mard*, / مرد کو *mard-ko*, } man.	{ مرد *mard*, / مردوں کو *mardoṅ-ko*, } men.
Ab.	مرد سي *mard-se*, from man.	مردوں سي *mardoṅ-se*, from men.
L.	مرد مين -پر *mard-meṅ*, *-par*, in, on, man.	مردوں مين -پر *mardoṅ-meṅ*, *-par*, in, on, men.
Ag.	مرد ني *mard-ne*, by man.	مردوں ني *mardoṅ-ne*, by men.
V.	اَي مرد *ai mard*, O man!	اَي مردو *ai mardo*, O men!

This class, throughout the singular, is exactly like class I., and in the plural the only difference consists in the absence of any termination added to the nominative, and consequently to the first form of the accusative, which is the same.

All the other cases in the plural are formed precisely as before. It must be admitted that the want of a distinct termination to distinguish the nominative plural from the singular, however, in Class II. is a defect in the language. This, however, seldom occasions any ambiguity, the sense being quite obvious from the context. The German is liable to a similar charge, and sometimes even the English, in the use of such words as 'deer,' 'sheep,' 'swine,' and a few others.

Class III.—Including Masculine Nouns purely Indian ending in ا *á*, a few ending in ان *áṅ*, and several words, chiefly from the Persian, ending in the imperceptible ه or short *a*.

Example, کُتّا *kuttá*, 'a dog.'

	Singular.	Plural.
N.	کُتّا *kuttá*, a dog.	کُتّے *kutte*, dogs.
G.	کُتّے کا - کے - کی *kutte-ká*, etc., of a dog.	کُتّوں کا - کے - کی *kuttoṅ-ká*, etc., of dogs.
D.	کُتّے کو *kutte-ko*, to a dog.	کُتّوں کو *kuttoṅ-ko*, to dogs.
Ac.	کُتّا *kuttá*, / کُتّے کو *kutte-ko*, } a dog	کُتّے *kutte*, / کُتّوں کو *kuttoṅ-ko*, } dogs.
Ab.	کُتّے سے *kutte-se*, from a dog.	کُتّوں سے *kuttoṅ-se*, from dogs.
Loc.	کُتّے مین - پر *kutte-meṅ, -par*, in, on, a dog.	کُتّوں مین - پر *kuttoṅ-meṅ, -par*, in, on, dogs.
Ag.	کُتّے نے *kutte-ne*, by a dog.	کُتّوں نے *kuttoṅ - ne*, *by* dogs.
Voc.	اے کُتّے *ai kutte*, O dog!	اے کُتّو *ai kutto*, O dogs!

a. In like manner may be declined many words ending in ه, as بنده *banda*, 'a slave,' gen. *bande-ká*, etc., nom. plur. *bande*, 'slaves,' gen. *bandoṅ-ká*, etc. Nouns in *áṅ* are not very numerous, and as the final *ṅ* is very little, if at all, sounded; it is often omitted in writing; thus بنیان *baniyáṅ* or بنیا *baniyá*, 'a trader,' gen. *baniyeṅ-ká* or *baniye-ká*, which last is the more common. In the ordinal numbers, such as دسوان *daswáṅ*, 'the tenth,' etc., the nasal *ṅ* generally remains in the inflection, as دسوین *daswеṅ-ká*, etc., 'of the tenth.' In the oblique cases plural, the ان *án*, is changed into وں *oṅ*. With regard to this third class of words, we have one remark to add; which is, that the vocative singular is often to be met with uninflected, like the nominative as اي بيٹا *ai beṭá* for اي بيٹے, 'O son!'

b. The peculiarity of Class III. is, that the terminations ا *á* and ه *a*, of the nominative singular, are entirely displaced in the oblique cases singular and nominative plural by ے *e*, and in the oblique cases plural by وں *oṅ*. This change or displacement of termination is called 'inflection,' and it is limited to masculine nouns only with the above terminations; for feminines ending in ا ان or ه, are never inflected, nor are all masculines ending in the same, subject to it. A considerable number of masculine nouns ending in ا *á*, purely Arabic, Persian, or Sanskrit, are not inflected, and consequently belong to Class II. On the other hand, masculine nouns purely Indian, such for example as the infinitives and participles of verbs used substantively or adjectively, are uniformly subject to inflection. In like manner, several masculine nouns ending in the imperceptible ه are not subject to inflection, and as these are not reducible to any rule, the student must be guided by practice.

c. Masculines in ه from the Persian often change the ه into ا in Hindústání; thus درجه *darja*, 'grade,' 'rank,' becomes درجا *darjá*; so مزه *maza*, 'taste,' becomes مزا *mazá*. All such words are subject to inflection, for by this change they become as it were 'Indianized.' The final ه is not inflected if in a state of construction (agreeably to the rules of Persian grammar) with another word, as ديدهٔ هوش ميں *dída-i hosh meṅ*, 'in the eye of prudence;' زبانِ ريخته ميں *zabán-i rekhta meṅ*, 'in the Rekhta or mixed dialect.'

26. *General rules for the Declension of Nouns.*— 1. In classes I. and II. the nominative singular remains unaltered throughout, the plural terminations being superadded. 2. In class III. the nominative singular is changed or inflected into ے *e*, for the oblique singular and nominative plural, and the terminations of the oblique cases plural are *substituted for*, not *added to*, the termination of the singular. 3. All plurals end in

ون *oṅ* in the oblique cases, that is, whenever a post-position is added or understood. 4. The vocative plural always ends in و *o*, having dropped the final ن *ṅ* of the oblique. 5. Words of the first and second classes, consisting of two short syllables, the last of which being *fatḥa*, drop the *fatḥa* on receiving a plural termination; thus طرف *ṭaraf*, 'aside,' nom. plur. طرفين *ṭarfeṅ*, gen. طرفون كا *ṭarfoṅ-ká*, etc., not *ṭarafeṅ*, etc.

a. A few words are subject to slight deviations from the strict rule, among which we may mention the following. 1. Words ending نو *ṅw*, preceded by a long vowel, as نانو *náṅw*, 'a name,' پانو *páṅw*, 'the foot,' and گانو *gáṅw*, 'a village;' reject the نو *ṅw*, and substitute the mark *hamza* on receiving a plural termination: thus, پاءون كا *pá,oṅ ká*, etc. 'of the feet.' 2. The word گاءي *gá,e*, 'a cow,' makes in the nominative plural گاءين *gá,eṅ*, and in the oblique plural گاءون *gá,oṅ*, thus resembling the oblique plural of گانو *gáṅw*, 'a village.' 3. A few feminine diminutives in يا *iyá*, like *randiyá*, *chiṛiyá*, etc. form the nominative plural by merely adding a nasal *ṅ*, as چڑيان *chiṛiyáṅ*, which is evidently a contraction for *chiṛiyá,eṅ*, the regular form. 4. Masculines of the third class ending in يه *ya*, may follow the general rule, or change the ي *y* into a *hamza* before the inflection; thus سايه *sáya*, 'a shade (of a tree),' gen. سايي كا *sáye-ká*, or ساءي كا *sá,e-ká*. 5. The word روپيه *rúpiya*, 'a rupee,' has generally رپئي *rupa,e*, for the nominative plural.

27. *Post-position.*—In this work, to avoid confusion, we apply the term post-position only to those inseparable particles or terminations which invariably follow the nouns to which they belong. They may be united with their substantives so as to appear like the case terminations in Latin, Greek, and Sanskrit, or they may be written separately, as we have given them in the examples for declension. The most useful and important of them are the following, viz.: كا *ká*, كي *ke*, كِي *kí*,

'of,' the sign of the genitive case; کو *ko* 'to,' the sign of the dative, and sometimes of the accusative or objective case; سي *se* 'from,' or 'with,' (also سون *soṅ*, سين *seṅ*, ستي, *siti*, are occasionally met with), the sign of the ablative and instrumental; پر *par* (sometimes in poetry په *pa*), 'upon,' 'on,' 'at,' مين *meṅ*, 'in,' 'into,' تک *tak*, تلک *talak*, لگ *lag*, 'up to,' 'as far as,' 'till,' one of the signs of the locative case; and, lastly, ني *ne*, 'by,' the sign of the agent.

a. The post-positions require the words to which they are affixed to be in the inflected form, if they belong to Class III.; and they are generally united with the oblique form in ون *oṅ* of all plurals. On the other hand, an inflected form in the singular can only occur in combination with a post-position, expressed or understood; and the same rule applies to all *bonâ fide* oblique forms in ون *oṅ* of the plural. There are a few expressions in which the oblique form in ون *oṅ* is used for the nominative plural; and when a numeral precedes, the nominative form may be used for the oblique, as will be noticed more fully in the Syntax.

OF ADJECTIVES.

28. Adjectives in Hindústání generally precede their substantives, and with the exception of those which are purely Indian words and ending in ا *á*, together with a few from the Persian ending in ه or short *a*, they are, as in English, indeclinable. Words purely Indian, ending in ا *á*, change the final ا *á* into ي *e*, when they qualify or agree with a masculine noun in any case except the nominative singular (or the first form of the accusative, which is the same); and the ا *á* is changed into ي *í* with feminine nouns. Thus, the adjective خوب *khúb*, 'good,' 'fair,' is the same before nouns of either gender or number in all cases, as *khúb jánwar*, 'a

fine animal;' *k͟húb laṛkí*, 'a fair girl'; *k͟húb randiyáṅ*, 'fine women,' *k͟húb ghoṛe*, 'beautiful horses.' Again the adjective كالا *kálá*, 'black,' is used in that form only before masculine nouns, in the nominative or the first form of the accusative singular; it will become كالي *kále*, before masculine nouns in the oblique cases singular and throughout the plural, as *kálá mard*, 'a black man,' *kále mard-ká*, 'of a black man,' *kále mard*, 'black men,' *kále mardoṅ-se*, 'from black men.' Lastly, before feminine nouns, *kálá* becomes كالي *kálí* for both numbers and in all cases, as *kálí rát*, 'the dark night,' *kálí rát-se*, 'from the dark night,' *kálí rátoṅ-ká*, 'of the dark nights,' etc.

a. Hence it appears, as a general rule:—1. That adjectives, before feminine nouns, have no variation on account of case or number. 2. That adjectives terminating like nouns of the first and second classes are indeclinable; and lastly, that adjectives, terminating like nouns of the third class, are subject to a slight inflection like the oblique singular of the substantives of that class.

b. The cardinal numbers, *ek*, 'one,' *do*, 'two,' etc., are all indeclinable when used adjectively. The ordinals above *pánchwáṅ*, 'the fifth,' inclusive, follow the general rule, that is, *pánchwáṅ* is inflected into *pánchweṅ* before the oblique cases of masculines, and it becomes *pánchwíṅ* before feminine nouns.

c. Adjectives ending in ة or short *a*, which are principally borrowed from the Persian; are, for the most part, indeclinable. There are some, however, which are inflected into ي *e* for the masculine, and ـِي *í* for the feminine, like those ending in ا *á*; among these may be reckoned رانّده *ránda*, 'rejected,' ساده *sáda*, 'plain,' عُمدَه *'umda*, 'exalted,' گندہ *ganda*, 'fetid,' مانّده *mánda*, 'tired,' خُرنّده *k͟hurinda*, 'gluttonous,' شرمنّده *sharminda*, 'ashamed, کمینه *kamína*, 'mean,' بیچاره *bechára*, 'helpless,' ناکاره *nákára*, 'useless,' نادِیده *nádída*, 'unseen,' حرامزاده *ḥarám-záda*, 'base-born,

یک ساله *yak-sálah,* 'annual,' 'one year old,' دو ساله *do sálah,* 'biennial,' and perhaps a few more.

d. The majority of adjectives purely Indian, together with all present and past participles of verbs, end in ا *á* (subject to inflection) for the masculine, and ـِي *í* for the feminine. All adjectives in ا *á*, purely Persian or Arabic, are indeclinable, with perhaps the sole exception of جُدا *judá,* 'separate,' 'distinct,' and a few that may have become naturalized in Hindústání by changing the final ﻩ of the Persian into ا *á*, like فُلانا *fulána,* 'such a one,' or 'so and so.'

29. *Degress of Comparison.*—The adjectives in Hindústání have no regular degrees of comparison, and the manner in which this defect is supplied will be fully explained in the Syntax. Suffice it here to say that when two objects are compared, that with which the comparison is made is put in the ablative case, like the Latin. Thus, for example, 'this house is high,' يِہ گھر بُلند هَي *yih ghar buland hai*; 'this house is higher thau the tree,' يِہ گھر درخْت سي بُلنْد هَي *yih ghar darakht-se buland hai,* literally 'this house (compared) with the tree is high.' The superlative degree is merely an extreme comparison formed by reference to the word سب *sab,* 'all,' as يِہ گھر سب سي بُلنْد هَي *yih ghar sab-se buland hai,* 'this house (compared) with all is high,' or 'this is the highest house of all.'

OF PRONOUNS.

Personal Pronouns.

30. The pronouns differ more or less from the substantantives in their mode of inflection. Those of the first and second persons form the genitive in را *rá,* ري *re,* and رِي *rí,* instead of کا *ká,* etc. They have a distinct

dative and accusative form in ي *e* (singular), and ين *eṅ* (plural), besides that made by the sign کو *ko*. They also form the oblique in a manner peculiar to themselves, and admit generally of the elision of the termination وں *oṅ*, in the oblique plural. They have the dative and accusative cases in both numbers the same; and lastly, the cases of the agent are never inflected in the singular, these being always *maiṅ-ne* and *tú-ne* or *taiṅ-ne;* never *mujh-ne*, or *tujh-ne*.

The first personal pronoun is thus declined:—

مَیں *main*, 'I.'

	Singular.		Plural.	
N.	مَیں *main*, I.		هم *ham*, We.	
G.	میرا میري *merá, mere* میرِي *merí*, f.	my, of me	همارا هماري *hamárá, hamáre* همارِي *hamárí*, f.	our.
D. & Ac.	مُجهي *mujhe*, مُجه کو *mujh-ko*,	me, *or* to me.	همين *hameṅ*, هم کو *ham-ko*, همون کو *hamoṅ-ko*,	us, *or* to us.
A.	مُجه سي *mujh-se*, from me.		هم سي *ham se*, همون سي *hamoṅ se*,	from us.
L.	مُجه مين *mujh-meṅ*, in me.		هم مين *ham-meṅ*, همون مين *hamoṅ meṅ*,	in us.
Ag.	مَین ني *maiṅ-ne*, by me.		هم ني *ham-ne*, همون ني *hamoṅ ne*,	by us.

In this example we have three forms essentially distinct from each other, viz., the nominative, genitive, and oblique modification in the singular, as مَین *maiṅ*, میرا *merá*, مُجه *mujh;* and in the plural هم *ham*, همارا *hamárá*, and هم *ham* or همون *hamoṅ*. From the oblique modifications,—مُجه *mujh*, and هم *ham* or همون *hamoṅ*,—the other oblique cases are formed by adding the requisite post-positions, except that the case denoting the agent is in the singular مَين ني *maiṅ ne.*

The second personal pronoun تُو *tú* or تَين *taiṅ* is declined in a similar manner.

	Singular.	Plural.
N.	تَين or تُو *tú* or *taiṅ*, Thou.	تُم *tum*, You.
G.	تيرا تيري *terá*, etc., thy.	تمهارا -ري -رِي *tumhárá*, etc., your.
D. & Ac.	تُجهي *tujhe*, تُجه كو *tujh-ko*, to thee, or thee.	تُمهين *tumheṅ*, to you. تُم كو تمهون كو *tum-ko*, or *tumhoṅ-ko*, you.
A.	تُجه سي *tujh-se*, from thee.	تُم سي تُمهون سي *tum-se*, or *tumhoṅ se*, from you.
L.	تُجه مين *tujh meṅ*, in thee.	تُم مين تُمهون مين *tum-meṅ*, or *tum-hoṅ-meṅ*, in you.
Ag.	تُو ني *tú-ne*, by thee.	تُم ني تُمهون ني *tum-ne*, or *tumhoṅ-ne*, by you.
V.	اَي تُو *ai tú*, O thou!	اَي تُم *ai tum*, O ye!

Demonstrative Pronouns.

31. In Hindústání the demonstrative pronouns, 'this, 'that,' 'these,' and 'those,' at the same time supply the place of our third person 'he,' 'she,' 'it,' and 'they.' They are the same for both genders, and the context alone determines how they are to be rendered into English. The word يِہ *yih*, 'this,' 'he,' 'she,' or 'it,' is used when reference is made to a person or object that is near; and وُہ *wuh*, 'that,' 'he,' 'she,' or 'it,' when we refer to that which is more remote. The

proximate demonstrative یہہ *yih*, 'he,' 'she,' 'it,' 'this,' is declined as follows:—

	Singular.	Plural.
N.	یہہ *yih*, this, he, *etc.*	یي *ye*, these, they.
G.	اِس کا-کي-کِي *is-ká*, *-ke*, *-kí*, of this, him, *etc.*	اِن کا-کي-کِي *in-ká*, *-ke*, *kí*, of these, of them.
D.	اِس کو اِسي *is-ko* or *ise*, to this, to him, *etc.*	اِن کو اِنهين انهون کو } *in-ko or inhen*, or *inhonko*, to these, *or* to them.
Ac.	یہہ اِس کو اِسي *yih*, *is-ko*, *ise*, this, him, *etc.*	یي اِن کو اِنهين *ye*, *in-ko*, or *inhen*, these, them.
Ab.	اِس سي *is-se*, from this, him, *etc.*	اِن سي *in-se*, from these, from them.
L.	اِس مين *is-men*, in this, *or* in him, *etc.*	اِن مين *in men*, in these, in them.
Ag.	اِس ني *is-ne*, by this, *or* by him, *etc.*	اِن ني *in-ne*, by these, by them.

In this example we see that the nominative *yih* is changed into *is* for the oblique cases singular, and the nominative plural *ye* becomes *in* for the oblique plural, just as in the English 'he' becomes 'him,' and 'they' 'them.' In the oblique cases plural, it may be mentioned that besides the form اِن *in*, we sometimes meet with انہ *inh* and انہون *inhon*, though not so commonly. The dative singular has two forms, one by adding *ko*, like the substantives, and another by adding ي *e*, as *is-ko* or *is-e*; in the plural we have *in-ko* and *in-hen*. The accusative is generally like the dative, but often the same as the nominative, as in the declension of substantives.

32. The demonstrative وُہ, 'that,' 'he,' 'she, 'it' the interrogative کون *kaun*, 'who?' 'what?' the relative

جو *jo*, 'he who,' 'she who,' etc., and the correlative سو *so*, 'that same,' are precisely similar in termination to يِہ in the foregoing example; hence it will suffice to give the nominatives, and one or two oblique cases of each, thus:—

Remote Demonstrative.

	Singular.	Plural.
N.	وُہ *wuh*, he, she, it, *or* that.	وي *we*, they, those.
G.	اُس كا[1] *us-ká*, etc.	اُن كا اُنهون كا *un-ká*, or *unhoṅ-ká*.
D.	اُس كو اُسي *us-ko*, or *use*.	اُن كو اُنهين *un-ko*, or *unheṅ*.

Interrogative (applied to persons or individuals).

	Singular.	Plural.
N.	كَون *kaun*, who, which.	كَون *kaun*, who, which.
G.	كِس كا *kis-ká*, etc.	كِن كا كِنهون كا *kin-ká*, or *kinhoṅ-ká*, etc.

Interrogative (applied to matter or quantity).

	Singular.	Plural.
N.	كِيا *kyá*, what.	Same as the singular.
G.	كاهي *káhe-ká*, etc.	

Relative.

	Singular.	Plural.
N.	جو *jo* or جَون *jaun*, He who, she who, that which.	جو *jo* or *jaun*, They who, those who, *or* which.
G.	جِس كا *jis-ká*, etc.	جِن كا جِنهون كا *jin-ká*, *jinhoṅ-ká*, etc.
D.	جِس كو جِسي *jis-ko*, etc.	جِن كو جِنهين *jin-ko*, or *jinheṅ*.

Correlative.

	Singular.	Plural.
N.	سو *so* or تَون *taun*, That same.	سو *so* or تَون *taun*, These same.
G.	تِس كا *tis-ká*, etc.	تِن كا تِنهون كا *tin-ká* or *tinhoṅ-ká*, etc.
D.	تِس كو تِسي *tis-ko*, *tise*.	تِن كو تِنهين *tin-ko*, *tinheṅ*.

[1] Sometimes وِس كا *wis ká*, etc.; and in the plur. وِن وِنه or وِنهون كا *win-*, *winh-*, or *winhoṅ-*, *ká*, etc.

POSSESSIVE PRONOUNS.

33. The genitives singular and plural of the personal and demonstrative pronouns are used adjectively as possessives, like the *meus*, *tuus*, *noster*, *vester*, etc., of the Latin, and in construction they follow the rule given respecting adjectives in ا *á*. There is, however, in addition to these, another possessive of frequent occurrence, viz. اپنا *apná*, اپني *apne*, اپني *apní*, 'own,' *or* 'belonging to self; which, under certain circumstances, supplies the place of any of the rest, as will be fully explained in the Syntax. The word آپ *áp*, 'self,' is used with or without the personal pronouns; thus, مَين آپ *main áp*, 'I myself,' which meaning may be conveyed by employing آپ *áp* alone. But the most frequent use of آپ *áp* is as a substitute for the second person, to express respect, when it may be translated, 'you,' 'sir,' 'your honour,' 'your worship,' etc. When used in this sense, آپ *áp* is declined like a word of the second class of substantives under the singular form, thus:—

N.	آپ	*áp*, your honour.
G.	آپ کا -کي -کِي	*áp-ká*, *-ke*, *-kí*, of your honour.
D. & Ac.	آپ کو	*áp-ko*, to your honour, your honour.
A.	آپ سي	*áp-se*, from your honour.
L.	آپ مين	*áp-meṅ*, in your honour.
Agt.	آپ ني	*áp-ne*, by your honour.

When the word آپ *áp* denotes 'self,' it is declined as follows:—

N.	آپ	*áp*, self, myself, *etc.*
G.	اپنا اپني اپِني	*apná*, *apne*, *apní*, own, of self, *etc.*

D. & A.	آپ كو اپني كو / اپني تئين	*áp-ko* or *apne-ko,* / or *apne ta,ín,*	to-self, self.

The phrase آپس مين *ápas-meṅ* denotes 'among ourselves,' 'yourselves,' or 'themselves,' according to the nominative of the sentence.

INDEFINITE PRONOUNS.

34. Under this head we class all those words which have more or less of a pronominal signification. The following are of frequent occurrence:—ايک *ek*, 'one;' دُوسرا *dúsrá*, 'another;' دونو *dono*, or دونون *donoṅ*, 'both;' اور *aur*, 'other (more);' غَير *ghair*, 'other, (different);' بعضي *ba'ẕe*, 'certain;' بہُت *bahut*, 'many,' 'much;' سب *sab*, 'all,' 'every;' هر *har*, 'each;' فُلانه *fulána* or فلانا *fulāná*, 'a certain one;' كوئي *ko'í*, 'any one,' 'some one;' كُچھ *kuchh*, 'any thing,' 'something;' كَئي *ka,í* and چَند *chand*, 'some,' 'several,' 'many;' كِتّنا *kitná* or كتّا *kittá*, 'how many?' جِتّنا *jitná* or جِتّا *jittá*, 'as many;' اتّنا *itná* or اتّا *ittá*, 'so many.' They are all regular in their inflections, with the exception of كوئي *ko,í*, 'any,' and كُچھ *kuchh*, 'some,' which are thus declined:—

كوئي *ko,í*.

	Singular.	Plural.
N.	كوئي *ko,í*, Any one, some one.	كوئي *ko,í* or كَئي *ka,í*, some. several.
Obl.	كِسي كا *kisí-ká*, etc.	*كِني كا *kiní-ká*, etc.

كُچھ *kuchh*.

N.	كُچھ *kuchh*, Any thing, something.	كُچھ *kuchh*, any, some, *etc.*
Obl.	كِسُو كا *kisú-ká*, etc.	*كِنُو كا *kinú-ká*, etc.

* We have given the oblique forms of the plural *kiní* and *kinú* on the authority of Mr. Yates; at the same time we must confess that we never met with either of them in the course of our reading.

a. The word *ko,í*, unaccompanied by a substantive, is generally understood to signify a person or persons, as *ko,í hai?* 'is there any one?' (vulgarly *qui hy*); and in similar circumstances *kuchh* refers to things in general, as *kuchh nahín*, 'there is nothing,' 'no matter.' When used adjectively, *ko,í* and *kuchh* may be applied to persons or things indifferently, particularly so in the oblique cases.

b. The following is a useful list of compound adjective pronouns; and as almost all of them have already been noticed in their simple forms, it has been deemed superfluous to add the pronunciation in Roman characters. They are for the most part of the indefinite kind, and follow the inflections of the simple forms of which they are composed; thus *ek ko,í*, 'some one,' *ek kisí-ká*, etc., 'of some one.' If both members be subject to inflection in the simple forms, the same is observed in the compound, as *jo-ko,í*, 'whosoever,' *jis-kisí-ká*, etc., 'of whomsoever,' so *jo-kuchh*, 'whatsoever,' *jis-kisú-ká*, etc., 'of whatsoever.'

The compound adjective pronouns of the indefinite kind are ایک اَور, ایک اَور *or* ایک دُوسرا, 'another,' ایک کوئي, 'some one,' دُوسرا کوئي *or* دُوسرا کُچھ, 'some other,' ایک نه ایک, 'one or other,' اَور کوئي, 'some one else,' اَور کُچھ, 'something else,' اَور سب, 'the rest,' بعضي کوئي *or* بعضي اَور, 'some others,' بُہت ایک, 'many a one,' بُہت کُچھ, 'much,' بُہت اَور, 'many more,' سب کوئي *or* هر کوئي, 'every one,' سب کُچھ *or* هر کُچھ, 'every thing,' سب ایک, هر ایک *or* هر کس, 'every one,' کوئي ایک 'whichever,' اَور کوئي, 'some other,' جو کوئي 'whoever,' جو کُچھ, 'whatever,' کوئي نه کوئي 'some one or other,' کُچھ ایک *or* کُچھ کُچھ, 'somewhat,' اَور کُچھ, 'some more,' کُچھ نه کُچھ, 'something or other. The use and application of all the pronouns will be fully explained under that head in the Syntax.

SECTION III.

OF THE VERB (فِعْل FI'L).

35. All verbs in Hindústání are conjugated in exactly the same manner. So far as terminations are concerned, there is not a single irregular verb in the language. There is, strictly speaking, but one simple tense (the aorist), which is characterized by distinct personal endings; the other tenses being formed by means of the present and past participles, together with the auxiliary 'to be.' The infinitive or verbal noun, which always ends in نا *ná* (subject to inflection), is the form in which verbs are given in Dictionaries; hence it will be of more practical utility to consider this as the source from which all the other parts spring.

36. From the infinitive are formed, by very simple and invariable rules, the three principal parts of the verb, which are the following:—1. The second person singular of the imperative or root, by rejecting the final نا *ná;* as from بولنا *bolná*, 'to speak,' comes بول *bol*, 'speak thou.' 2. The present participle, which is always formed by changing the final نا *ná* of the infinitive into تا *tá*, as بولنا *bolná*, 'to speak,' بولتا *boltá*, 'speaking.' 3. The past participle is formed by leaving out the ن *n* of the infinitive, as بولْنا *bolná*, 'to speak,' بولا *bolá*, 'spoken.' If, however, the نا *ná* of the infinitive be preceded by the long vowels ا *á* or و *o*, the past participle is formed by changing the ن *n* into ي *y*, in order to avoid a disagreeable hiatus; thus from لانا *láná*, 'to bring,' comes لايا *láyá* (not لاا *lá-á*) 'brought;' so رونا *roná*, 'to weep,' makes

رويا *royá* in the past participle. These three parts being thus ascertained, it will be very easy to form all the various tenses, etc., as in the examples which we are about to subjoin.

37. As a preliminary step to the conjugation of all verbs, it will be necessary to learn carefully the following fragments of the auxiliary verb 'to be,' which frequently occur in the language, not only in the formation of tenses, but in the mere assertion of simple existence.

Present Tense.

Singular.	Plural.
مَين هُون *maiṅ húṅ*, I am.	هم هَين *ham haiṅ*, we are.
تُو هَي *tú hai*, thou art.	تُم هو *tum ho*, you are.
وُه هَي *wuh hai*, he, she, it is.	وي هَين *we haiṅ*, they are.

Past Tense.

مَين تها *maiṅ thá*, I was.	هم تهي *ham the*, we were.
تُو تها *tú thá*, thou wast.	تُم تهي *tum the*, you were.
وُه تها *wuh thá*, he *or* it was.	وي تهي *we the*, they were.

a. The first of these tenses is a curiosity in its way, as it is the only present tense in the language characterized by different terminations, and independent of gender. Instead of the form هَي *hai*, in the second and third persons singular, هَيگا *haigá* is frequently met with in verse; and in the plural, هَينگے *hainge* for هَين *haiṅ* in the first and third persons. In the past tense, تها *thá* of the singular becomes تهِي *thí* when the nominative is feminine, and in the plural تهِين *thíṅ*. We may here remark that throughout the conjugation of all verbs, when the singular terminates in *á* (masculine), the plural becomes *e;* and if the nominative be feminine, the *á* becomes *í* for the singular, and *íṅ* (contracted for *iyáṅ*) for the plural. If several feminine terminations in the plural follow in succession, the *íṅ* is added only to the last, but even here there are exceptions.

38. We shall now proceed to the conjugation of an intransitive or neuter verb, and with a view to assist the memory, we shall arrange the tenses in the order of their formation from the three principal parts already explained. The tenses, as will be seen, are nine in number—three tenses being formed from each of the three principal parts. A few additional tenses of comparatively rare occurrence will be detailed hereafter.

Infinitive, بولنا *bolnā*, To speak.

Principal parts.			
	Imperative and root	بول	*bol,* speak (thou).
	Present participle	بولتا	*boltá,* speaking.
	Past participle	بولا	*bolá,* spoke *or* spoken.

1. TENSES FORMED FROM THE ROOT:

Aorist.

English—'I may speak,' *etc.*

مَين بولُون *maiṅ bolúṅ.*	هم بولين *ham boleṅ.*
تُو بولي *tú bole.*	تُم بولو *tum bolo.*
وُہ بولي *wuh bole.*	وي بولين *we boleṅ.*

Future.

English—'I shall *or* will speak,' *etc.*

مَين بولُونگا *maiṅ bolúṅgá.*	هم بولينگي *ham boleṅge.*
تُو بوليگا *tú bolegá.*	تُم بولوگي *tum bologe.*
وُہ بوليگا *wuh bolegá.*	وي بولينگي *we boleṅge.*
fem. *bolúṅgí,* etc.	fem. *boleṅgíṅ,* etc.

Imperative.

English—'Let me speak, speak thou,' *etc.*

مَين بولُون *maiṅ bolúṅ.*	هم بولين *ham boleṅ.*
تُو بول *tú ból.*	تُم بولو *tum bolo.*
وُہ بولي *wuh bole*	وي بولين *we boleṅ.*

2. TENSES FORMED FROM THE PRESENT PARTICIPLE:

Indefinite.

English (as a present tense)—'I speak, thou speakest,' *etc.*; (conditional)—'If I spoke, had I spoken,' *etc.*; (habitual)—'I used to speak.'

مَین بولتا *main boltá.*	هم بولتي *ham bolte.*
تُو بولتا *tú boltá.*	تُم بولتي *tum bolte.*
وُه بولتا *wuh boltá.*	وي بولتي *we bolte.*

Present.

English—'I speak *or* am speaking,' *etc.*

مَین بولتا هُون *main boltá hún.*	هم بولتي هَين *ham bolte hain.*
تُو بولتا هَي *tú boltá hai.*	تُم بولتي هو *tum bolte ho.*
وُه بولتا هَي *wuh boltá hai.*	وي بولتي هَين *we bolte hain.*

Imperfect.

English—'I was speaking, thou wast,' *etc.*

مَین بولتا تها *main boltá thá.*	هم بولتي تهي *ham bolte the.*
تُو بولتا تها *tú boltá thá.*	تُم بولتي تهي *tum bolte the.*
وُه بولتا تها *wuh boltá thá.*	وي بولتي تهي *we bolte the.*

3. TENSES FORMED FROM THE PAST PARTICIPLE:

Past.

English—'I spoke, thou spokest,' *etc.*

مَین بولا *main bolá.*	هم بولي *ham bole.*
تُو بولا *tú bolá.*	تُم بولي *tum bole.*
وُه بولا *wuh bolá.*	وي بولي *we bole.*

Perfect.

English—'I have spoken, thou hast,' *etc.*

مَین بولا هُون *main bolá hún.*	هم بولي هَين *ham bole hain.*
تُو بولا هَي *tú bolá hai.*	تُم بولي هو *tum bole ho.*
وُه بولا هَي *wuh bolá hai.*	وي بولي هَين *we bole hain.*

Pluperfect.

English—'I had spoken, thou hadst spoken,' *etc.*

مَیں بولا تها *main bolá thá.*	هم بولي تهي *ham bole the.*
تُو بولا تها *tú bolá thá.*	تُم بولي تهي *tum bole the.*
وُہ بولا تها *wuh bolá thá.*	وي بولي تهي *we bole the.*

4. MISCELLANEOUS VERBAL EXPRESSIONS:

Respectful Imperative or *Precative.*

بولِئِي *boliye* or بولِيُو *boliyo,* 'You, he, *etc.*, be pleased to speak.'
بولِئِيگا *boliyegá,* 'You, he, *etc.*, will have the goodness to speak.'

Infinitive (used as a gerund *or* verbal noun).

Nom. بولْنا *bolná,* 'Speaking:' gen. بولْني كا *bolne-ká,* etc., 'Of speaking,' *etc.*, like substantives of the third class.

Noun of Agency.

بولْني والا *bolne-wálá,* and sometimes بولْني هارا *bolne-hárá,* 'A speaker,' 'one who is capable of speaking.'

Participles, used adjectively.

Singular.	Plural.
Pres. بولْتا *boltá* or بولْتا هُؤا *boltá hú,á,* fem. *boltí* or *boltí hú,í.*	بولْتي *bolte* or بولْتي هُؤي *bolte hú,e,* fem. *boltín* or *boltí hú,ín.*
Past. بولا *bolá* or بولا هُؤا *bolá hú,á,* fem. *bolí* or *bolí hú,í.*	بولي *bole* or بولي هُؤي *bole hú,é,* fem. *bolín* or *bolí hú,ín.*

Conjunctive (indeclinable). بول *bol,* بولي *bole,* بولْكي *bolke,* بولْكر *bolkar,* بول كرْكي *bol kar-ke,* or بول كركر *bol karkar,* 'having spoken.'

Adverbial participle (indeclinable). بولْتي هِي *bolte-hi,* 'On speaking, *or* on (the instant of) speaking.'

a. We may here briefly notice how the various portions of the verb are formed. The aorist, it will be seen, is the only part worthy of the name of tense, and it proceeds directly from the ***root*** by adding the terminations *ún*, *e*, *e*, for the singular, and *en*, *o*, *en*, for the plural. The future is formed directly from the aorist by adding *ga* to the singular and *ge* to the plural for masculines, or by adding *gí* and *giyáṅ* (generally contracted into *gíṅ*) when the nominative to the verb is feminine. The imperative differs from the aorist merely in the second person singular, by using the bare root without the addition of the termination *e*. Hence, the future and imperative are mere modifications of the aorist, which we have placed first, as the tense *par excellence*. It is needless to offer any remark on the tenses formed from the present participle, as the reader will easily learn them by inspection. The three tenses from the past participle are equally simple in all neuter or intransitive verbs; but in transitive verbs they are subject to a peculiarity of construction, which will be noticed further on. The proper use and application of the various tenses and other parts of the verb will be fully treated of in the Syntax.

b. As the aorist holds the most prominent rank in the Hindústání verb, it will be proper to notice in this place a few euphonic peculiarities to which it is subject. 1. When the root ends in *á*, the letter *w* is optionally inserted in the aorist between the root and those terminations that begin with *e;* thus لانا *láná*, 'to bring,' root لا *lá*, *Aorist*, لاوي *láwé* or لاءي *lá,e*. 2. When the aorist ends in *o*, the letter *w* is optionally inserted, or the general rule may be observed, or the initial vowels of the termination may all vanish, as will be seen in the verb *honá*, which we are about to subjoin. Lastly, when the root ends in *e*, the letter *w* may be inserted between the root and those terminations which begin with *e*, or the *w* being omitted, the final *e* of the root is absorbed in the terminations throughout. Thus دينا *dená*, 'to give,' root دي *de*, *Aorist*, *deúṅ*, *dewe*, *dewe; deweṅ de,o, deweṅ;* or, contracted, *dúṅ*, *de*, *de; deṅ*, *do*, *deṅ*. It is needless to add that the future and imperative of all such verbs are subject to the same modification. With regard to the respectful form of the imperative and future, we see at once that it comes from the root by adding *íye*, *íyo*, or *íyegá;* if, however, the root happens to end in the long vowels *í* or *ú*, the letter *j* is inserted between the root and the termination. Thus پينا *píná*, 'to drink,' root, *pí*, respectful form, *píjiye*, *píjiyo*, and *píjiyegá*.

39. We now come to the verb هونا *honá*, 'to be, *or* become,' which, being of frequent occurrence, is worthy of the reader's attention. It is perfectly regular in the formation of all its tenses, etc., and conjugated precisely like *bolná*, already given. The past participle changes the *o* of the root into *ú*, instead of retaining the *o* and inserting the euphonic *y* (No. 36), thus هُوا *hú,á*, 'been *or* become,' not هويا *hoyá;* so the respectful imperative is *hújiye*, etc.; but these slight peculiarities do not in the least affect the regularity of its conjugation, as will be seen in the paradigm.

Infinitive, هونا *honá*, 'To be, *or* become.'

Root هو *ho*, present participle هوتا *hotá*, past participle هُوا *hú,á*.

Aorist.

'I may, *or* shall be, *or* become.'

هون- مَیں هوُون *main ho,ún*, or *hoṅ*.
هو- هؤي- تُو هووي *tú howe, ho,e* or *ho*.
هو- هؤي- وُہ هووي *wuh howe, ho,e,* or *ho*.
هون- هوئِن- هم هووين *ham howeṅ, ho,eṅ,* or *hoṅ*.
هو- تُم هؤو *tum ho,o* or *ho*.
هون- هؤين- وي هووين *we howeṅ, ho,eṅ,* or *hoṅ*.

Future.

'I shall *or* will be, *or* become.'

هُونگا- مَیں هوُونگا *main ho,úngá,* or *húngá*.
هوگا- هؤيگا- تُو هوويگا *tú howegá, ho,egá,* or *hogá*.
هوگا- هؤيگا- وُہ هوويگا *wuh howegá, ho,egá,* or *hogá*.
هونگي- هؤينگي- هم هووينگي *ham howeṅge, ho,eṅge,* or *hoṅge*.
هوگي- تُم هؤوگي *tum ho,oge,* or *hoge*.
هونگي- هؤينگي- وي هووينگي *we howeṅge, ho,eṅge,* or *hoṅge*.

Imperative.

'Let me be, be thou,' *etc.*

مَین ہوُون -ہون *main ho-ún*, or *hon*.

تُو ہو *tú ho.*

وُہ ہووي -ہوئي -ہو *wuh howe, ho,e,* or *ho.*

ہم ہووین -ہوئین -ہون *ham howen, ho-en,* or *hon.*

تم ہوُو -ہو *tum ho,o,* or *ho.*

وي ہووین -ہوئین -ہون *we howen, ho,en,* or *hon.*

Indefinite.

'I am, I might be, I used to be, *or* become.'

ہوتا	مَین *main* / تُو *tú* / وُہ *wuh*	*hotá.*	ہوتي	ہم *ham* / تُم *tum* / وي *we*	*hote.*

Present.

'I am, *or* I become,' *etc.*

مَین ہوتا ہُون *main hotá hún.*	ہم ہوتي ہَین *ham hote hain.*
تُو ہوتا ہَي *tú hotá hai.*	تُم ہوتي ہو *tum hote ho.*
وُہ ہوتا ہَي *wuh hotá hai.*	وي ہوتي ہَین *we hote hain.*

Imperfect.

'I was becoming,' *etc.*

ہوتا تھا	مَین *main* / تُو *tú* / وُہ *wuh*	*hotá thá.*	ہوتي تھي	ہم *ham* / تُم *tum* / وي *we*	*hote the.*

Past.

'I became,' *etc.*

ہُوا	مَین *main* / تُو *tú* / وُہ *wuh*	*hú,á.*	ہُوي	ہم *ham* / تُم *tum* / وي *we*	*hú,e.*

Perfect.

'I have become,' *etc.*

Singular.	Plural.
مَین هُؤا هُون *main hú,á hún.*	هم هُؤي هَین *ham hú,e hain.*
تُو هُؤا هَي *tú hú,á hai.*	تُم هُؤي هو *tum hú,e ho.*
وُہ هُؤا هَي *wuh hú,á hai.*	وي هُؤي هَین *we hú,e hain.*

Pluperfect.

'I had become,' *etc.*

Singular.	Plural.
مَین *main* / تُو *tú* / وُہ *wuh* } هُؤا تها *hú,á thá.*	هم *ham* / تُم *tum* / وي *we* } هُؤي تهي *hú,e the.*

Respectful Imperative, etc.

هُوجِيي *hújiye,* هُوجِيو *hújiyo,* or هُوجِئيگا *hújiyegá,* 'be pleased to be, *or* to become.'

Infinitive, or *Verbal Noun.*

هونا *honá,* 'being,' *hone-ká,* etc., 'of being.'

Noun of Agency or *Condition.*

هونيوالا *honewálá,* 'that which is, *or* becomes.'

Participles.

Pres. هوتا *hotá,* or هوتا هُؤا *hotá hú,á,* 'being, becoming.'

Past. هُؤا *hú,á,* 'been, or become.'

Conjunctive Participle.

هو هوكر هوكي *ho, hokar, hoke,* etc., 'having been, *or* become.'

Adverbial Participle.

هوتي هِي *hote-hí,* 'on being, *or* becoming.'

a. We may here observe that the aorist, future, and indefinite of هونا *honá,* 'to be,' are sometimes used as auxiliaries with the present and past participles of other verbs, so as to give us three additional tenses. These, from their nature, are not of very frequent occurrence, and some forms of them we confess we have never met with in any work, printed or manuscript, except in grammars. They are, however, considered as distinct parts of the verb by native grammarians, therefore it is but right that they should find a place here. We therefore subjoin them, together with their native appellations, reserving the account of their use and application till we come to the Syntax.

1. *Hál-i mutashakki*, literally, 'present dubious.'
English—'I may *or* shall be speaking.'

مَین بولتا هوُون -هوُونگا *main boltá ho,ún* or *ho,úngá.*
تُو بولتا هووي -هوويگا *tú boltá howe* or *howegá.*
وُہ بولتا هووي -هوويگا *wuh boltá howe* or *howegá.*
هم بولتي هووين -هووينگي *ham bolte howeṅ* or *howeṅge.*
تُم بولتي هوُو -هووگي *tum bolte ho,o* or *ho,oge.*
وي بولتي هووين -هووينگي *we bolte howeṅ* or *howeṅge.*

2. *Máẓí mutashakki* or *Mashkúk*, 'past dubious.'
English—'I may *or* shall have spoken.'

مَین بولا هوُون -هوُونگا *main bolá ho,úṅ* or *hoúṅgá.*
تُو بولا هووي -هوويگا *tú bolá howe* or *howegá.*
وُہ بولا هووي -هوويگا *wuh bolá howe* or *howegá.*
هم بولي هووين -هووينگي *ham bole howeṅ* or *howeṅge.*
تُم بولي هوُو -هوُوگي *tum bole ho,o* or *ho,oge.*
وي بولي هووين -هووينگي *we bole howeṅ* or *howeṅge.*

3. *Máẓí sharṭiya* or *máẓí mutamanní.*

Past Conditional.

English—'Had I been speaking,' *or* 'had I spoken.'

بولتا هوتا ـ بولا هوتا { مَین *main*, تُو *tú*, وُہ *wuh* } *boltá hotá,* or *bolá hotá.*

بولتي هوتي ـ بولي هوتي { هم *ham*, تم *tum*, وي *we* } *bolte hote,* or *bole hote.*

b. Of these three tenses, the first is of rare occurrence; the second is more common, and the future form of the auxiliary is more usual than the aorist in both tenses. The third tense, or past conditional, is of very rare occurrence under the above form, its place being generally supplied by the simpler form مَیں بولتا *maiṅ boltá*, the first of the tenses from the present participle, which on account of its various significations we have given under the appellation of the *Indefinite Tense*. In the 'Father of Hindústání Grammars,' that of Dr. Gilchrist, 4to. Calcutta, 1796, and also in two native treatises in our possession, the various forms '*maiṅ boltá*,' '*maiṅ boltá hotá*,' '*maiṅ boltá hú,á hotá*,' and '*maiṅ bolá hotá*,' are all included under the appellation of *máẓí sharṭí*, or *máẓí mutamanní*, that is, 'Past Conditional.' It is true, the form '*maiṅ boltá*' has occasionally a present signification, but to call it a present tense, as is done in some of our grammars, is leading the student into a gross error, as we shall shew hereafter.

40. We shall now give an example of a transitive verb, which, as we have already hinted, is liable to a peculiarity in those tenses which are formed from the past participle. The full explanation of this anomaly belongs to the Syntax. Suffice it here to say that the construction resembles to a certain extent the passive voice of the corresponding tenses in Latin. Thus for example, the sentence, 'He has written one letter,' may in Latin, and in most European tongues, be expressed in two different ways, by which the assertion amounts to exactly the same thing, viz., '*Ille unam epistolam scripsit*,' or '*Ab illo una epistola scripta est*.' Now these two modes of expression convey the same idea to the mind, but in Hindústání the latter form only is allowed; thus '*us-ne ek chiṭhí likhí hai*,' literally, 'by him one letter has been written.' Hence, in Hindústání those tenses of a transitive verb which are formed from the past

participle, will have their nominative cases changed into that form of the ablative expressive of the agent. What ought to be the accusative of the sentence will become the real nominative, with which the verb agrees accordingly, except in some instances when it is requisite that the accusative should have the particle *ko* affixed, in which case the verb is used in its simplest form of the masculine singular, as we have given it below.

a. It is needless to say that in all verbs the tenses from the root and present participle are formed after the same manner, and the peculiarity above alluded to is limited to transitive verbs only,— and to only *four tenses* of these,—which it is particularly to be wished that the student should well remember. In the following verb, مارنا *márná*, 'to beat *or* strike,' we have given all the tenses in ordinary use, together with their various oriental appellations, as given in a treatise on Hindústání Grammar, compiled by a munshí in the service of Mr. Chicheley Plowden. It is a folio volume, written in Hindústání, but without author's name, date, or title.

Infinitive (*maṣdar*) مارنا *márná*, 'To beat.'

مار *már*, 'beat thou; مارتا *mártá*, 'beating'; مارا *márá*, 'beaten.'

1. TENSES OF THE ROOT:—

Aorist (*muẓári'*).

Singular.	Plural.
مَیں ماروں I may beat.	ہم مارین we may beat.
تو ماري thou mayst beat.	تم مارو you may beat.
وہ ماري he may beat.	وي مارين they may beat.

Future (*mustaḳbil*).

مَیں مارونگا I shall *or* will beat.	ہم مارینگي we shall *or* will beat.
تو ماريگا thou shalt *or* will beat.	تمماروگي you shall *or* will beat.
وہ ماريگا he shall *or* will beat.	وي مارينگي they shall *or* will beat.

Imperative (*amr*).

Singular.	Plural.
مَیں ماروں let me beat.	ہم ماریں let us beat.
تو مار beat thou.	تم مارو beat ye or you.
وہ ماري let him beat.	وي ماریں let them beat.

Respectful form—Máriye, máriyo, or *máriyegá.*

2. TENSES OF THE PRESENT PARTICIPLE :—

Indefinite, or *Past Conditional (mází sharṭí* or *mází mutamanní).*

مَیں مارتا I beat, *etc.*	ہم مارتي we beat.
تو مارتا thou beatest.	تم مارتي ye beat.
وہ مارتا he beats.	وي مارتي they beat.

Present (*ḥál*).

مَیں مارتا ہوں I am beating.	ہم مارتي ہَیں we are beating.
تو مارتا ہَي thou art beating.	تم مارتي ہو you are beating.
وہ مارتا ہَي he is beating.	وي مارتي ہَیں they are beating

Imperfect (*istimrárí*).

مَیں مارتا تھا I was beating.	ہم مارتي تھي we were beating
تو مارتا تھا thou wast beating.	تم مارتي تھي you were beating
وہ مارتا تھا he was beating.	وي مارتي تھي they were beating.

Present Dubious (ḥál i mutashakkí).

English—'I may, shall, *or* will be beating.'

مَیں مارتا ہوُونگا	ہم مارتي ہووینگي
تو مارتا ہوویگا	تم مارتي ہوُوگي
وہ مارتا ہوویگا	وي مارتي ہووینگي

3. TENSES OF THE PAST PARTICIPLE :—

Peculiarity.—All the nominatives assume the case of the agent, characterised by the post-position ني *ne,* the verb agrees with the object of the sentence in gender and number, or is used impersonally in the masculine singular form.

Past Absolute (*mází mutlak*).

English—'I beat *or* did beat,' *etc.* Literally, 'It is *or* was beaten by me, thee, him, us, you, *or* them.'

	Singular.			Plural.	
مارا	مَين ني *main ne*	*márá.*	مارا	هم ني *ham ne*	*márá.*
	تُو ني *tú ne*			تُم ني *tum ne*	
	اُس ني *us ne*			اُن ني *un ne*	

Perfect or *Past Proximate* (*mází karíb*).

English—'I have beaten.' Literally, 'It has been, (is) beaten, by me, thee, him,' *etc.*

مِارا	مَين ني *main ne*	*márá*	مِارا	هم ني *ham ne*	*márá*
هي	تُو ني *tú ne*	*hai.*	هي	تُم ني *tum ne*	*hai.*
	اُس ني *us ne*			اُن ني *un ne*	

Pluperfect, or *Past Remote* (*mází ba'íd*).

English—'I had beaten.' Literally, 'It was beaten by me, thee, him,' *etc.*

مارا	مَين ني *main ne*	*márá*	مارا	هم ني *ham ne*	*márá*
تها	تُوني *tú ne*	*thá.*	تها	تُم ني *tum ne*	*thá.*
	اُس ني *us ne*			اُن ني *un ne*	

Past Dubious (*mází mashkúk*).

English—'I shall have beaten,' *i.e.* 'It shall have been beaten by me, thee,' *etc.*

مارا	مَين ني *main ne*	*márá*	مارا	هم ني *ham ne*	*márá*
هوگا	تُوني *tú ne*	*hogá.*	هوگا	تُم ني *tum ne*	*hogá.*
	اُس ني *us ne*			اُن ني *un ne*	

All the other parts formed as in the verb *bolná.*

41. We have now, we trust, thoroughly explained the mode of conjugating a Hindústání verb. There is no such thing as an irregular verb in the language; and six words only are slightly anomalous in the formation of the past participle, which last being known, the

various tenses unerringly follow according to rule. We here subjoin the words to which we allude, together with their past participles.

INFINITIVES.		PAST PARTICIPLES.			
		Singular.		Plural.	
		Mas.	Fem.	Mas.	Fem.
جانا *jáná*,	To go	گیا *gayá*	گئِي *ga,í*	گئي *ga,e*	گئِين *ga,ín*
كرنا *karná*,	to do	كِيا *kiyá*	كِي *kí*	كِيئي *kí,e*	كِين *kín*
مرنا *marná*,	to die	مُوا *mú,á*	مُوِي *mú,í*	مُوي *mú,e*	مُوِين *mú,ín*
هونا *honá*,	to be	هُوا *hú,á*	هُوِي *hú,í*	هُوي *hú,e*	هُوِين *hú,ín*
دينا *dená*,	to give	دِيا *diyá*	دِي *dí*	دِيئي *dí,e*	دِين *dín*
لينا *lená*,	to take	لِيا *liyá*	لِي *lí*	لِيئي *lí,e*	لِين *lín*

a. Of these, *jáná* and *marná* are neuter or intransitive, and conjugated like *bolná*. The conjugation of *honá* we have already given in full, and that of *karná*, *dená*, and *lená*, is like *márná*, 'to beat.' It would be utterly ridiculous, then, to call any of these an irregular verb; for, at the very utmost, the deviation from the general rule is not so great as in the Latin verbs, *do, dedi, datum*; or *cerno, crevi*, etc., which no grammarian would on that account consider as irregular.

b. The peculiarities in the past participles of *honá*, *dená*,[1] and *lená*, are merely on the score of euphony. The verb *jáná* takes its infinitive and present participle evidently from the Sanskrit root या *yá*, the *y* being convertible into *j*, as is well known, in the modern tongues of Sanskrit origin. Again, the past participle *gayá*, seems to have arisen from the root गम्, which also denotes 'to go.' In the case of *karná*, 'to do, make,' it springs naturally enough from the modified form *kar*, of the root कृ *kri*, and at the same time there would appear to have been another infinitive, *kíná*, directly from the Sanskrit root, by changing the *ri* into *í*,; hence the respectful imperative of this verb has two forms, *kariye* and *kíjiye*, while the past participle *kiyá* comes from *kíná*, the same as *piyá* from *píná*, 'to

[1] The verb *dená* makes *díjiye*, etc., and *lená*, *líjiye*, etc., in the respectful imperative.

drink.' Lastly, *marná, mar,* is from the modified form of मृ *mri*; at the same time the form *múná,* whence *mú,á,* may have been in use; for we know that in the Prákrit, which is a connecting link between the Sanskrit and the present spoken tongues of Northern India, the Sanskrit vowel *ri* began to be generally discarded, and frequently changed into *u,* and the Prákrit participle is *mudo,* for the Sanskrit *mrito;* just as from the Sanskrit verbal noun *prichhana,* we have the Hindústání *púchhná,* 'to ask,' through the Prákrit *puchhana.*

42. *Passive Voice.*—In Hindústání the use of the passive voice is not nearly so general as it is in English and other European languages. It is regularly formed by employing the past (or passive) participle of an active or transitive verb along with the neuter verb جانا *jáná,* 'to go,' or 'to be.' The participle thus employed is subject to the same inflection or variations as an adjective purely Indian (*v.* page 33), ending in ا *á.* Of the verb *jáná* itself, we have just shown that its past participle is *gayá,* which of course will run through all the tenses of the past participle, as will be seen in the following paradigm.

Infinitive, مارا جانا *márá jáná,* 'To be beaten.'

Imperative,	مارا جا	*márá já,* 'be thou beaten.'
Present Participle,	مارا جاتا	*márá játá,* 'being beaten.'
Past Participle,	مارا گیا	*márá gayá,* 'beaten.'

TENSES OF THE ROOT.

Aorist.

Singular.	Plural.
مَیں مارا جاؤں I may be beaten.	ہم ماري جاوين we may be beaten.
تُو مارا جاوي thou mayest be beaten.	تُم ماري جاؤ you may be beaten.
وُہ مارا جاوي he may be beaten.	وي ماري جاوين they may be beaten.

Future.

Singular.	Plural.
مَين مارا جاؤنگا I shall *or* will be beaten.	هم ماري جاوينگي we shall *or* will be beaten.
تُو مارا جاويگا thou shalt *or* wilt be beaten.	تُم ماري جاؤگي you shall *or* will be beaten.
وُه مارا جاويگا he shall *or* will be beaten.	وي ماري جاوينگي they shall *or* will be beaten.

Imperative.

مَين مارا جاؤن let me be beaten.	هم ماري جاوين let us be beaten.
تُو مارا جا be thou beaten.	تُم ماري جاؤ be ye beaten.
وُه مارا جاوي let him be beaten.	وي ماري جاوين let them be beaten.

TENSES OF THE PRESENT PARTICIPLE.

Conditional.

اگر مَين مارا جاتا if I be, *or* had been, beaten.	اگر هم ماري جاتي if we be, *or* had been, beaten.
اگر تُو مارا جاتا if thou be, *or* hadst been, beaten.	اگر تُم ماري جاتي if you be, *or* had been, beaten.
اگر وُه مارا جاتا if he be, *or* had been, beaten.	اگر وي ماري جاتي if they be, *or* had been, beaten.

Present.

مَين مارا جاتا هُون I am being beaten.	هم ماري جاتي هَين we are being beaten.
تُو مارا جاتا هَي thou art being beaten.	تُم ماري جاتي هو you are being beaten.
وُه مارا جاتا هَي he is being beaten.	وي ماري جاتي هَين they are being beaten.

Imperfect.

Singular.	Plural.
مَین مارا جاتا تھا I was beaten *or* being beaten.	ہم ماري جاتي تھي we were beaten.
تُو مارا جاتا تھا thou wast beaten.	تم ماري جاتي تھي you were beaten.
وُہ مارا جاتا تھا he was beaten.	وي ماري جاتي تھي they were beaten.

TENSES OF THE PAST PARTICIPLE.

Past.

مَین مارا گیا I was beaten.	ہم ماري گئي we were beaten.
تُو مارا گیا thou was beaten.	تم ماري گئي you were beaten.
وُہ مارا گیا he was beaten.	وي ماري گئي they were beaten.

Perfect.

مَین مارا گیا ہون I have been beaten.	ہم ماري گئي ہَین we have been beaten.
تُو مارا گیا ہَي thou hast been beaten.	تم ماري گئي ہو you have been beaten.
وُہ مارا گیا ہَي he has been beaten.	وي ماري گئي ہَین they have been beaten.

Pluperfect.

مَین مارا گیا تھا I had been beaten.	ہم ماري گئي تھي we had been beaten.
تُو مارا گیا تھا thou hadst been beaten.	تُم ماري گئي تھي you had been beaten.
وُہ مارا گیا تھا he had been beaten.	وي ماري گئي تھي they had been beaten.

a. Muhammad Ibrahím Munshí, the author of an excellent Hindústání grammar entitled 'Tuhfae Elphinstone,' printed at Bombay, 1823, would seem to conclude that the Hindústání has no passive voice at all. He says, p. 44, "Dr. Gilchrist and Mr. Shakspear are of opinion that there is a passive voice in Hindústání, formed by compounding the past participle of active verbs with the verb جانا; but the primitive signification of this verb ('to go') seems so irreconcileable with the simple state of 'being,' as to render it improbable that it could ever be used in the same manner as the substantive verbs of other languages." Now, the fact is, that the worthy Munshí is carried too far, principally from a strong propensity to have a slap at his brother grammarians, Messrs. Gilchrist and Shakespear, whom he hits hard on every reasonable occasion; and, in addition to this, the passive voice in his native language is of rare occurrence. But there is undoubtedly such a thing as a regular passive voice occasionally to be met with, and it is formed with the verb جانا *jáná*, 'to go,' as an auxiliary. Nor is the connection of *jáná*, 'to go,' with the passive voice so very *irreconcileable* as the Munshí imagines. In Gaelic, the very same verb, viz., 'to go,' is used to form the passive voice, though in a different manner, the verbal noun denoting the action being used as a nominative to the verb 'to go;' thus the phrase, "he was beaten," is in Gaelic literally "the beating of him went," *i. e.*, 'took place,' which is not very remote from the Hindústání expression. Again, in Latin, the phrase, "I know that letters will be written," is expressed by "Scio literas scriptum iri," in which the verb 'to go,' enters as an auxiliary: to say nothing of the verb *veneo* (*ven* + *eo*), 'to be sold.'

b. We have seen in the conjugation of *márná*, 'to beat,' that those tenses which spring from the past participle, have a construction similar to the Latin passive voice. This construction is always used when the agent is known and expressed; as اُس سپاهِي نے ايک مرد مارا هے *us sipáhí-ne ek mard márá hai*, 'that soldier has beaten a man,' or (more literally) 'by that soldier a man has been beaten.' Again, if the agent is unknown or the assertion merely made in general terms, the regular form of the passive is used; as, *ek mard márá gayá*, 'a man has been beaten,' and even this might be more idiomatically expressed by saying *ek mard-ne mar khá,í hai*, 'a man has suffered a beating.'

c. One cogent reason why the passive voice does not frequently occur in Hindústání is, that the language abounds with primitive simple verbs of a passive or neuter signification which are rendered active by certain modifications which we are about to state. Thus جلنا *jalná* signifies 'to burn,' or 'take fire,' in a neuter sense; and becomes an active or transitive verb by inserting the vowel ا *á*, between the root and the termination نا *ná* of the infinitive as, جلانا *jalána*, 'to kindle *or* set on fire;' and this becomes causal or doubly transitive by assuming the form جلوانا *jalwáná*, 'to cause to be set on fire,' as will be more amply detailed in the next paragraph.

DERIVATIVE VERBS.

43. In Hindústání a primitive verb, if neuter, is rendered active, as we have just hinted, by certain modifications of, or additions to, its root. In like manner, an active verb may, by a process somewhat similar, be rendered causal or doubly transitive. The principal modes in which this may be effected are comprised under the following

Rules.

1. By inserting the long vowel ا *á* between the root and the نا *ná* of the infinitive of the primitive verb; thus, from پکنا *pakná*,—a neuter verb, 'to grow ripe,' 'to be got ready' (as food),—becomes پکانا *pakáná* (active), 'to ripen, *or* make ready,' 'to cook.' Again, this active verb may be rendered causal or doubly transitive by inserting the letter و *w* between the root and the modified termination انا *áná;* thus, from پکانا *pakáná*, 'to make ready,' inserting the letter و *w*, we get the causal form پکوانا *pakwáná*, 'to cause (another) to make (any thing) ready.' To show the use of the three forms of the verb, we will add a few plain examples. 1. کهانا پکتا هي *khána paktá hai*, 'the dinner is getting ready, cooking, or being cooked.' 2. باورچي کهانا پکاتا هَي *báwarchí khána pakátá hai*, 'the cook is (himself) cooking the dinner *or* food;' 3. مہماندار کهانا پکواتا هَي *mihmándár khána pakwátá hai*, 'the host is causing dinner to be cooked.' These examples show the copiousness of the Hindústání verb as compared with the English. For whereas we are obliged to employ the same verb both as neuter and active, like the word 'cooking' in the first and second examples, the Hindústání has a distinct expression for each. And the form پکوانا *pakwáná* in the last example is much more neat and concise

than the English 'is having,' 'is getting,' or 'is causing' the dinner (to be) 'cooked.' In like manner, the neuter جلنا *jalná*, 'to burn,' *jaláná*, 'to kindle,' and *jalwáná*, 'to cause to be kindled;' for example, *battí jaltí hai*, 'the candle burns;' a man will say to his servant, *battí-ko jaláo*, 'light the candle (yourself),' but he may say to his munshí, *battí-ko jalwáo*, 'cause the candle to be lit (by others).'

2. When the root of the primitive verb is a monosyllable with any of the long vowels ا *á*, و *o* or *ú*, and ي *e* or *í*, the latter are shortened in the active and causal forms, that is, the ا of the root is displaced by fatḥa, the و by ẓamma, and the ي by *kasra*; as, جاگنا *jágná*, 'to be awake,' جگانا *jagáná*, 'to awaken,' or 'rouse up,' جگوانا *jagwáná*, 'to cause to be roused up;' بولنا *bolná*, 'to speak,' بُلانا *buláná*, 'to call,' بُلوانا *bulwáná*, 'to cause to be called, to send for;' so بهولنا *bhúlná*, 'to forget,' بهلانا *bhuláná*, 'to mislead,' بهلوانا *bhulwáná*, 'to cause to be misled;' ليٹنا *leṭná*, 'to lie down,' لِٹانا *liṭáná*, 'to lay down,' لِٹوانا *liṭwáná*, 'to cause to be laid down;' بهيگنا *bhígná*, 'to be wet,' بهگانا *bhigáná*, 'to wet, بهگوانا *bhigwáná*, 'to cause to be made wet.' When the vowel-sound of the root consists of the strong diphthongs ـَو *au*, and ـَي *ai*, these undergo no change, and consequently such words fall under Rule 1; as, دَوڑنا *dauṛná*, 'to run,' دَوڑانا *dauṛáná*; پَيرنا *pairná*, 'to swim,' پَيرانا *pairáná*. The verb بَيٹهنا *baiṭhná*, 'to sit,' makes بِٹهانا *biṭháná* or بَيٹهانا *baiṭháná*, also بِٹهلانا *biṭhláná*, etc. *Vide* No. 4, below.

3. A numerous class of neuter verbs, having a short vowel in the last syllable of the root, form the active by changing the short vowel into its corresponding long; that is, fatḥa becomes ا *á*; as ẓamma becomes و *o*[1] (or *ú*), and *kasra* becomes ي *e* (or *í*): as, پلنا *palná*, 'to

[1] The forms *e* and *o* are by far the most common; the *í* and *ú* comparatively rare.

thrive, *or* be nourished,' پالنا *pálná*, 'to nourish;' کھلنا *khulná*, 'to open (of itself'), کھولنا *kholná*, 'to open (any thing).' These form their causals regularly, according to Rule 1; as, کھلوانا *khulwáná*, 'to cause (another) to open (any thing).'

4. A few verbs add لانا *láná* to the root, modified as in Rule 2; thus, سیکھنا *sīkhná*, 'to learn,' سکھانا *sikhána*, and سکھلانا *sikhláná*, 'to teach;' کھانا *khána*, 'to eat,' کھلانا *khiláná*, 'to feed;' سونا *soná*, 'to sleep,' سلانا *suláná*, 'to lull (asleep);' بیٹھنا *baiṭhná*, 'to sit,' 'to be placed,' has a variety of forms, viz., *biṭháná*, *baiṭháná*, *biṭhláná*, and *baiṭhláná;* also *baiṭhálná and baiṭhárná*, 'to cause to sit,' 'to set,' or 'cause to be seated.'

5. The following are formed in a way peculiar to themselves:— بکنا *bikná*, 'to be sold,' بیچنا *bechná*, 'to sell;' رهنا *rahná*, 'to stay,' رکھنا *rakhná*, 'to keep, *or* place;' ٹوٹنا *ṭúṭná*, 'to burst,' 'to be broken,' توڑنا *toṛná*, 'to break;' چھٹنا *chhuṭná*, 'to cease,' 'to go off (as a musket, etc.), چھوڑنا *chhoṛná*, 'to let off,' 'to let go;' پھٹنا *phaṭná*, 'to be rent,' پھاڑنا *pháṛná*, 'to rend,' پھوٹنا *phúṭná*, 'to crack, *or* split,' پھوڑنا *phoṛná*, 'to burst open' (actively).

6. Verbs are formed from substantives or adjectives by adding انا *áná* or نا *ná;* as from پاني *páni*, 'water,' پنیانا *paniyáná*, 'to irrigate;' so from چوڑا, 'wide,' *chauṛáná*, 'to widen.' A few infinitives spring, as Hindústání verbs, regularly from Arabic and Persian roots, by merely adding نا *ná*. If the primitive word be a monosyllable ending with two consonants, a *fatḥa* is inserted between the latter, on adding the نا *ná;* as from ترس *tars*, 'fear, pity,' comes ترسنا *taras-ná*, 'to fear;' so from لرز *larz*, 'trembling,' لرزنا *laraz-ná*; and from بحث *baḥs*, 'argument,' *baḥas-ná*, 'to dispute,' etc.

General Rule.—Primitive words consisting of two short syllables, the last of which is formed by the vowel *fatḥa*, on the accession of an additional syllable beginning with a vowel, whether for the purpose of declension, conjugation, or derivation, reject the *fatḥa* of the second syllable. Conversely, primitive words ending in two consecutive consonants, on adding a verbal termination beginning with a consonant, generally insert a *fatḥa* between the two consonants, as we have just seen in Rule 6.

COMPOUND VERBS.

44. The Hindústání is peculiarly rich in compound verbs, though it must be admitted that our grammarians have needlessly enlarged the number. We shall, however, enumerate them all in the following list, and, at the same time, point out those which have no title to the appellation. Compound verbs are formed in various ways, as follows:—

I. FROM THE ROOT.

1. INTENSIVES, so called from being more energetic in signification than the simple verb. *Ex.* مار ڈالنا *már-ḍálná*, 'to kill outright,' from مارنا *márná*, 'to strike,' and ڈالنا *ḍálná*, 'to throw down;' رکھ دینا *rakh-dená*, 'to set down,' from رکھنا *rakhná*, 'to place,' and دینا *dená*, 'to give; کھا جانا *khá-jáná*, 'to eat up,' from کھانا *kháná*, 'to eat,' and جانا *jáná*, 'to go,' etc. The main peculiarity of an intensive verb is, that the second member of it has, practically speaking, laid aside its own primary signification, while at the same time the sense of the first member is rendered more emphatic, as in our own verbs 'to run off,' 'to march on,' 'to rush away,' etc.; thus, *wuh háthí par se gir-paṛá*, 'he fell down from off (or, as the Hindústání has it, more logically, *from upon*) the elephant.'

2. POTENTIALS, formed with سکنا *sakná*, 'to be able;' as بول سکنا *bol-sakná*, 'to be able to speak,' جا سکنا *já-sakná*, 'to be able to go,'

etc. The using the root of a verb in composition with *sakná* in all its tenses may be viewed as the potential mood of such verb; thus, *maiṅ bol-saktá húṅ*, 'I am able to speak,' or 'I can speak;' so *maiṅ bol-saká*, 'I could speak.'

3. Completives, formed with چُکنا *chukná*, ' 'to have done;' as کھا چُکنا *khá-chukná*, 'to have done eating,' لِکھ چُکنا *likh-chukná*, 'to have finished writing.' The root of a verb with the future of *chukná*, is considered, very properly, as the future perfect of such root; thus, *jab maiṅ likh-chukúngá*, 'when I shall have done writing,' that is, 'when I shall have written,' 'postquam scripsero.' So, *agar maiṅ likh-chukúṅ*, 'if I may have written, or have done writing,' 'si scripserim.'

II. FROM THE PRESENT PARTICIPLE.

1. Continuatives, as بکتا جانا *baktá jáná*, or بکتا رهنا *baktá rahná*, 'to continue chatting.' This is not a legitimate compound verb; it is merely a sentence, the present participle always agreeing with the nominative in gender and number, as, *wuh mard baktá játá hai*, 'that man goes on chatting;' *we mard bakte játe hain*, 'these men go on chatting;' *wuh randi baktí jáṭí hai*, 'that woman goes on chatting.'

2. Statisticals, گاتي آنا *gáte áná*, 'to come singing,' *or* 'in singing;' روتي دوڑنا *rote daurná*, 'to run crying.' Here the present participle always remains in the inflected state, like a substantive of the third class, having the post-position *meṅ*, 'in,' understood, hence this is no compound verb properly speaking.

III. FROM THE PAST PARTICIPLE.

1. Frequentatives: مارا کرنا *márá-karná*, 'to make a practice of beating;' جایا کرنا *jáyá-kárná*, 'to make a practice of going.'

2. Desideratives, as بولا چاهنا *bolá-cháhná*, 'to wish, *or* to be about, *or* like to speak.'

IV. FROM SUBSTANTIVES OR ADJECTIVES, HENCE TERMED NOMINALS.

From substantives, as from جمع *jam'*, 'collection,' جمع کرنا

jam' karná, 'to collect, *or* bring together,' and جمع هونا *jam' honá*, 'to be collected, *or* come together;' also from غوطه *ghoṭa*, 'a plunge,' غوطه مارنا *ghoṭa márná*, 'to dive,' غوطه کہانا *ghoṭa khánā*, 'to be dipped.' From adjectives, as from چهوٹا *chhoṭá*, 'small,' چهوٹا کرنا *chhoṭá karná*, 'to diminish;' کالا *kálá*, 'black,' کالا کرنا *kálá karná*, 'to blacken,' such forms of expression, however, are scarcely to be considered as compound verbs.

a. There is a very doubtful kind of compound called a reïterative verb, said to be formed by using together two verbs, regularly conjugated, etc., as بولنا چالنا *bolná chálná*, 'to converse;' but the use of these is generally confined to tenses of the present participle, or the conjunctive participle; and they are not regularly conjugated, for the auxiliary is added to the last only, as *we bolte chálte hain̉*, not *bolte hain̉ chálte hain̉*, 'they converse (chit-chat) together;' so *bol-chál-kar*, not *bol-kar chál-kar*, 'having conversed.' Those which are called Inceptives, Permissives, Acquisitives, etc., given in most grammars, are not properly compound verbs, since they consist regularly of two verbs, the one governed by the other, in the inflected form of the Infinitive, according to a special rule of Syntax; as, وه بولنے لگا *wuh bolne lagá*, 'he began to say;' وه جانے دیتا هے *wuh jáne detá hai*, 'he gives (permission) to go;' وه جانے پاتا هے *wuh jáne pátá hai*, 'he gets (permission) to go;' all of which expressions are mere sentences, and not compound verbs.

b. Hence the compound verbs in the Hindústání language are really five in number, viz.: the Intensive, Potential, Completive, Frequentative and Desiderative. In these, the first part of the compound remains unchanged throughout, while the second part is always conjugated in the usual way. But among such of the nominals as are formed of an adjective with a verb, the adjective will agree in *gender* with the object of the verb, unless the concord be cut off by کو *ko*. Thus: گاڑی کهڑی کر *gáṛí khaṛí kar*, or گاڑی کو کهڑا کر *gáṛí-ko khaṛá kar*, 'stop the carriage.' In the latter case only can the verb کهڑا کرنا *khaṛá-karná* be regarded as belonging to the class of compounds.

SECTION IV.

ON THE INDECLINABLE PARTS OF SPEECH—CARDINAL AND ORDINAL NUMBERS—DERIVATION AND COMPOSITION OF WORDS.

I. ADVERBS.

45. THE adverbs in Hindústání, like the substantives, adjectives, and verbs, are to be acquired mainly by practice. Hence it would be a mere waste of space to swell our volume with a dry detached list of such words, which in all probability no learner would ever peruse. We shall therefore notice only those which have any peculiarity in their character or formation. As a general rule, most adjectives may be used adverbially when requisite, as is the case in German, and often in English. A series of pure Hindústání adverbs of frequent use is derived from five of the pronouns, bearing to each other a similar relation, as will be seen in the following table. Dr. Gilchrist's old pupils will no doubt recollect with what pains the learned Doctor used to impress upon them the necessity of learning this 'quintuple series,' or, as he called it, 'The philological harp.'

a. Adjectives and adjective pronouns, when used adverbially, remain uninflected in the simplest form, viz., that of the nominative singular masculine; as, وُہ بہُت اچّھا لکھْتا هَي *wuh bahut achchhá likhtá hai*, 'he writes very well.' This is exactly the rule in German, 'er schreibt sehr gut.' In the following series, accordingly, numbers 5, 6, and 7, are merely the adjective or indefinite pronouns, formerly enumerated, employed as adverbs.

TABLE OF A QUINTUPLE SERIES OF ADVERBS OF TIME, PLACE, MANNER, QUANTITY, AND NUMBER, FORMED FROM THE FIVE PRONOUNS, یہہ YIH, وُہ WUH, کَون KAUN, جَون JAUN, تَون TAUN, AS UNDER:

	NEAR.	REMOTE.	INTERROGATIVE.	RELATIVE.	CORRELATIVE.
	یہہ *yih*, this.	وُہ *wuh*, that.	کَون *kaun*, who?	جَون *jaun*, who, which.	تَون *taun*, that same.
1	اب *ab*, now.	اُسوقت *us-waḳt*, then.	کب *kab*, کد *kad*, } when?	جب *jab*, جد *jad*, } when.	تب *tab*, تد *tad*, } then.
2	یہاں *yaháṅ*, here.	وہاں *waháṅ*, there.	کہاں *kaháṅ*, where?	جہاں *jaháṅ*, wherever.	تہاں *taháṅ*, there.
3	اِدّھر *idhar*, hither.	اُدّھر *udhar*, thither.	کدّھر *kidhár*, whither?	جِدّھر *jidhar*, whither.	تدّھر *tidhar*, thither.
4	یُوں *yúṅ*, this.	وُوں *wúṅ*, in that way.	کیُّوں *kyúṅ*, how?	جیُّوں *jyúṅ*, as.	تیُّوں *tyúṅ*, so.
5	اَیسا *aisá*, like this.	وَیسا *waisá*, like that.	کَیسا *kaisá*, like what?	جَیسا *jaisá*, like which.	تَیسا *taisá*, like that same.
6	اِتّا *ittá*, ایتا *etá*, } this much.	اُتّا *uttá*, اوتا *otá*, } that much.	کِتّا *kittá*, کیتا *ketá* } how much?	جِتّا *jittá*, جیتا *jetá*, } as much.	تِتّا *tittá*, تیتا *tetá*, } so much.
7	اِتّنا *itná*, ایتّنا *etná*, } this many.	اُتّنا *utná*, اُوتّنا *útná*, } that many.	کِتنا *kitná*, کیتّنا *ketná*, } how many?	جِتّنا *jitná*, جیتّنا *jetná*, } as many.	تِتّنا *titná*, تیتّنا *tetná*, } so many.

a. From the first class we have other adverbs rendered more emphatic by the addition of هِي *hí*, etc. Thus: ابِهي *abhí*, 'just now,' كبِهي *kabhí*, كبِهُو *kabhú*, or كدّهِي *kadhí*, 'ever,' *etc.* From the second class, by changing ان *án* into يِن *ín*: thus, يہِين *yahín*, 'exactly here,' كہِين *kahín*, 'whereabouts, somewhere,' etc. From the fourth, by adding هِين *hín*: يُونہِين *yúnhín*, 'in this very way,' وُونہِين *wúnhín*, 'thereupon, at that very time, exactly, the same as before,' etc.

b. From among these may also be formed, by means of post-positions, etc., a number of useful compounds; as اب تك *ab-tak*, or اب تلك *ab-talak*, 'till now;' كب تك *kab-tak*, 'till when,' etc.; كبِهي كبِهي *kabhí kabhí*, 'sometimes;' كبِهي نه كبِهي *kabhí na kabhí*, 'some time or other;' جهان تهان *jahán tahán* 'here and there;' جهان كہِين *jahán káhín*, 'wherever;' اَور كہِين *aur kahín*, 'somewhere else;' جب كبِهي *jab kabhí*, 'whenever;' كيُون كر *kyún kar*, 'how?'

c. A few adverbs of time have a twofold signification, *i.e.* past or future, according to circumstances; thus, كل *kal*, 'to-morrow, *or* yesterday;' پرسون *parson*, 'the day after to-morrow, *or* the day before yesterday;' ترسون *tarson*, 'the third day from this, past, *or* to come;' نرسون *narson*, 'the fourth day from this.' The time is restricted to past or future by the tenses of the verb and by the context of the sentences in which such words are found.

d. Many adverbs occur from the Arabic and Persian languages; as قصارا *kazárá* (or قصاكار *kazákár*), 'by chance,' from قضا *kazá*, 'fate,' etc., and را *rá*, the sign of the objective case; چگونه *chigúna*, 'how;' باري *báre*, 'once, at last;' بارها *bárhá* (pl.), 'often (times);' شايد *sháyad*, 'perhaps (Hindústání هو تو هو *ho to ho*, it may be);' خواه نه خواه *khwáh na khwáh*, 'volens-nolens, positively, at all events;' و غيره *wa ghaira*, 'et-cetera,' etc.; فقط *fakat*, 'merely, finis.'

e. Adverbs purely Arabic occur chiefly as follows: 1. Simply a noun with the article; thus, القصّه *alkissa* (literally, 'the story'); and الغرض *algharaz* (literally, 'the end, purport,' *etc.*), 'in short;' الحال *alhál* (the present), 'at this time;' البتّه *albatta*, 'certainly;' *etc.*

2. The Arabic noun in the accusative case, marked with the termination اً *an̲* (p. 20); thus, اتّفاقاً *ittifákan̲*, 'by chance,' (from اتّفاق *ittifák*, 'fortune, accident,' *etc.*); اصْلاً *aslan̲* (or اصْلا *aslá*), 'by no means;' مثْلاً *mislan*, 'for example,' (from مِثْل *misl*, 'parable, similitude'); خُصُوصاً *khusúsan̲*, 'especially,' *etc.* Lastly, a noun with a proposition; as, بِالفعل *bi-l-fi'l*, 'in fact;' فِي آلحال *fi-l-hál*, (in the present), فِي آلفَور *fi-l-faur* (in the heat), all signifying 'instantly, immediately;' فِي آلحقِيقت *fi-l-hakikat* (in truth), 'really;' يعْنِي *ya'ni*, 'that is to say, to wit, viz.'

f. Many adverbial expressions occur consisting of a pronoun and substantive governed by a simple postposition understood, as, اِس طرح *is tarah*, 'in this manner;' كِس طرح *kis tarah*, 'how?' *etc.*; كِس واسطي *kis wáste*, 'why?' *i.e.* 'for what reason?' and so on, with many other words of which the adverbial use is indicated by the inflection of the accompanying pronoun.

g. The pluperfect participle may also very often be elegantly applied adverbially; as, هنْسْكر *hanskar*, 'laughingly,' سوچْكر *soch-kar*, 'deliberately,' from هنْسْنا *hansná*, 'to laugh,' سوچْنا *sochná*, 'to think,' اُس ني هنْسْكر كها *us-ne hanskar kahá*, 'he laughingly (or having laughed) said.'

II. PREPOSITIONS.

46. The prepositions in Hindústání are mere substantives in the locative case, having a postposition understood and sometimes expressed. Most of them are expressive of situation with regard to place, and thence figuratively applied to time, and even to abstract ideas. Hence as substantives, they all govern the genitive case, those of them which are masculine (forming the majority) require the word which they govern to have the postposition كي *ke* after it; as, مرْد كي آگي *mard-ke áge*, 'before the man,' literally, 'in front of the man'; while those that are feminine require the word they govern to have كِي *kí*; as, شهْركِي طرف *shahr-kí taraf*,

'towards the city,' literally, 'in the direction of the city.' It is optional to put the preposition before or after the noun which it governs; thus in the foregoing example we might have said *áge mard-ke*, or *mard-ke áge*, with equal propriety.

The following is an alphabetical list of masculine prepositions requiring the nouns which they govern to have the genitive with *ke*, for reasons explained in the beginning of the Syntax.

آگي *áge*, before, in front.
اندر *andar*, within, inside.
اوپر *úpar*, above, on the top.
باعث *bá'is*, by reason of.
باهر *báhar*, or *báhir*, without (not within.)
بجاي *ba-já,e*, instead.
بدلي *badle*, or بدل *badal*, instead.
بدون *bidún*, without, except.
برابر *barábar*, equal to, opposite to.
براي *bará,e*, for, on account of.
بعد *ba'd*, after (as to time).
بغير *baghair*, without, except.
بن *bin*, بنا *biná*, without.
بيچ *bích*, in or among.
پار *pár*, over (other side).
پاس *pás*, by, near.
پيچهي *píchhe*, behind, in the rear.
تلي *tale*, under, beneath.
تئين *ta,ín*, to, up to.
خارج *khárij*, without, outside.
درميان *dar-miyán*, in the midst, between, among.
ساته *sáth*, with (in company).
سامهني *sámhne*, before, in front.
سبب *sabab*, by reason of.
سوا *siwá* or *siwá,e*, except.
عوض *'iwaz*, instead, for.
قبل *kabl*, before, (time).
قريب *karíb*, near.
كني *kane*, near, with.
گرد *gird*, round, around.
لئي *liye*, for, on account of.
ماري *máre*, through (in consequence of).
مطابق *mutábik*, conformable to.
موافق *múáfik*, according to.
موجب *mújib*, or بموجب *ba-mújib*, by means of.
نزديك *nazdík*, near.
نيچي *níche*, under, beneath.
واسطي *wáste*, for, on account of.
هاته *háth*, in the power of, by means of.

The following prepositions being feminine, require the words they govern to have the genitive with *kí*.

بابت *bábat*, respecting, concerning.

بدَولت *ba-daulat*, by means of.

بمدد *ba-madad*, by aid of.

جِهت *jihat*, on account of.

خاطِر *khatir*, for the sake of.

طرح *tarah*, after the manner of, like.

طرف *taraf*, towards.

معْرِفت *ma'rifat*, by, or through.

نِسْبت *nisbat*, relative to.

Some of the feminine prepositions, when they come *before* the word they govern, require such word to have the genitive in *ke*, instead of *kí*. This is a point well worthy of examination, and we reserve the investigation of it till we come to the Syntax.

a. We have applied the term preposition to the above words with a view to define their *use* and *meaning*, not their mere *situation*. In most grammars they are absurdly called *Compound Post-positions*, on the same principle, we believe, that *lucus*, 'a *dark grove*,' is said to come from *lucere*, 'to shine,' or *lux*, 'light.' But in sober truth, what we have called prepositions here, are neither compounds, nor necessarily *post-positive*; and we make it a rule never to countenance a new term unless it be more explicit than those already established and familiar. In Greek, Latin, and Old English, the prepositions frequently follow the word which they govern, but this does not in the least alter their nature and use.

b. Besides the above prepositions, the following Arabic and Persian prefixes are occasionally employed with words from those languages.

از *az*, from, by.

اِلّا *illá*, except, besides.

با *bá*, with (possessed of).

به or بِ *ba* (or *bi*), in, by.

بي *be*, without (deprived of).

بر *bar*, on, in, at.

براي *bará,e*, for (on account of).

بِلا *bilá*, without (*sine*).

در *dar*, in, within.

علي *'alá*, upon, above.

عن *'an*, from.

عِند *'ind*, near, with.

في *fí*, in.

ك *ka*, according to, like.

ل *la* or *li*, to, for

مع *ma'*, with

مِن *min*, from.

III. CONJUNCTIONS.

47. The conjunctions have no peculiarity about them; we shall therefore add a list of the more useful of them in alphabetical order.

از بسکه *az bas-ki*, since, for as much as.

اگر *agar*, گر *gar*, if.

اگرچه *agarchi*, although.

امّا *ammá*, but, moreover.

اور *aur*, and, also.

بلکه *balki*, but, on the contrary.

بهي *bhí*, also, indeed.

پر *par*, but, yet.

پس *pas*, thence, therefore.

تو *to*, then, consequently.

جبتک *jabtak*, until, while.

جو *jo*, if, when.

حال آنکه *hál-ánki*, whereas, notwithstanding.

خواه *khwáh*, either, or.

که *ki*, that, because, than.

تاکه *táki*, that, in order that.

کیونکه *kyúnki*, because.

گویا *goyá*, as if.

گوکه *go-ki*, although.

لیکن *lekin*, but, however.

مگر *magar*, except, unless.

نهین تو *nahín-to*, otherwise.

نیز *níz*, also, likewise.

و *o*, وَ *wa*, and, but.

ور *war*, for, وگر *wa-gar*, and if.

ورنه *war-na*, and if not, unless.

هم *ham*, also, likewise.

هرچند *harchand*, although.

هنوز *hanoz*, yet, still.

یا *yá*, or, either.

IV. INTERJECTIONS.

48. These scarcely deserve the appellation of 'part of speech;' we shall therefore content ourselves by enumerating a few of common occurrence.

شاباش *shábásh* (i. e. شاد باش *shád básh*,) 'happiness *or* good luck to you!' آفرین *áfrín* 'blessings on you,' واه واه *wáh wáh* 'admirable!' کیا خوب *kyá khúb* 'how excellent!' دهن دهن *dhan-*

dhan 'how fortunate!' واه جي *wáh jí*, كيا بات هَي *kyá bát hai* 'what an affair!' all express joy, admiration and encouragement, like 'bravo! well done!' etc. But باپ ري *báp re* (*lit.*, O father) 'astonishing! dreadful!' هاءي هاءي *h,áe h,áe*, or هَي هَى *hai hai*, واءي واءي *wá,e wá,e*, وَاءي وَيلا *wá,e wailá*, 'alas, alas! alackaday! woe is me!' هت *hat*, چهي چهي *chhí chhí*, 'tush, pshaw, pish, fie fie!' دُر *dur*, 'avaunt!' express sorrow, contempt, and aversion. اَي *ai*, او *o*, 'Oh!' ري *re* or اري *are*, 'holla you!' are used in calling attention: the two last in a disrespectful way. ري *re* (m.) or رِي *rí* (f.) agrees in gender with the object of address; as, لَونڈي ري *launḍe re*, 'you boy!' لَونڈِي رِي *launḍí rí*, 'you girl!'

NUMERALS.

49. The Hindústání numeral adjectives, 'one,' 'two,' 'three,' etc., up to a hundred, are rather irregular, at least in appearance, though it would not be very difficult to account for the seeming irregularity on sound etymological principles. This, however, would not greatly benefit the student, who must, in the meantime, learn them by heart as soon as he can.

FIGURES.			NAMES.	FIGURES.			NAMES.
	ARABIC.	INDIAN.			ARABIC.	INDIAN.	
1	١	१	ايک *ek.*	6	٦	६	چهه *chha.*
2	٢	२	دو *do.*	7	٧	७	سات *sát.*
3	٣	३	تِين *tín.*	8	٨	८	آٹه *áṭh.*
4	٤	४	چار *chár.*	9	٩	९	نَو *nau.*
5	٥	५	پانچ *pánch.*	10	١٠	१०	دس *das.*

	FIGURES.		NAMES.		FIGURES.		NAMES.
	ARABIC.	INDIAN.			ARABIC.	INDIAN.	
11	۱۱	११	اِگاره *igárah.*	31	۳۱	३१	اِکتِیس *iktís.*
12	۱۲	१२	باره *bárah.*	32	۳۲	३२	بتِیس *batís.*
13	۱۳	१३	تیره *térah.*	33	۳۳	३३	تیتِیس *tétís.*
14	۱۴	१४	چَوده *chaudah.*	34	۳۴	३४	چَوتیس *chautís.*
15	۱۵	१५	پنْدْره *pandrah.*	35	۳۵	३५	پَینْتیس *paiṅtís.*
16	۱۶	१६	سوله *sólah.*	36	۳۶	३६	چھتِّیس *chhattís.*
17	۱۷	१७	سْتره *satrah.*	37	۳۷	३७	سَینْتِیس *saiṅtís.*
18	۱۸	१८	اٹھاره *aṭhárah.*	38	۳۸	३८	اٹھْتِیس *aṭhtís.*
19	۱۹	१९	اُنِیس *unís.*	39	۳۹	३९	اُنْتالِیس *untális.*
20	۲۰	२०	بِیس *bís.*	40	۴۰	४०	چالِیس *chális.*
21	۲۱	२१	اِکّیس *ikkís.*	41	۴۱	४१	اِکْتالِیس *iktális.*
22	۲۲	२२	بائِیس *bá,ís.*	42	۴۲	४२	بیالِیس *bé,ális.*
23	۲۳	२३	تِیئیس *té,ís.*	43	۴۳	४३	تیتالِیس *tétális.*
24	۲۴	२४	چَوبیس *chaubís.*	44	۴۴	४४	چَوالِیس *chau,ális.*
25	۲۵	२५	پچِیس *pachís.*	45	۴۵	४५	پَینْتالِیس *paiṅtális.*
26	۲۶	२६	چھبِّیس *chhabbís.*	46	۴۶	४६	چھِیالِیس *chhi,ális.*
27	۲۷	२७	ستائِیس *satá,ís.*	47	۴۷	४७	سَینْتالِیس *saiṅtális.*
28	۲۸	२८	اٹھائِیس *aṭhá,ís.*	48	۴۸	४८	اٹھْتالِیس *aṭhtális.*
29	۲۹	२९	اُنْتِیس *untís.*	49	۴۹	४९	اُنْچاس *unchás.*
30	۳۰	३०	تِیس *tís.*	50	۵۰	५०	پچاس *pachás.*

FIGURES.			NAMES.	FIGURES.			NAMES.
	ARABIC.	INDIAN.			ARABIC.	INDIAN.	
51	٥١	५१	اِکاون *ikáwan.*	71	٧١	७१	اِکہتر *ikhattar.*
52	٥٢	५२	باون *báwan.*	72	٧٢	७२	بہتر *bahattar.*
53	٥٣	५३	تِرپن *tirpan.*	73	٧٣	७३	تِہتر *tihattar.*
54	٥۴	५४	چَوّن *chauwan.*	74	٧۴	७४	چَوہتر *chauhattar.*
55	٥٥	५५	پچپن *pachpan.*	75	٧٥	७५	پچہتر *pachhattar.*
56	٥٦	५६	چھپن *chhappan.*	76	٧٦	७६	چھِہتر *chhihattar.*
57	٥٧	५७	ستاون *sattáwan.*	77	٧٧	७७	ستہتر *sathattar.*
58	٥٨	५८	اٹھاون *aṭháwan.*	78	٧٨	७८	اٹھہتر *aṭhhattar.*
59	٥٩	५९	اُنسٹھ *unsaṭh.*	79	٧٩	७९	اُناسِی *unásí.*
60	٦٠	६०	ساٹھ *sáṭh.*	80	٨٠	८०	اسِّی *assí.*
61	٦١	६१	اِکسٹھ *iksaṭh.*	81	٨١	८१	اِکاسِی *ikásí.*
62	٦٢	६२	باسٹھ *básaṭh.*	82	٨٢	८२	بیاسِی *bé,ásí.*
63	٦٣	६३	تِرسٹھ *tirsaṭh.*	83	٨٣	८३	تِراسِی *tirásí.*
64	٦۴	६४	چَوسٹھ *chausaṭh.*	84	٨۴	८४	چوراسِی *chaurásí.*
65	٦٥	६५	پَینسٹھ *paiṅsaṭh.*	85	٨٥	८५	پچاسِی *pachásí.*
66	٦٦	६६	چھِیاسٹھ *chhí,ásaṭh.*	86	٨٦	८६	چھِیاسِی *chhí,ásí.*
67	٦٧	६७	سَتسٹھ *satsaṭh.*	87	٨٧	८७	ستاسِی *satásí.*
68	٦٨	६८	اٹھسٹھ *aṭhsaṭh.*	88	٨٨	८८	اٹھاسِی *aṭhásí.*
69	٦٩	६९	اُنہتر *unhattar.*	89	٨٩	८९	نَواسِی *nau,ásí.*
70	٧٠	७०	ستّر *sattar.*	90	٩٠	९०	نَوّے *nauwé.*

FIGURES.			NAMES.	FIGURES.			NAMES.
	ARABIC.	INDIAN.			ARABIC.	INDIAN.	
91	٩١	९१	اِکانَوي *ikánawé.*	96	٩٦	९६	چھِيانَوي *chhi,ánawé*
92	٩٢	९२	بانَوي *bánawé.*	97	٩٧	९७	ستانَوي *satánawé.*
93	٩٣	९३	تِرانَوي *tiránawé.*	98	٩٨	९८	اٹھانَوي *aṭhánawé.*
94	٩٤	९४	چَورانَوي *chauránawé*	99	٩٩	९९	نِنانَوي *ninánawé.*
95	٩٥	९५	پچانَوي *pachánawé.*	100	١٠٠	१००	سَو *sau* or سَي *sai*

a. Some of these have names slightly differing from the preceding, which we here subjoin :

11	گيارہ *gyárah*	51	ايکاوَن *ékáwan.*	85	پَنْچاسِي *panchási.*
18	اٹھارا *aṭhárá.*	54	چَوپن *chaupan.*	86	چھاسِي *chhási.*
19	اُنِّيس *unnís*	55	پچاوَن *pacháwan.*	90	نَوّد *nauwad.*
21	ايکِيس *ékís.*	61	ايکْسَٹھ *éksaṭh.*	91	ايکانَوي *ékánawé* or اِکانَوّي *ikánauwé.*
31	ايکَتِيس *éktís.*	66	جھاچھٹ *chhâchhat* or چھسٹھ *chha-saṭh.*	92	بانَوّي *bánauwé* or بِرانَوّي *biránauwé.*
33	تَينْتِيس *taintís.*	68	اَڑسٹھ *arsaṭh.*	93	تِرانَوّي *tiránauwé.*
34	چَونْتِيس *chauntís.*	71	ايکْہتّر *ékhattar.*	95	پَنْچانَوي *panchánawé.*
38	اَڑتِيس *artís.*	73	تِرْہتّر *tirhattar.*	96	چھانَوي *chhánawé.*
39	اُنْچالِيس *unchális.*	76	چھہتّر *chha-hattar*	99	نَوانَوي *nau,ánawe* or نِنانَوّي *ninánauwé.*
41	ايکْتالِيس *éktális.*	81	ايکاسِي *ékásí.*		
43	تَينتالِيس *taintális.*	82	باسِي *básí* or بِراسِي *birásí.*		
46	چھتالِيس *chhatális.*				
48	اَڑتالِيس *artális.*				

a. The numbers above one hundred proceed somewhat like our own, only the conjunction is generally suppressed; as ایک سَو پانچ *ek sau pánch*, 'one hundred (and) five;' دو سَو دس *do sau das*, 'two hundred (and) ten,' etc. The present year, 1855, may be expressed as with us, ایک هزار آٹھ سَو پچپن *ek hazár áṭh sau pachpan*, or اٹھارہ سَو پچپن *aṭhárah sau pachpan*, that is, 'one thousand eight hundred,' etc., *or* 'eighteen hundred,' etc.

b. The following are used as collective numbers:

گنڈا *ganḍá*, a group of four.	سَیکڑا *saikṛá*, a hundred.
گاهي *gáhí*, a five.	هزار *hazár*, a thousand.
کوڑي *koṛí*, a score.	لاکھ *lákh*, a hundred thousand.
چالِیسا *chálísá*, a forty.	کڑوڑ *karoṛ*, one hundred lákhs, *or* ten millions.

c. The Ordinals proceed as follows:

پہلا *pahlá* or *pahilá*, or پیہلا *paihlá*, 1st.	چَوتھا *chauthá*, 4th.
دُوسرا *dúsrá*, 2nd.	پانچوان *pánchwáṅ*, 5th.
تیسرا *tísrá*, 3rd.	چھٹوان *chhaṭwáṅ*, چھٹھا *chhaṭhá*, 6th.

The 'seventh' and upwards are regularly formed from the Cardinals by the addition of وان *wáṅ*. The ordinals are all subject to inflection like adjectives in ا *á* or *áṅ*, that is, *á* becomes *e* for the oblique masculine, and *í* for the feminine. In like manner, *áṅ* becomes *eṅ* and *íṅ*.

d. Fractional Numbers.

پاؤ *pá,o*, چَوتھ *chauth*, چَوتھائِي *chauthá,í*, ¼	پَون *paun*, پَونا *pauná*, ¾.
تہائِي *tihá,í*, ⅓.	سَوا *sawá*, 1¼.
آدھا *ádhá*, ½.	ڈیڑہ *ḍeṛh*, 1½.
	اڑھائِي *aṛhá,í*, 2½.

In the use of the fractional numbers, a few peculiarities occur which it will be well to notice; thus, پونے *paune*, when prefixed to a number, signifies 'a quarter less' than that number; سوا *sawá*, 'a quarter more;' ساڑھے *sáṛhe*, 'one half more,' etc. To the collective numbers for a hundred, a thousand, etc., they are similarly applied; thus, پونے سو *paune sau* = 75; سوا سو *sawá sau* = 125. The words *ḍeṛh* and *aṛhá,í* denote multiplication; as, ڈیڑھ هزار *ḍeṛh hazár* = 1500, i. e. (1000 × 1½); اڑھائی هزار *aṛhá,í hazár* = 2500, or (1000 × 2½).

e. It will be seen then, that altogether the management of the numerals, whole and fractional, is no easy matter. The *sure* plan is to commit them carefully to memory up to 100. As a check upon this the learner should get the first ten, and the multiples of 10, as 20, 30, 40, etc.; then, if he is not *quite certain* of any number (not an unlikely occurrence), for example 35, he may safely say تیس پر پانچ *tís par pánch*, 'five over thirty.' Lastly, let him get the first twenty thoroughly, and then count by scores کوڑی *koṛí*; thus, 35 is *ek koṛí pandrah*; but the more scientific mode is, of course, to carry the hundred numerals in his head, and be quite independent.

DERIVATION OF WORDS.

50. The Hindústání abounds with derivative words both of native origin and of foreign importation. Those from the Arabic are generally single words modified from a triliteral root, according to the grammatical rules of that language. From the Persian, on the other hand, not only derivative words are freely borrowed, but also a multitude of compounds, for the formation of which the Persian language has a peculiar aptitude, and to the number of which there is no limit. In like manner, compositions in the Hindí dialect abound in Sanskrit words both derivative and compounded according to the genius of that highly-cultivated language. Hence, in order to know Hindústání on sound etymological principles, a slight knowledge of Arabic, Persian, and

Sanskrit is absolutely requisite. To the majority of students in this country, however, this is impracticable, their time being necessarily occupied in the acquisition of those essential branches of knowledge usually taught at schools. As a general rule, then, we may take it for granted that an acquaintance with the words of the Hindústání language, whether native or foreign, primitive or derivative, must be ultimately acquired by practice in reading, with the aid of a vocabulary or dictionary, together with exercises in composition. This being the case, it will not be necessary for us to enter deeply into the subject of derivation or composition; the reader, if inclined, may consult Dr. Gilchrist's quarto Grammar, edit. 1796, where he will find twenty-nine goodly pages devoted to this department.

NOUNS DENOTING AGENCY OR POSSESSION.

51. We have already seen that the agent of a verb is denoted by adding the termination والا *wálá* (sometimes هارا *hárá*) to the inflected form of the infinitive, as *bolne-wálá* or *bolne-hárá*, 'a speaker.' The same terminations added to a substantive denote in general the possessor of such substantive, real or temporary; as گھر والا *ghar-wálá*, 'the master of the house;' بَیل والا *bail-wálá*, 'the owner of the bullock;' or, simply, 'the man with the bullock.' A noun of the third class is inflected on the addition of والا *wálá*, thus, گدھے والا *gadhe-wálá*, 'the owner of the ass;' or 'the man with the donkey.' Various nouns of agency, etc. are also formed by adding the following terminations, thus:—

بان	to	باغ a garden,	باغبان	*bágh-bán*, a gardener.
باز	—	ٹھٹھا a jest,	ٹھٹھے باز	*thatthe-báz*, a jester.

بر to	راه	a road,	راه‌بر	*ráh-bar*, a guide.
بردار —	حقه	a pipe,	حقه بردار	*hukka-bardár*, a pipe-bearer.
بند —	نعل	a horse-shoe,	نعلبند	*na'l-band*, a farrier.
چي —	مشعل	a torch,	مشعلچي	*mash'al-chí*, a torch-bearer.
دار[1] —	زمين	land,	زمين دار	*zamín-dár*, a landholder.
ر —	لوها	iron,	لوهار	*lohár*, a blacksmith.
كار —	بد	bad,	بدكار	*bad-kár*, an evil-doer.
گر —	زر	gold,	زرگر	*zar-gar*, a goldsmith.
گار —	گناه	crime,	گناه گار	*gunáh-gár*, a sinner.
وار —	اميد	hope,	اميدوار	*ummed-wár*, an expectant.
وان —	در	door,	دروان	*dar-wán*, a porter.
ي —	سپاه	army,	سپاهي	*sipáhí*, a soldier.

NOUNS DENOTING THE MEANS OR INSTRUMENT.

52. These signify the thing by which the action may be performed, and are derived from verbal roots by affixing

ن as	بيل	rolling,	بيلن	*belan*, a rolling-pin.
نا —	رم	playing,	رمنا	*ramná*, a park.
ني —	كتر	clipping,	كترني	*katarní*, a pair of scissors.
و —	جهاڑ	sweeping,	جهاڑو	*jhárú*, a broom.

Others are formed from nouns, by affixing

ال as	گهڑي	an hour,	گهڑيال	*gharíyál*, an hour-bell
آنه —	دست	the hand,	دستانه	*dastána*, a glove.
ك —	چشم	the eye,	چشمك	*chashmak*, spectacles.
ه —	دست	the hand,	دسته	*dasta*, a handle.

[1] The terminations *dár*, *báz*, and perhaps a few more, require the noun to be inflected, if of the third class; as, *maze-dar*, tasteful, *ṭhaṭṭhe-báz*, a jester.

NOUNS DENOTING PLACE OR SITUATION.

53. These are formed partly by uniting two nouns together, and also by adding certain terminations; as,

آباد a city,	حَيدر Ḥaidar,	حَيدراباد *ḥaidar-ábád*, the city of Ḥaidar.
باڑِي واڑِي a garden,	پھُول a flower,	پھُلواڑِي *phúl-wáṛí*, a flower-garden.
پُور a city,	غازِي Ghází,	غازِي پُور *Ghází-pur*, the city of Ghází.
زار multitude,	لاله a tulip,	لاله زار *lála-zár*, a tulip-bed.
سال or سالا a place,	گھوڑا a horse,	گھُڑسال *ghuṛ-sál*, a stable.
ستان a place,	قبر a grave,	قبرِستان *kabr-istán*, a burying-ground.
شن a place,	گُل a rose,	گُلشن *gul-shan*, a rose-bower.
گاه a place,	آرام rest,	آرامگاه *árám-gáh*, a resting-place.
نگر city,	کِشن Kishn,	کِشن نگر *Kishn-nagar*, the town of Krishna.

ABSTRACTS.

54 Abstract nouns are formed chiefly from adjectives, by affixing some termination, of which the following are of common occurrence:

ا to	گرم warm,	گرما *garmá*, warm weather.
تا تِي —	کم little,	کمتِي *kamtí*, deficiency.
پا ,پن ,or پنا —	لڑکا a child,	لڑکپن *laṛak-pan*, childhood.
س —	مِيٹھا sweet,	مِٹھاس *miṭhás*, sweetness.
گي —	تازه fresh,	تازِگي *tázagí*, freshness.

ن to اونچا high, اونچان *únchán*, height.

ئي — برا bad, برائي *burá,í*, badness.

هٹ — کڑوا bitter, کڑواهٹ *kaṛwáhaṭ*, bitterness.

To Arabic nouns ت is generally added to form abstracts; as, حکم *hukm*, 'a command,' حکومت *ḥukúmat*, 'dominion;' so حجام *ḥajjám*, 'a barber,' *ḥajjámat*, 'shaving.' A few abstracts are formed by a repetition of the word, with a slight alteration in the last, as جهوٹه موٹه *jhúṭh-múṭh*, 'falsehood.'

VERBALS.

55. The verbal noun denoting the action (in progress) is generally expressed by the infinitive. The action, in the abstract, is frequently expressed by the mere root; as, بول *bol*, 'speech,' چاه *cháh*, 'desire,' etc. Others are formed from the root by adding certain terminations; as,

ا to کهه speak, کها *kahá*, a saying.

ائي — بو sow, بوائي *bo,á,í*, a sowing.

آپ — مل mix, ملاپ *miláp*, a mixing or union.

اس — پي drink, پياس *piyás*, desire to drink, thirst.

ِش — دان know (Pers.) دانش *dánish*, knowledge.

ن — جل burn, جلن *jalan*, a burning.

وا — بهلا deceive, بهلاوا *bhuláwá*, a deception.

وٹ — سجا prepare, سجاوٹ *sajáwaṭ*, preparation.

ائي — کهل feed, کهلائي *khilá,í*, a feeding.

هٹ — بلا call, بلاهٹ *buláhaṭ*, a calling.

DIMINUTIVES.

56. These are formed from other nouns, by adding to them various terminations; as,

ا to	بيٹي a daughter,	بٹيا *biṭiyá*, a little daughter.
چه or چي —	ديگ a cauldron,	ديگچي *degchí*, a kettle.
ڑي —	پلنگ a bedstead,	پلنگڑي *palangṛí*, a small bedstead.
ک —	توپ a cannon,	توپک *topak*, a musket.
وا —	مرد a man,	مردوا *mardú,á*, a little man.
يٹا —	برهمن a brahman,	برهمنيٹا *brahmaneṭá*, a young brahman.
وٹا —	هرن a deer,	هرنوٹا *hiranoṭá*, a fawn.
يل or يلا —	مور a peacock,	موريلا *morelá*, a pea-chicken.
يچه —	باغ a garden,	باغيچه *baghícha*, a kitchen-garden.

FEMININES FORMED FROM MASCULINES.

57. Names of males ending in ا *á* or ه *a*, of the third class, have the corresponding females in ـي *í*; as بيٹا *beṭá*, 'a son;' بيٹي *beṭí*, 'a daughter;' گهوڑا *ghoṛá*, 'a horse;' گهوڑي *ghoṛí*, 'a mare.' In a similar manner names of lifeless objects of the third class have sometimes a feminine form, generally significant of diminution, as گولا *golá*, 'a bullet;' گولي *golí*, 'a pill.' Substantives of the first and second classes form the corresponding feminine by adding either ـي *í*, ني *ní*, or ـن *in*, as follows:—

ملا *mullá*, a teacher,	ملاني *mullání*.
شير *sher*, a lion,	شيرني *sherní*.
مهتر *mihtar*, a sweeper,	مهترانی *mihtarání*.

براهمن *bráhman*, a Brahman, براهمِني *bráhmaní*.

سُنار *sunár*, a goldsmith, { سُنارِن *sunárin*, or سُنارِني *sunární*. }

a. A few are irregular in their formation; thus, from بهائي *bhá,í*, 'brother,' بہن *bahin*, 'sister;' بيگ *beg* or خان *khán*, 'lord,' بيگم *begam* or خانم *khánam*, 'lady;' راجا *rájá*, 'king,' رانِي *rání*, 'queen;' هاتِهي *háthí*, m. 'an elephant,' هتهِني *hathní*, f. In other cases, as باپ *báp*, 'father,' ما *má*, 'mother,' the words are totally different, as in our own language, and often taken from different tongues, as مرد *mard*, 'man' (Persian), عَورت *'aurat*, 'woman' (Arabic).

ADJECTIVES.

58. Adjectives are formed from substantives by the addition of certain terminations, most of which will be found in the following alphabetical list: their ordinary meaning will be obvious from the various examples; thus, by adding

ا to	بهُوكه hunger,	بهُوكها *bhúkhá*, hungry.
انه —	طِفل a child,	طِفلانه *tiflána*, childish.
اور —	زور strength,	زوراور *zor-áwar*, strong.
بند —	هتهيار arms,	هتهياربند *hathyár-band*, armed.
دار —	وفا fidelity,	وفادار *wafá-dár*, faithful.
زا —	ولايت foreign country,	ولايتزا *wiláyat-zá*, foreign-born.
سار —	كوه a mountain,	كوهسار *koh-sár*, mountainous.
گير —	دِل the heart,	دِلگير *dil-gír*, grieved.
گين —	غم sorrow,	غمگين *gham-gín*, sorrowful.
لا or لو —	پچها behind,	پچهلا *pichhlá*, hindermost.
مند —	دَولت wealth,	دَولتمند *daulat-mand*, wealthy.

نا to	دو two,	دُونا *dúná*, double.
ناک —	هَول terror,	هَولناک *haul-nák*, terrible.
و —	دِیدار view,	دِیدارو *dídárú*, slightly.
وار —	سوگ grief,	سوگوار *sog-wár*, grievous.
ور —	نام name,	نامور *nám-war*, renowned.
ه —	دوسال two years,	دوساله *do-sála*, biennial.
ي —	بازار a market,	بازارِي *bázárí*, of the market.
يل or يلا —	دانت tooth,	دنتيل *dantel*, tusked.
ين يِنه or يانه to	چوب wood,	چوبِين *chobín*, wooden.

فام *fám* and گُون *gún* are added to words to denote colour; as, زعفران فام *za'farán-fám*, 'saffron-coloured,' نِيل گُون *níl-gún*, 'blue-coloured.' كونا *koná* and گوشه *gosha* are added to numerals to express the figure of things; as, چَوكونا *chau-koná*, 'quadrangular, شش گوشه *shash-gosha*, 'hexagonal,' *etc.* وَش *wash* and وار *wár* are added to express likeness; as, برق وَش *bark-wash*, 'like lightning,' مردانه وار *mardána-wár*, 'like a brave man.'

a. Many adjectives are formed by prefixing certain words; as follows:—

ان to	ديكها seen,	انديكها *an-dekhá*, unseen.
با —	وفا trust,	باوفا *bá-wafá*, trusty.
بي —	صبر patience,	بيصبر *be-sabr*, impatient.
بد —	نام a name,	بدنام *bad-nám*, infamous.
غَير —	حاضِر present,	غَيرحاضِر *ghair-házir*, absent.
خِلاف —	عقل wisdom,	خِلاف عقل *khiláf-'akl*, foolish.
کم —	بخت fortune,	کم بخت *kam-bakht*, unfortunate.
لا —	چارہ help,	لاچارہ *lá-chára*, helpless.

نا to خوش pleased, ناخوش *ná-khush*, displeased.

هم — عمر age, همعمر *ham-'umr*, coeval.

59. In concluding our remarks on the derivation of words, we would particularly direct the student's attention to the various uses of the termination ـِي *í*. 1. It may be added to almost every adjective of the language, simple or compound, which then becomes the corresponding abstract substantive. 2. It may be added to all substantives denoting country, city, sect, tribe, physical substances, etc., which then become adjectives, signifying *of* or *belonging to*, or *formed from*, etc., the primary substantive. Lastly. It is used in forming feminines from masculines; and it is the characteristic of the feminine gender in all present and past participles, as well as in all adjectives purely Indian ending in ا *á*.

COMPOUND WORDS.

60. In all works written in the Urdu or mixed dialect of Hindústání, a vast number of compound words from the Persian may be met with in almost every page. These are generally formed by the union of two substantives, or of an adjective with a substantive. Many of them are given in dictionaries, but as there is no limit to their number, the student must not place much reliance on that source. A few weeks' study of Persian will make the matter clearer than any body of rules we could lay down on the subject; we shall therefore notice here only the more important compounds, referring the student for further information to our Persian Grammar, last edition.

SUBSTANTIVES.

a. A Persian or Arabic substantive with its regimen is of frequent occurrence in Hindústání; as, آبِ حَيات *áb-i-ḥaiyát*, 'water of immortality;' ديدۀ دانش *dída,i-dánish*, 'the eye of discernment;' رُوي زمين *rú-e-zamín*, 'the face of the earth.' In a similar form a Persian substantive with its adjective occasionally occurs; as, مردِ نكو *mard-i-nikú*, 'a good man;' عالمِ فاني *'álam-i-fání*, 'the perishable world.' These, when introduced into Hindústání, are viewed as single words, and form their various cases by adding the post-positions like nouns of the first or second classes; as, *áb-i-ḥaiyát ká*, *áb-i-ḥaiyát se*, etc.

b. A numerous class of Compound Substantives is formed by the mere juxta-position of two nouns; as, باوَرچِي خانه *báwar-chí-khána*, 'cook-house, or kitchen,' from باوَرچِي 'cook,' and خانه 'a house;' so, رَزْم گاه *razm-gáh*, 'the battle-field,' from رَزْم 'contest,' and گاه 'a place;' in like manner, جهان پناه *jahán-panáh*, 'the asylum of the world,' *i. e.* 'your majesty,' from جهان 'the world,' and پناه 'refuge;' so, روز نامه *roz-náma*, 'a day-book,' خِرَدْنامه *khirad-náma*, 'the book of wisdom,' etc. In compounds of this kind, the two words are generally written separate, though they may also be united into one. These are upon the whole like our own compounds, *book-stall*, *coffee house*, *newspaper*, etc., of which it is customary to write some with a hyphen between, others quite separate, and a few united into one word.

c. There is a class of verbal Nouns, not very numerous, consisting, 1st. Of two contracted infinitives, connected with the conjunction و; as, گُفْت و شنُود *guft o shanúd*, 'conversation,' literally, 'speaking and hearing;' آمد و رفْت *ámad o raft* or *ámad o shud*, 'coming and going,' 'intercourse.' 2ndly. A contracted infinitive, with the corresponding root; as جُسْت و جُو *just o jú*, 'searching;' گُفْت و گُو *guft o gú*, 'conversation.' The conjunction و in such cases is occasionally omitted; as, گُفْت گُو, آمد شُد, the same as آمد و شُد, *etc.*

d. There are a few compounds similar to the preceding, consisting of two substantives, sometimes of the same, and sometimes of different signification; as, مرْز و بُوم or مرْز و کِشْور *marz o búm* or *marz o kishwar*, 'an empire' or 'kingdom,' literally, 'boundary and region;' so, آب و هَوا *áb o hawá*, 'climate,' literally, 'water and air;' نشْو و نما *nashw o namá*, 'rearing *or* bringing up' (a plant or animal). In these, also, the conjunction و may be omitted, as نشْو نما, مرْز بُوم, *etc.*

e. Compounds purely Hindústání or Hindí are not nearly so numerous as those borrowed from the Persian; the following are occasionally met with: 1st. A masculine and feminine past participle, generally the same verb, though sometimes different; as, کہا کہِي *kahá-kahí*, 'altercation,' کہا سُنِي *kahá-suni*, 'disputation.' 2nd. Two nouns of the same, or nearly the same signification; as, نَوکر چاکر 'servants,' رِيت رسْم 'a custom *or* mode,' etc. Such expressions are very common in the 'Bágh o Bahár,' which is the standard work of the language. 3rd. Two words having something of alliteration about them, or a similarity of rhyme; as, دْھُوم دْھام 'hurly-burly,' شور زور 'uproar,' مکر چکر 'trickery,' *etc.*, all of which we should of course vote to be vulgarisms, only that they occur in the very best writers. Lastly, the Hindústání is particularly rich in imitative sounds, such as جھن جھن 'jingling,' سن سن 'simmering.'

f. Arabic phrases, such as we described in p. 19 (No. 18), are occasionally met with, such as مُسَبِّبُ ٱلْأَسْباب, 'the Causer of causes,' 'God,' *etc.*; but we believe that all such are explained in good dictionaries.

ADJECTIVES.

a. A very numerous class of epithets is formed by the union of two substantives; as, لاله رُخ *lála rukh*, 'having cheeks like the tulip;' پري رُوئي *párí-rú,e* or *parí-rú*, 'having the face of a fairy;' سنگ دِل *sang-dil*, 'having a heart like stone;' شكر لب *shakar-lab*, 'having lips (sweet) as sugar.' In English we have many instances, in the more familiar style, of this kind of compound; as, 'iron-hearted,' 'bull-headed,' 'lynx-eyed,' *etc.*

b. Another numerous class, similar to the preceding, is formed by prefixing an adjective to a substantive; as, خُوب رُوئي *khúb-rú,e*, 'having a fair face;' پاك رائي *pák-rá,e*, 'of pure intention;' تنگ دل *tang-dil*, 'distressed in heart.' We make use of many such compounds in familiar conversation and newspaper style, such as 'clear-sighted,' 'long-headed,' 'sharp-witted,' 'hard-hearted,' *etc.*

c. Perhaps the most numerous class of the epithets is that composed of verbal roots, joined to substantives or adjectives; as, عالم گِير *'álam-gír*, 'world-subduing;' فِتنه انگيز *fitna-angez*, 'strife-exciting;' جان آسا *ján-ásá*, 'giving rest to the soul;' دِل سِتان *dil-sitán*, 'ravishing the heart;' سُبُك رَو *subuk-raw*, 'moving lightly.' Our best English poets frequently indulge in compounds of this class; thus, 'the night-tripping fairy,' 'the temple-haunting martlet,' 'the cloud-compelling Jove,' *etc.*

d. A knowledge of these Persian compounds will be absolutely necessary, in order to peruse with any advantage the finest productions of the Hindústání language. The poets in general freely use such terms; nor are they of less frequent occurrence in the best prose works, such as the 'Bágh o Bahár,' the 'Ikhwánu-ṣ-ṣafá,' the 'Khirad

Afroz,' etc., for the thorough understanding of which, a slight knowledge of the Persian is absolutely requisite. In proof of this, we could point out many compounds which occur in our own selections from the 'Khirad Afroz,' not to be found in any dictionary, the meaning at the same time being quite obvious to any one who knows Persian. Such, for example, are مرہم بہا *marham-bahá*, 'medicine-money;' نفس کُشي *nafas-kushí*, 'mortifying of the passions;' صُوفِي مِزاج *ṣúfí-mizáj*, 'of philosophic disposition,'

e. We may reckon among the compounds such expressions as ما باپ *má-báp*, 'parents,' لاڑ کپُور *láṛ-kapúr*, 'Lár and Kapúr,' names of two brother minstrels who lived at the court of Akbar. It is barely possible that this may be an imitation of the Sanskrit compound called Dwandwa; though the probability is in favour of its being an idiomatic omission of the conjunction اَور 'and,' between two such words as are usually considered to be associated together. In works purely Hindí, translated from the Sanskrit, such as the 'Prem Ságar,' it is most likely that such phrases as نند جسودا *nanda-jasodá*, 'Nanda and Jasodá;' کرِشن بلرام *krishna-balarám*, 'Krishna and Balarám,' are boná-fide Dwandwas; but it would savour of pedantry to apply the term to such homely expressions as روٹي مکھن 'bread and butter,' or the very *un-classical* beverage commonly called برنڈِي پانِي, videlicet, 'brandy and water.'

SECTION V.

SYNTAX, OR THE CONSTRUCTION OF SENTENCES.

61. In all languages a simple sentence must necessarily consist of three parts, expressed or understood: 1st, a nominative or subject; 2nd, a verb; and 3rd, a predicate or attribute; as, 'fire is hot,' 'ice is cold.' In many instances the verb and attribute are included in one word; as, 'the man sleeps,' 'the horse runs,' 'the snow falls,' in which case the verb is said to be neuter or intransitive. When the verb is expressive of an action, and at the same time the sense is incomplete without stating the object acted upon, it is called an active or transitive verb, as, 'the carpenter made a table,' 'the masons built a church.' In each of these sentences it is evident that something is required beyond the verb to complete the sense, for if we merely said 'the carpenter made,' 'the masons built,' the hearer would instantly ask, 'made what?' 'built what?' In Hindústání and several of its kindred dialects, it is of the utmost importance that the learner should discriminate the active or transitive from the neuter or intransitive verb, in order that he may adopt that mode of construction peculiar to each. In a sentence whose verb is active or transitive, we shall designate the three parts as agent, verb, and object; thus, *the carpenter* is the agent; *made*, the verb; and *a table*, the object.

a. In the arrangement of the three parts of a sentence, different languages follow rules peculiar to themselves; for instance, in the sentence, 'the elephant killed the tiger,' the Latin, Greek, and Sanskrit languages have the option of arranging the words in any order. The Arabic and the Gaelic put the verb first, then the nominative, and lastly the object. The English and French follow the logical order as we have given it, and the Hindústání and Persian have also an arrangement of their own, which we shall now proceed to explain, as our first rule of Syntax or construction.

62. The general rule for the arrangement of the parts of a sentence in Hindústání is, first, the nominative or agent; secondly, the predicate or object; and, last of all, the verb; thus, آگ گرم هے *ág garm hai*, 'fire is hot,' پرهيز اچّهي دَوا هے *parhez achchhí dawá hai*, 'abstinence is good physic,' هاتهِي نے شير كو مار ڈالا هے *háthí-ne sher-ko már-ḍálá hai*, 'the elephant has killed the tiger.'

a. Though the above rule holds in short sentences, such as those we have just given, yet it is by no means of stringent application. In the first place, poets are freely allowed the proverbial license of the *genus;* that is, to adopt that arrangement of the words which best pleases the ear, or suits the metre. In prose, also, it may sometimes be more emphatic to put the object first; as, اُن بتُون كو تُو چُرا لايا 'thou hast stolen those images.' Sometimes the object is, for the sake of contrast or emphasis, put last, in the place usually occupied by the verb; as follows, جاهِل طلب كرّتا هے مال كو — اور عاقِل كمال كو 'the fool seeks for wealth, and the sage for excellence,' where *mál-ko* and *kamál-ko* are put last.

b. The Hindústání makes no difference in the arrangement of a sentence, whether it be interrogative or affirmative. In conversation, the tone of the voice, or the look, suffices to indicate whether or not a question is asked, and in reading it must be inferred from the context; thus, تُم جاوگے may signify 'you will go,' or 'will you go?' There are, however, several words which are used only in asking a question, such as those given in the middle column of p. 68. These, when used, come immediately before the verb, as تُم كهان جاوگے 'where will you go?' The word كيا is sometimes employed at the beginning of a sentence to denote interrogation, like the Latin *num* or *an*; as, كيا تم ني يهہ مثل نهين سني 'have you not heard this proverb?'

CONCORD OF ADJECTIVES WITH SUBSTANTIVES.

63. The adjective, as in English, generally precedes its substantive. If the adjective be capable of inflection, that is, if it be a purely Indian word ending in ا *á*, the following rule holds: The termination ا *á* is used before all masculine nouns in the nominative (or first accusative) case singular; the termination ي *e* is used before masculine nouns in any other case singular, or in the plural number; and the termination ـِي *í* is used before all feminine nouns, in any case, singular or plural; thus, وہ بهلا مرد هي *wuh bhalá mard hai*, 'he is a good man,' بهلي مرد سي *bhale mard-se*, 'from a good man,' بهلي مرد *bhale mard*, 'good men,' بهلي مردون سي *bhale mardoṅ-se*, 'from good men,' بهلِي عورت *bhalí 'aurat*, 'a good woman,' بهلِي عورتون كا *bhalí 'auratoṅ-ká*, 'of good women.'

a. The same rule applies to such adjectives in ان *áṅ* and ہ *a*, as admit of inflection; as, دسوان مرد 'the tenth man,' دسوين مرد كا 'of the tenth man,' دسوِين رات 'the tenth night;' so, بيچارہ مسافِر 'the helpless traveller,' بيچاري مسافِر كو 'to the helpless traveller,' بيچارِي رانِي 'the helpless queen.'

b. If adjectives, capable of inflection, be separated by means of the particle كو from the noun which they qualify, and united with the verb, they undergo no change; as, اسكي منهہ كو كالا كرو 'blacken his face;' but in this sentence *kálá-karná* is to be reckoned a compound verb (p. 66, *b*). Adjectives, ending with any letter except ا, ہ and ان, restricted as above, do not undergo any change;

as, پاك آدمي 'a pure man, پاك عورت 'a pure woman,' نا پاك چيز 'an unclean thing.'

c. As a general rule, adjectives, when followed by their substantives, never receive the nasal terminations (*áṅ*, *eṅ*, or *oṅ*) of the plural; and the same rule applies to such tenses as are formed of participles with or without an auxiliary verb, it being deemed sufficient to add the nasal *ṅ* to the last word only; as اچهي كتابين *achchhí* (not *achchhí,áṅ*) *kitáben*, 'good books;' بهلي آدميون ني *bhale* (not *bhaloṅ*) *ádmiyoṅ-ne*, 'by good men;' وي چلي جاتي رهتي تهين *we chalí játi rahtí thíṅ*, 'they (females) continued going along.' Sometimes, however, the participle takes the plural termination; as پهرتيان هين and كرتيان هين. When the adjective comes last (which may happen in verse), it sometimes receives the plural termination; as, راتين بهاريان 'heavy (tedious) nights.' (Yates's Grammar).

d. If an adjective qualify two or more nouns, some of which are masculine, and others feminine, the adjective is used in the masculine form, and the same rule applies to the participles and future tenses of verbs; as, اسكي ما باپ موئي هين 'his mother and father are dead;' اسني اپني بيتي بيتي كو موا ديكهكر كها 'he seeing his son and daughter dead, said,' etc. If, however, the substantives be names of inanimate things, the adjective generally agrees with that to which it stands nearest; thus, كپڙي باسن اور كتابين بهت اچهي هين 'the clothes, plates, and books are very good.'

CONCORD OF THE GENITIVE WITH ITS REGIMEN; ETC.

64. We have seen (p. 27, etc.,) that the genitive case has three distinct terminations, *ká*, *ke*, and *kí*, and the rule which determines the choice of these is exactly similar to that which regulates the termination of the

adjective; in fact, all genitives in Hindústání are *possessive adjectives*, subject to inflection, and, like adjectives, they are generally placed before the substantive which governs them. If the governing word be masculine and in the nominative case (or first form of the accusative) singular, کا *ká* is used, as, مرد کا گھر *mard-ká ghar*, 'the man's house,' or 'the house of the man,' مرد کا کُتا وفادار هَي *mard-ká kuttá wafádár hai*, 'the man's dog is faithful,' مرد کا کُتا مت مارو *mard-ká kuttá mat máro*, 'do not beat the man's dog.' If the governing word be masculine, and in an oblique case singular, or in any case plural, کي *ke* is used, as, مرد کي گھرسي *mard-ke ghar-se*, 'from the man's house,' مرد کي گھرون کو *mard-ke gharoṅ-ko*, 'to the man's houses.' Lastly, if the governing word be feminine, in whatever case or number, کِي *kí* is used; as, مرد کِي بيٹي *mard-kí beṭí*, 'the man's daughter,' مرد کِي کِتابين *mard-kí kitábeṅ*, 'the man's books.'

a. Although the general rule is to put the genitive case before its regimen, yet the reverse is of frequent occurrence, particularly in such works as have been translated or imitated from the Persian; as قَيد بدن کِي 'the thraldom of the body,' سِجّدہ شُکر کا 'the worship of thanksgiving.' We may here state that the Persian genitive is formed by placing the governing word first, having its last letter marked with the vowel *kasra*; as, گنجِ دانِش *ganj-i dánish*, 'the treasury of wisdom,' where the short vowel *i* is the sign of the genitive, similar in its use to our particle *of* in English. Persian words ending with ہ and ـِي take ٔ; and those ending with ا or و take ي for the sign of the genitive; as, بندۂ خُدا 'a servant of God,' هَواي بحر 'air of the sea.'

b. The genitive sign is employed *idiomatically* in such expressions as سب کا سب *sab-ká sab*, 'one and all,' کهیت کا کهیت *khet-ká khet*, 'the whole (field) of the field,' بات کِي بات *bát-kí bát*, 'mere talk;' and *adjectively* to convert a substantive into an attributive; thus, سوني کا تختہ *sone-ká takhta*, 'a golden plate,' or 'plate of gold;' بڑي سِر کا چهوکرا 'a boy with a large head.'

c. In some cases it is idiomatically omitted; as دریا کناري *daryá kanáre*, 'on the river bank,' for دریا کي کناري مين *daryá-ke kanáre-meṅ*, 'on the bank of the river.' It is also omitted in many expressions in which the governing words denote weight or measure; as, ایک سیر گوشت 'one pound of flesh,' ایک بِیگها زمین 'a bíghá of ground,' where the words are used merely in apposition, the same as in German.

d. The genitive is also used to signify possession, value, etc.; as, پادشاه کي ایک بیٹا تها *pádsháh*-KE [*pás* or *yaháṅ* understood] *ek beṭá thá*, 'the king had a son;' in like manner, اُسکي بهي ایک بیٹي تهي *us*-KE [*pás*, etc.] *bhí ek beṭí thí*, 'he had also a daughter;' ایک رُوپِیئي کا چاوَل *ek rúpí,e-ká cháṅwal*, 'one rupee's (worth of) rice.'

e. Compounds formed of two common substantives in English will in Hindústání be expressed by the genitive case; as لِکهني کِي میز *likhne-kí mez*, 'a writing-table;' کهاني کا وقت *kháne ká wakt*, 'dinner time;' and sometimes the genitive sign is used in Hindústání when in English it is inadmissible, as فِکر کا لفظ *fikr ká lafẓ*, 'the word FIKR.'

f. Instances sometimes occur in which a genitive case is used in consequence of a noun or preposition understood; such as تم اُسکي سُنو 'hear ye him,' *i.e.* اُسکِي بات 'his word;' so in the tale of the First Darwesh ('Bágh o Bahár,' p. 34,) we have اب هماري تُمهاري دوستي جانِي هُوئي (where the word بیچ or درمِیان is understood), 'between you and me there has arisen a sincere friendship.' The editors of a recent Calcutta edition have made an *amendment* here, by using *hamárí tumhárí!*

GOVERNMENT OF PREPOSITIONS, ETC.

65. The list of prepositions, page 71, beginning with آگي *áge*, etc., govern the genitive with كي *ke;* as گهر كي آگي *ghar-ke áge*, 'before (in front of) the house;' دريا كي پار *daryá-ke pár*, 'over (on the other side of) the river,' etc. The less numerous list, beginning with بابت *bábat*, etc., page 72, govern the genitive with كي *kí;* as, شهر كي طرف *shahr-kí taraf*, 'towards (in the direction of) the city.' All the prepositions may be optionally put before or after the word which they govern, their effect on the substantive, with few exceptions, remaining the same.

a. The prepositions being all substantives in an oblique case whose termination is (No. 64, *c*) idiomatically omitted, it is easy to see from what we have just stated why they should govern the genitive in *ke* or *kí*, but never in *ká*. There is however one peculiarity attending some of the feminine prepositions which custom seems to have established; though the *rationale* of it be not at all evident. We have excellent authority for saying that the words بمدد, بيمرضي, طرف, and مانند, when they precede the substantive, require the genitive in كي *ke;* and when they follow, they require كي *kí*. In the second volume of the 'Khirad Afroz,' p. 277, we have بمدد عقل كي *bamadad 'akl-ke,* 'by aid of the understanding.' In the 'Bágh o Bahár,'[1] p. 40, we have بي مرضي حضور كي

[1] Whenever reference is made to the 'Bágh o Bahár,' it is understood to be the edition recently edited by me, at the desire and expense of the Honourable the East-India Company. It is not only the cheapest, but in every respect the best work that the student can peruse, after he has gone through the Selections appended to this Grammar.—D. F.

be-marẓí ḥuẓúr-ke, 'without consent of her highness the princess;' and in page 188 of the same work, we have ايک طرف شہرکي *ek ṭaraf shahr-ke,* 'on one side of the city;' all of them with *ke* in every edition and copy, printed or manuscript. The wonder is, how it escaped the *critical amendments* of the Calcutta editors already alluded to; but so it has, for even *they* have here followed the established reading.

b. The preposition مانند *mánand* or *mánind* has been amply discussed by Dr. Gilchrist in several of his works, but it must be confessed that the learned doctor does not in this instance appear as a sound and fair critic. He assumes that one of the Munshís used *ke* instead of *ki* by *mistake,* and that he had sufficient influence with all the other learned natives of the country to make them take his part, and sanction the error. This argument is so very ridiculous that refutation is superfluous. Use is everything in language, and if in Hindústání custom has ordained that several of the prepositions when they precede the word which they govern, require the genitive with *ke,* and when they follow require *ki,* then it is the duty of the grammarian fairly to state the fact. It is quite probable that many instances of this mode of construction, in addition to those which we have shown above, may yet be detected.

c. The adverbs يہان 'here,' and وہان 'there,' govern the genitive with *ke,* like nouns or prepositions. When thus used, they convey idiomatically the signification of '*at, to,* or *in* the house of,' or 'in the possession of.' صاحِب کي يہان جاؤ 'go to the gentleman's house,' which is not unlike the use of the French particle *chez.* The prepositions پاس and نزديک are used in the same general sense as اسکي پاس 'near *or* with him,' and more generally 'in his possession,' '*chez lui.*' The word نزديک denotes idiomatically 'in the opinion of,' as عقلمندون کي نزديک 'in the opinion of the wise;' 'apud sapientes.'

d. Several of the prepositions, when they follow their substantives, may dispense entirely with the genitive signs *ke* and *kí*, thus shewing a tendency to become real postpositions; as, قاضِي پاس 'near *or* before the judge.' If the word they govern be a noun of the third class, or a pronoun, the inflected form remains the same as if *ke* or *kí* had been expressed; as, لڑکي پاس 'near the boy;' اُس بِنا 'without him *or* her;' and if the word governed be the first or second personal pronoun, when the genitive is thus dispensed with, the oblique forms *mujh* and *tujh* are used; as, مُجھ پاس 'near me;' تُجھ پاس 'near thee.'

DATIVE CASE.

66. The use and application of this case is very nearly the same as in most European languages. As a general rule, an English noun, governed by the prepositions *to* or *for*, will be expressed in Hindústání by means of the dative case.

a. The Hindústání dative sometimes corresponds with the Latin accusative, expressive of motion to a place; for instance, مَیں گھر کو چلُونگا 'I will go home,' 'ibo domum.' In this last sense also, the sign *ko* is often omitted, which brings it still nearer the Latin; as, مَیں گھر جاتا ہُون 'I am going home,' 'eo domum.' The dative case is also used to express time when; as, دِن کو 'by day;' رات کو 'by night;' شام کو 'at evening.' In such expressions the post-position *ko* is frequently and even elegantly omitted; as, ایک دِن 'one day;' and if the word expressive of time be accompanied by an adjective or pronoun subject to inflection, the inflected form of the latter remains the same as if *ko* had been expressed; as, اُس دِن 'on that day;' کِس وقت 'at what time?'

ACCUSATIVE CASE.

67. The accusative in Hindústání, as in English, is generally like the nominative, but when it is desirable to render the object of an active verb very definite or specific, then the termination *ko* (of the dative) is added to the object.

a. We believe this rule to be quite sound as a general principle, though by no means of rigid application. Many words are sufficiently definite from accompanying circumstances, such as an adjective, a genitive case, a pronoun, etc., so as not to require any discriminative mark. Others again, though sufficiently definite in themselves, generally require the particle *ko*; such are proper names, names of offices, professions, etc.; as, مانِک کو بُلاؤ 'call Mánik;' سرّدار کو بُلاؤ 'call the Sardár.' In these instances, however, the Hindústání assimilates with the Greek, which would employ the definite article in like cases.

b. The use of the particle *ko* to denote the object of an active verb forms one of the niceties of the Hindústání, which can only be arrived at by practice. A well-educated native, and many Europeans who have studied the language and associated much with natives, will without effort supply the particle *ko* in its proper place, and nowhere else. It follows then that there must be some principle to regulate all this, though it may be difficult to lay hold of, or to express within a short compass. The rule given by Muḥammad Ibráhím of Bombay, and we assuredly know of no better authority, is in substance the same as we have just stated.—*Vide* 'Tuḥfae Elphinstone,' page 80.

c. When a verb governs an accusative and also a dative, both being substantives, the first or nominative form of the accusative is generally used, as the repetition of *ko* in both cases would not only sound ill, but in many instances lead to ambiguity; thus, مرّد کو گھوڑا دو 'give the horse to the man.' If, however, it be deemed essential to add *ko* to the accusative, even this rule must give way; as in the following sentence : اُس ني اپني بهاءي كي حِصّي كو اُسكي بيبي كو دِيا 'he gave his brother's share to his (brother's) wife.' When the dative is a pronoun, the repetition of *ko* is easily avoided by using the termination *e* or *eṅ* for the latter ; as, قاضِي ني لڑكي كو اُسي سِپُرد كيا 'the judge gave up to her the child.'

ABLATIVE AND LOCATIVE.

68. The ablative denotes the source from which any thing proceeds; the locative, as its name imports, denotes situation. In their use and application, they generally correspond with the Latin ablative.

a. The ablative sign سي *se* signifies 'from' and 'with.' It is applied to the instrument *with which*, but very seldom to the agent *by whom*, any act is done, unless in connection with a neuter verb. *Example*: جلّاد ني قَيدِي كو تلوار سي مارا 'the executioner smote the prisoner *with* a sword.' In Dr. Gilchrist's Story-Teller (No. 97), we have an instance of *se* denoting the agent, the *only one* we have ever met with in our reading ; تُجهه سي رُوكهي روتِي كيُونكر كهاءِي گئِي تهِي 'how is it that stale bread was eaten by thee?' With a neuter verb *se* may be used to denote the source or origin of the event described ; as follows, كِسِي شاعِر سي كُچهه قُصُور سرزد هُوا 'by some poet (*or* through some poet) a fault took place.'

b. With the verb كهنا *kahná*, 'to say' or 'tell,' the particle سي *se* seems to be used idiomatically, and must often be translated in English by 'to ;' as, مَين اُس سي سچ كهتا هُون 'I am saying *to* him,' or 'telling him, truth ;' because the sentence مَين اُس كو سچ كهتا هُون will mean, 'I declare him (*or* her, *or* it) to be true,' or 'I call that truth ;' so اُسكو لوگ مرد نہين كهتي means 'people do not call him a man.' The use of سي *se* with كهنا therefore is obvious.

c. The locative sign مين *meṅ* generally denotes *in*, sometimes *to* or *into*; as, وُہ شہْر مین هَي 'he is in the city;' شہْر مین گیا 'he is gone to (into) the city.' The locative signs مین and پر have frequently the post-position سي joined to them; as, شہْر مین سي تلوار لایا 'he brought a sword from *in* the city;' وُہ اَپني گھوڑي پر سي گِر پڑا 'he fell down from *on* his horse.' Here the English idiom is 'from off' his horse, which is less logical.

CASE OF THE AGENT.

69. The case of the agent, characterized by the particle ني *ne*, is never used except with transitive verbs, and when used it is confined to those tenses only which are formed of the past participle (No. 40, page 55). The verb then agrees with the object in gender and number, unless it be deemed requisite to render the object definite by the addition of the particle کو *ko* (No. 67), in which case the verb remains in the simple form of the third person singular masculine.

a. In further illustration of this very simple rule, we here subjoin a sufficient number of examples; اُس ني ایک کُتا دیکھا 'he saw a dog,' or, literally, 'by him a dog (was) seen;' likewise, اُس ني تین گھوڑي دیکھي 'he saw three horses,' or, 'by him,' etc.; اُس ني ایک لومْڑي دیکھِي 'he saw a fox;' اُس ني بہُت لومْڑِیان دیکھِین 'he saw many foxes;' in all which phrases the construction agrees precisely with the Latin passive voice. Again, if it be deemed necessary or elegant to add *ko* to the object, then the verb will be always the same, that is, the masculine singular form; thus, هم ني کُتّي کو دیکھا 'we have seen the dog;' تُم ني گھوڑون کو دیکھا 'have you seen the horses?' جب اُس مرْد ني لومْڑي کو دیکھا 'when that man saw the fox;' هم ني لومْڑِیون کو دیکھا 'we have seen the foxes.'

The same rule applies to all the tenses into which دیکھا enters (page 55); as, اس نے ایک کتا دیکھا ہے 'he has seen a dog;' so, اس نے تین گھوڑے دیکھے تھے 'he had seen three horses.' As this is a subject of great importance in the language, we would advise the student to repeat each of the above phrases in all the tenses given in page 55.

b. It must be remembered that the case denoting the agent in the personal pronouns *I* and *thou*, are مین نے *main-ne* and تو نے *tú-ne* or تین نے *tain-ne;* as مین نے اسکو دیکھا 'I saw him (her *or* it);' تو نے یہہ مثل نہین سنی 'hast thou not heard this proverb?' If, however, the pronouns be followed by a qualifying word (substantive or adjective), the inflected forms مجھ *mujh* and تجھ *tujh* are used; thus, in the 'Bágh o Bahár,' page 20, مجھ فقیر نے ما باپ کے سائے مین پرورش پائی 'I poor (or wretched) obtained nourishment under the shelter of my parents.'

c. The student should endeavour to remember the limited and restricted use of this case of the agent. 1st. It is never used before a neuter or intransitive verb. 2nd. It is never used before any of the tenses formed from the root or from the present participle of any verb whatever. 3rd. It is never used before the verb بولنا *bolná,* 'to speak *or* say,' nor before لانا *láná,* 'to bring,' although they both seem according to our notion to be intransitive. *Bolná* appears to differ very little from کہنا *kahná,* which last requires the use of the agent with *ne.* The verb *láná* is a compound of *le-áná,* the last member of which is neuter or intransitive, and this leads us to a general rule, which is, that 'compound verbs, such as Intensives, of which the last member is neuter, though really transitive in signification, do not require the agent with *ne;*' thus, وے مسافر کھانی کو کھا گئے ہین 'those travellers have eaten up the dinner.'

d. When two sentences having the same nominative or agent are coupled by the conjunction اور *aur,* 'and,' the first of which has a neuter verb, and the following a verb transitive, it is not necessary to express the agent with *ne* in the second sentence, but the construction goes on the same as if *ne* had been expressed; thus, وُہ جھٹ پھر آئي اور کہا *wuh jhaṭ phir á,í aur* (*us-ne*) *kahá*, 'she quickly returned and said.'

e. This very peculiar use of the particle *ne* to denote the agent prevails, with slight modifications, throughout an extensive group of dialects spoken in Hindústán Proper. It is found in the Maráthí, the Guzerátí, and the Panjábí, in the West. In the Nepalese it assumes the form لي *le*; and it may be inferred that it prevails in most of the intermediate dialects of Hindí origin, amounting to nearly twenty in number. It does not exist in the group of dialects connected with the Bengálí, nor in those of the Deccan. In the grammars of the Maráthí language, it is called the *Instrumental case*, a term inapplicable in Hindí, as it never is used with the *instrument*, but solely with the *agent*. What is called the instrumental case in Sanskrit, is applied indifferently to the agent or instrument; but in the modern dialects above alluded to, particularly the Hindústání, *ne* is restricted to the agent only.

f. Our *great* grammarians have succeeded wonderfully well in mystifying the very simple (though singular) use and application of this particle *ne*. Dr. Gilchrist, in the first edition of his grammar, seems to have felt greatly embarrassed by it, without exactly knowing what to make of it. Those who have merely followed the learned doctor, with very few ideas of their own, have contented themselves by calling it an *expletive*, which luminous explanation has stood for years in one of the books hitherto read by beginners. Now, the term 'expletive' in philology is as convenient, in its way, as that of *the humours* in the jargon of quack doctors; it solves every difficulty, and forms a ready answer to all questions: it may mean anything or nothing. To account philosophically for the mode in which this particle is applied does not fall within our province; suffice it merely to say, that it is a form of construction very common in Sanskrit. With regard, however, to its practical use and application, we trust that all difficulty has been removed. The fact is, that the only real difficulty likely to arrest the progress of the learner consists, not in the use of *ne* to express the agent, but in that of *ko* to define the object of a transitive verb.

NUMERALS.

70. When a noun is accompanied by a numeral adjective, the plural termination *on* of the oblique cases is generally dispensed with. If the noun be of the third class, the inflected form in *e* is generally used.

a. Thus, تین سِپاهِي نے چار مرْد کو مارا 'three soldiers beat four men.' We have reason to believe that the addition of the termination *oṅ* would render the substantives more pointed or definite; thus, *tín sipáhiyoṅ-ne* would signify 'the three soldiers (aforesaid).' In the grammar prefixed to Dr. Gilchrist's Dictionary (London ed.), we have سَو گهوڑا نَوّاب کي یہان تها 'a hundred horses were at the Nawwáb's,' which ought to be translated 'a hundred horse,' *i. e.* 'a troop or collective body of one hundred,' whereas, 'a hundred horses,' or 'a hundred boys,' would be سَو گهوڑے and سَو لڑکے.

b. Collective numbers add *oṅ* to denote multiplication or repetition; as, سَیکڑون لڑائیان 'hundreds of battles;' ہزارون شہْر 'thousands of cities.' Any numeral by adding *oṅ* becomes more emphatic or definite; as, وے چارون شخْص 'those four persons.' Words expressive of time, as year, month, day, etc., add *oṅ* in the nominative plural; as, برْسون گذْرے 'years have passed away.'

c. In Hindústání the conjunction, etc., is idiomatically omitted in such phrases as دو تِین 'two (or) three,' دس بِیس '(from) ten (to) twenty.' A doubtful number is expressed by adding ایک to the numeral; as, دس ایک آدْمي 'about ten men;' سَو ایک برس 'about a hundred years.' To signify 'fold,' چند or گنا is added to numerals; as دوچنْد 'two-fold;' دس گنا 'ten-fold.' Distributives are formed by doubling the number; as, دو دو 'two by two,' or 'two apiece.' Thus, suppose we wish to say, 'give these men three rupees each,' or 'three rupees apiece,' the Hindústání will be اُن آدمِیون کو تِین تِین رُپئي دو 'to these men, *three three* rupees give.'

COMPARISON OF ADJECTIVES.

71. We have already observed that adjectives in Hindústání do not admit of comparison by any regular or systematic terminations. The comparative degree is indicated by merely putting the standard of comparison in the ablative, and the superlative by prefixing to that the word *sab*, 'all.'

a. The comparative and superlative are to be inferred in general from the context, as the adjective has only one form, that of the positive or simple word, thus سخِي سي سُوم بهلا جو تُرّت دي جَواب 'the miser is better than the liberal man if he (the miser) give an answer quickly.' It is obvious that if the standard of comparison should include the whole class spoken of, the adjective will express the superlative degree. *Ex.* سب هُنرون مين سي دو خُوب هَين 'of all accomplishments two are best' (viz. learning and the art of war).

b. To express the comparative degree, the particles اَور *aur*, and زِيادہ *siyáda*, 'more,' may also be employed exactly as in French and English; as, وي لوگ کُتون سي زِيادہ خراب هَين 'those people are worse than dogs.' The adjective is sometimes doubled to express the superlative degree; as, اچّها اچّها 'very good;' but the words most commonly used and prefixed for this purpose are بڑا 'great, very;' بہُت 'much;' حدّ 'beyond bounds;' نہايت 'extremely;' سخْت 'very' (generally in a bad or disagreeable sense); and سا 'most, very,' which last is added. It is to be further observed that

بڑا, though thus used apparently as an adverb, agrees in gender and number with the substantive; as, وُه بڑا خراب لڑکا هَي 'he is a very wicked boy;' and again, وُه بڑي خراب لڑکي هَي 'she is a very wicked girl.'

c. The particle سا *sá* (*se*, *si*), when added to a substantive, converts such substantive into an adjective denoting similitude; as, کُتّا سا ناپاک جانور 'a dog-like unclean animal.' When added to an adjective, it seems to render the same more intensive, though frequently it is difficult to find for it an equivalent English expression; as, تھوڑا سا پاني لي آؤ 'bring a little water;' بہُت سي ھتھیار وھاں تھي 'there were many weapons there.' When the comparison made by سا alludes to one thing out of many, it governs the genitive case; as in the sentence تُمھارا بِھي اُنہي کا سا جِسْم هَي 'you also have a body exactly like theirs;' شیرکِي سِي صُورت 'a form like that of a tiger.'

USE OF THE PERSONAL PRONOUNS.

72. The personal pronouns, as in Latin, are very often merely understood, particularly before such tenses of the verb as possess distinct personal terminations; and as a general rule, the pronouns need not be expressed when the sense is quite clear without them, except it be by way of contrast or emphasis.

a. When the third personal pronouns become the object of an active verb, they are generally used in the second (or dative) form of the accusative; as, اُسکو مارو 'beat him;' اُنکو بُلاؤ 'call them;' اِسي اُٹھا 'take this away.' If, however, they are employed as adjectives, along with their substantives, they may be used in the nominative form: as, تُم یِہ بات سُنتي هو 'you hear this word.' With the conjunctive participle, they are elegantly used in the nominative form; as, يہہ کہکر 'having said this.' Sometimes, though rarely, the nominative form may be used when a dative follows; as, مَین وُہ تُجھي دُون 'I will give that to thee.' When the first or second personal pronouns are governed by an active verb, the dative form is always used; as, وُہ مُجھي مارتا هَي or وُہ مُجھکو مارتا هَي 'he is beating me;' مَین تُجھي (تُجھکو) دیکھتا هُون 'I see thee.'

b. It may be observed that the personal, relative, and interrogative pronouns have two distinct terminations for the dative and accusative cases, viz. *ko* or *e* for the singular, and *ko* or *eń* for the plural. Hence, when an active verb governs an accusative (second form) and dative at the same time, it will be easy to avoid a repetition of the termination *ko* by employing *e* or *eń* in the one case, and *ko* in the other; thus, مَین اُسي تُمکو دُونگا I will give it to you; قاضِي نے لڑکي کو اُسي سُپُرد کِیا 'the judge gave up the child to her.' In sentences of this kind, the accusative is generally put before the dative, but not always; thus, in the 'Baitál Pachísí,' a very sagacious young lady says to her father, پِتا جو سب گُن جانتا هو مُجھي اُسي دِیجو 'O father, whosoever may be acquainted with all the sciences, give me to him,' or 'bestow me upon him in marriage,' but then, in another part of the same work, we have a similar expression differently arranged, as پِتا اُسي مُجھي دینا where the dative is placed first.

c. When the first and second personal pronouns are accompanied by a qualifying word, the genitive of the whole expression is made by *ká, ke, kí,* not *rá, re, rí,* and the pronouns are used in the inflected forms *mujh* and *tujh*; as, مُجھ فقِیر کا 'of me wretched;' تُجھ دانا کا 'of thee wise.' This oblique form is also used when the particle *sá, se, sí* is added to denote similitude; as, تُجھ سا عقلمند 'a sensible man like thee.'

d. In Hindústání, as in English, it is customary to address an individual generally in the second person plural, the singular being used in prayer to a deity, or to express familiarity or contempt; but in the vulgar tongue they go a step further, and the speaker uses the plural هم 'we,' when it really refers to no more than himself. This abuse has led to the nesessity of adding the word لوگ 'people,' to denote a genuine plural, as *ham log*, 'we (people),' *tum log*, 'you (people).' Thus, هم جانتي هَين 'I know' (literally 'we know'); and if a real plural is meant, then they say *ham log jánte hain;* so, کِتاب هم کو دو 'give me (us) the book.' To testify great respect, the third person must also be used in the plural when speaking of a king, saint, or any illustrious or respected man in general; as, وي سچ فرماتي هَين 'he is speaking truth' (literally, 'they,' *etc.*). When the plural is thus used for the singular, it is generally uninflected; but when a still higher degree of respect, or a more decided plural is intended, it receives the inflection; as, اُنهون ني کها 'they *or* he (his honour, majesty, etc.) said.'

e. This confusion of numbers may have given rise to the following idioms: هماري تُمهاري هاتهہ 'into our and your hands,' that is, 'into the hands of us two;' هم تُم چلينگي *ham tum chalenge*, 'we and you (*i.e.* I and thou) will go,' meaning, 'we shall go.' The speaker *politely* assumes precedence to himself; and when two different persons thus occur in a sentence, the verb agrees with the first person in preference to the second, and with the second in preference to the third; as, هم تُم جاوينگي 'we and you will go;' تُم وي جاؤگي 'you and they will go.'

f. We here subjoin the rules laid down by Muḥammad Ibráhím of Bombay respecting the *etiquette* to be observed in the use of the pronouns. "1. When the speaker and the person whom he addresses are of the same rank, each should speak of himself in the singular number, and address the other in the second person plural. 2. A person of superior rank may speak of himself in the plural number, but this is not considered to be polite, nor is it thought correct to address even the lowest rank in the singular number. 3. The pronouns of the third person may be used in the singular when speaking of any person in their presence, unless they be of superior rank, when they ought to be spoken of in the plural. 4. When one person of rank addresses another of the same or superior rank, or speaks of him in his presence, it is most correct to make use of the respectful pronoun آپ, or the great man's title, or some respectful phrase, as خُداوَنْد 'your honour,' حضرت 'honour, highness,' etc., and the like, with the third person plural (of the pronouns and verbs); and when an inferior addresses a superior, he ought at all times to use similar expressions of respect, suitable to the rank of the person addressed." We may further add, that an inferior at the same time speaks of himself in the third person singular, under the appellation of غُلام 'your servant' or 'slave;' فِدْوِي 'your devoted;' بنْده 'your bondsman;' مُخْلِص 'your sincere friend,' etc.

g. When a person relates the speech of another, he makes use of the identical words which the person whose speech is reported is supposed to have used. *Example*, He said he should go next day, اُس نے کہا کِہ مَیں کل جاؤنْگا (*lit.* 'he said, I will go to-morrow.') So in the sentence, He told me to go home, اُس نے کہا کِہ گھر جاؤ (*lit.* 'he said, go home.') This idiomatic use of the pronouns, and consequently of the persons and tenses of the verb, is well worthy of the student's attention. It is perhaps that point in which the Hindústání differs most widely from the English, as will be seen in the following sentence, which to save room we shall give in the Roman character. *Kal main-ne áp-ke beṭe-ko shahr-men dekhá, wuh yahán áyá-cháhtá thá tum-se milne-ko, par kahá ki ghoṛá merá mar-gayá, aur hamen ishára kiyá ki áp-se ẓáhir karná ki apní pálkí mere wáste bhej-dená; fi-l-ḥál jo tumhárí pálkí maujúd na ho, to mukhlis apní pálkí us-ke wáste bhej-degá.* 'I saw your son yesterday in the city, he wished to come here to see you, but mentioned that his horse was dead, and desired me to tell you to send your pálkí for him; if your pálkí be not now at hand, I shall despatch mine for him.' From the preceding sentence it will appear that considerable attention and experience will be necessary before the student can readily apply the pronouns agreeably to the rules of grammar, idiom, and *etiquette*, which last is a point of great importance among the Orientals.

USE OF THE POSSESSIVE 'APNÁ.'

73. When there occurs in the complement of a sentence a possessive pronoun belonging to the nominative or agent, such possessive is expressed in Hindústání by اپنا *apná* (*-ne* or *-ní*).

a. We may define the complement of a sentence in general, as that portion of it which in English follows the verb; thus, in the sentences, 'he returned to his house,' 'he was transacting his business,' the phrases 'to his house,' and 'his business,' form the complement. Again, in each of these, the possessive pronoun *his*, if it refers solely to the nominative *he*, will be expressed by *apná* in Hindústání; as, وُہ اپني گھر پھِر آیا and وُہ اپنا کام کرتا تھا; but if the pronoun *his* refers to another person, then it will be expressed by اُسکا *us-ká* (*-ke*, *-kí*); for instance, وُہ اُسکي گھر آیا 'he came to his house,' meaning not his own house, but the house of some other third person.

b. When the nominative of a sentence consists of the first or second personal pronoun, and its possessive occurs in the complement, the matter admits of no hesitation; as, 'I am going to see my father;' 'we have seen our new house;' 'you are destroying your health;' in all of which *apná* would be used for 'my,' 'our,' and 'your,' respectively. In the use of the third person, however, the English language is liable to an ambiguity, for example, the sentence 'he was beating his slave' has two meanings; it might be his *own* slave, or another man's. The Hindústání is much more explicit; 'his own slave' would be expressed by *apne ghulám-ko*, and 'another man's slave' by *us-ke ghulám-ko*; hence, as a practical rule, if the possessive in the complement of a sentence denotes *own*, it will be expressed in Hindústání by *apná* (*-ne*, *-ní*). Sometimes, *apná* is elegantly repeated, to denote separation or distinction; as follows, وي دونون اپني اپني گھر گئي 'they both went, each to his own house,' whereas *apne ghar* would merely denote 'their own house,' as common to both.

c. It is needless to add, that if a possessive pronoun occurs in the nominative part of a sentence, the use of *apná* is inadmissible; as, مَین اَور میرا باپ اپني مُلک مین جائینگي 'I and my father will go to our own country.' Here *maiṅ aur merá báp* is the nominative of the sentence, and *apne mulk meṅ* is the complement; in the former, the regular possessive *merá* is used, and in the latter, *apná*, according to our rule above stated.

d. When in the first clause of a sentence there occurs the conjunctive participle, the possessive in it will be *apná*; as مَین اپني باپ کو ساتهه لیکر اپني مُلک مین جاؤنگا 'I, having taken my father with me, will go to my own country.' Here, the use of *apná* is strictly according to rule, for the sentence is equivalent to 'I will take my father with me; and I will go to my own country.'

e. We occasionally meet with *apná* used irregularly instead of the other possessives; as, اپنا بهي مِزاج بهک گیا 'my own disposition even was led astray.' ('Bágh o Bahár,' p. 21.) In ordinary discourse, according to Dr. Gilchrist, we may hear such expressions as the following, namely, جو اپنا بیٹا ایسا کرتا 'if my son had done so.' Lastly, *apná* is used substantively in the general sense of 'one's people, friends,' etc., like the Latin expression 'apud suos;' thus, وُہ اپنون کي پاس آیا ـ پر اپنون ني اُسي قبُول نہ کیا 'he came to his own, but his own received him not.'

DEMONSTRATIVE PRONOUNS.

74. The demonstratives یہ *yih*, 'this,' and وُہ *wuh*, 'that,' together with their plurals, are sometimes used in the same sense as our definite article 'the.' They are applicable to both genders, and agree with their substantives in case, and generally in number.

a. We have seen it stated in some grammar, 'that a demonstrative pronoun in the singular may be used with an Arabic plural,' etc., from which the reader is left to infer that it is not used with any other plural. Now, the fact is, that *yih* and *wuh* are frequently used with any plural, and represent the plural even without the substantive; as, يِہہ دونون بهائي حاكِم كي پاس گئي 'these two brothers went to the magistrate;' and again, وُہ بہ طرِيق خيرات كي كُچهہ ديتي هَين 'they by way of alms give something.'[1] It would be needless to multiply examples, as they may be met with in any author. We have reason to believe, however, that when the singular is thus used, it is either to denote a collective group, or in a disrespectful sense; on a principle analagous to that of applying the plural to one person in order to denote respect or reverence.

INTERROGATIVES.

75. The interrogative كَون *kaun*, when used by itself, generally applies to persons, and كيا *kyá* to irrational or lifeless beings; but if the substantive be expressed, *kaun* will agree with it adjectively in case and number, whereas the inflection of *kyá* is never used adjectively.

a. For example, in the phrase كَون هَي 'who is there?' the inference is, 'what person?' so, كيا هَي signifies 'what (thing) is it?' At the same time we may not only say كَون مرد 'what man?' كِس مرد كو 'to what man?' but also كَون چيز 'what thing?' كِس چيز كا 'of what thing?' We can also say, كيا چيز 'what thing?' but we cannot say كاهي چيز كا to denote 'of what

[1] Here is another instance of a feminine preposition requiring the genitive in *ke*, agreeably to what we stated page 98, *a*. The example is from the 'Bágh o Bahár,' p. 144. It is the reading of half-a-dozen different copies (two of them manuscript), as well as of the Calcutta edition, 1836, printed in the Roman character.—D. F.

thing.' The oblique form *káhe* is used only as a substantive; as, کاهي كِي گهڑي 'a watch of what (substance, etc.)?' the answer to which may be سوني كِي 'of gold,' etc. Sometimes *kyá* is applied to a person or thing by way of exclamation; as, كِيا حرامزاده 'what a rogue!' كِيا بات 'what an affair!' When *kyá* is repeated, it seems to convey the idea of 'what various?' as, كِيا كِيا عجائِب 'what various wonders?' Sometimes, *kyá* is used as a conjunction, meaning 'whether,' 'or;' like the Latin '*sive*;' as, كِيا باغ كِيا كهيت مين 'whether in the garden or in the field.'

b. The interrogative is used for the relative in such sentences as مَين جانْتا هُون كِه كَون هَي 'I know who it is.' Also adverbs derived from the interrogative (*vide* page 68) are in a similar manner substituted for those from the relative; for instance, مَين نہِين جانْتا هُون كِه وُه كب جاٸيگا 'I do not know when he will go.'

c. Sometimes a question is used to denote negation or surprise; as, اِتْنا مُلْك جو لِيا تيري كِس كام آويگا 'all the territory which thou hast taken will be of no use to thee;' literally, 'of what use will it be to thee?' and again, كہان راجا كا بيتا كہان يِہ شُہره 'where is the king's son? and where this report?' meaning 'the king's son has nothing to do with this report.'

RELATIVE AND CORRELATIVE.

76. Strictly speaking, the Hindústání does not possess a relative pronoun corresponding with our 'who,' 'which,' and 'that,' and as this want is a source of much perplexity to the learner, we shall endeavour in the following paragraphs to explain fully how the place of the relative is supplied.

a. In page 38 we have given the declension of جو and سو which from want of a better term we called *relative* and *correlative,* respectively. The word جو signifies 'he who,' 'she who,' or 'that which,' and refers, not to an antecedent, like our relative 'who,' but to a noun following, like our words 'whosoever,' 'whatsoever,' 'whoso.' Hence جو usually begins the sentence, and is followed in a second clause by سو and the use of the two together generally forms a substitute for our relative pronouns 'who,' 'which,' and 'that,' as will be seen by the following examples; جو گھوڑي تُم ني بھيجي تھي - سو راجا ني بہُت پسنْد کِئي 'the king much approved of the horses which you sent,' literally, 'what horses you sent, the king much approved of the same;' جو تُم ني کہا هَي ـ سو سب سچ هَي 'that is all true which you have said,' literally, 'whatever you have said, that is all true.' In like manner, the relative and correlative adverbs usually accompany each other; جہان گنْج تہان مار - جہان پھُول تہان خار 'where the treasure is, there is the snake; and where there is a flower there is a thorn.'

b. Sometimes, the remote demonstrative may be used instead of the correlative, both pronominally and adverbially; as follows, جِسْکِي ديغ اُسْکِي تيغ 'he who has the pot has the sword' (he who pays best, is best served); جَيسا دوگي وَيسا پاٶگي 'as you shall give, so shall you get.' In the following sentence, the demonstrative adverb وهان is used; whereas in a few sentences before, the author uses the correlative تہان for the same expression (*vide* Selections in Devanágari, page 8, lines 3 and 10); جہان نِنانَوي گھڑي دُودْه کي هونْگي ـ وهان ايکْ گھڑا پانِي کا کيا جانا جايگا 'where there shall be ninety-nine pitchers of milk, how will a single pitcher of water be there discovered?' We may here at the same time see the negative effect of the question, as the speaker means that 'there is no chance of detecting one pitcher full of water among ninety-nine of milk.'

c. The conjunction كه frequently accompanies the relative, and sometimes occupies its place entirely; as in the phrases, جو اذيت كه هم كو پهنچي هَي خاطِر مين نه لاوين 'let us not bring into mind the trouble which has come upon us;' so also, دانا وُه هَي كه كام سي پهلي انجامِ كار كو سوچي 'he is a wise man, who, before the commencement, thinks of the end of his work;' وُه شخص كه جِس ني خط لِكها 'the man who wrote the letter.' Sometimes, the demonstrative is substituted, in imitation of the Persian; thus, بُتخانه هَي كه اُس مين كَئي بُت سوني كي هَين 'there is a temple in which there are several idols of gold.'

d. In many instances the relative جو corresponds with our 'who,' 'which,' or 'that,' but the student must be careful not to consider this as a rule, for it is only the exception; as follows, دو روٹي جو بيٹي كهاتي هَين 'the two loaves which my children eat.' Here the word جو is not put first, because there is another word دو already used to define *roṭí*; but suppose the sentence were 'the bread which I ate was very good,' we should have to say in Hindústání, '*jo roṭí main-ne khá,í, so* (or *wuh*) *bahut achchhí thí.*'

INDEFINITES.

77. The indefinite كوئي *ko,í*, 'somebody' or 'anybody,' when used alone, refers to a person, whereas كچه *kuchh*, 'something,' 'anything,' refers to matter in general. As an adjective, however, *ko,í* may agree with any substantive, as, كوئي آدمي 'any *or* some man,' كوئي چيز 'any *or* some thing.' كچه is seldom applied to persons in

the nominative, but in the oblique cases; *kisí* or *kisú* seems to be equally applicable to persons or things.

a. The indefinites *ko,í*, and *kuchh*, as well as the numeral ایک *ek*, 'one,' frequently supply the place of our articles 'a,' 'an,' or 'a certain;' as, ایک دانشمند کِسي شہر مین وارِد ہُوا 'a sage arrived in a certain city;' کِسي وقت ایک شیر بیمار پڑا 'on a certain time a tiger fell sick.' The indefinite article frequently occurs more than once at the beginning of a story, and it is a point of good taste to use *ko,í* and *ek* alternately, as in the preceding examples, so as to avoid the clumsy repetition of the same word. The emphatic particle ـِي *í* or هِي *hí* may be affixed to many of the pronouns; as, آپ هِي 'my (your, etc.) own self;' یِہِي 'this same;' وُهِي 'that same.' Also in the oblique cases اُسِي, اِسِي etc., as in اُسِي کو, اِسِي کو 'to this *or* that self-same person *or* thing.' Sometimes هِين is added with the same effect.

CONCORD OF THE VERB WITH THE NOMINATIVE.

78. As a general rule, the Hindústání verb agrees with its nominative in number, person, and gender, subject, however, to the following exceptions: 1. To mark respect, a singular nominative has a verb in the plural; 2. If the nominative consist of different irrational objects in the singular number, they may take a singular verb; 3. If the nominatives be of various genders, the verb takes the masculine form, or agrees with that next to it; Lastly. If the verb be transitive, and in any tense formed of the past participle, the nominative assumes the case of the agent, and the verb follows a special rule already illustrated, p. 103, No. 69, etc.

a. We shall here add a few examples in illustration of the preceding rule, embracing, as it does, the whole subject of verbal concord, which differs in some respects from that of the European languages. Thus, وُہ لِکھتا ہَي 'he is writing;' وُہ ناچتي ہَي 'she is dancing;' وي بولتي ہَين 'they (males) are talking;' and وي گاتي ہَين 'they (females) are singing.' The following examples refer to the exceptions: 1. بادشاہ دیکھکر آبدیدہ ہُوي 'the king having seen (this), became tearful,' or 'wept;' where the verb ہُوي is plural, expressive of respect to 'the king,' which is in the singular nominative. In like manner we have مُناسِب نہین کِہ جہان پناہ عاجِزي کرین 'it is not proper that your majesty should submit.' 2. In the following sentences we have two nouns in the singular number, coupled by a conjunction, whilst the verb is in the singular, agreeing with the nearest noun; as, ابھِي بَیل اَور گھوڑا پہنچا ہي 'the bullock and horse have just now arrived;' جن ڈھن اَور راج میرا کیون نہ سب گیَا آج 'my people, my wealth, and my kingdom, why are they not all gone (from me) this day?' 3. Several nouns of different genders occur in the next two sentences, but the verb takes the masculine plural in preference to the feminine; as, اُسکي ما باپ بھائِي تینون اُسکي شادِي کي فِکر مین تھي 'her father, mother, and brother, were all three meditating the accomplishment of her marriage;' اُسکي ہاتھِي اُونٹ گاڑِي لادي جاتي ہَین 'his elephant, camel, and carriage are being loaded.'

GOVERNMENT OF VERBS.

79. In this department the Hindústání differs very little from the English. Actives or transitives naturally govern the accusative case, which, as we have shewn, is generally like the nominative, and sometimes like the dative (*vide* p. 101, No. 67.)

a. Causal verbs, verbs of clothing, giving, etc., may be considered as governing two accusative cases, or the accusative and the dative; as, لڑکي کو کہانا کہِلاکر گھر جاؤ 'having given the child food, go home;' اُسکو ايک رُوپيه دو 'put on him these clothes;' and اسي يِہ کپڑا پہنا؛ 'give him a rupee.'

b. Some neuter verbs, as آنا 'to come,' بنْنا 'to become,' بھانا 'to suit,' پڑنا 'to fall,' پہنچنا 'to arrive,' بھنْنا 'to become,' چاہْنا 'to be desirable,' رہْنا 'to remain,' سُوجھنا 'to appear,' لگنا 'to unite,' مِلْنا 'to meet, to occur,' and ھونا 'to be,'. govern the dative case, and are frequently used impersonally; as follows, مُجھي رحْم آتا ھَي 'I feel compassion;' مُجھي اِس بات مين شُبْہہ ھَي 'I have some doubt in this matter;' ھمکو چاھِئي که وھان جاوين 'it is desirable that we should go there.' We may here observe that the form چاھِئي from *cháhná*, is frequently used impersonally in the sense of 'it is proper,' 'it is fit;' like the Latin 'decet,' 'oportet.' When thus employed, governs the dative of the person, and either the past participle or the aorist of the accompanying verb, as in the preceding example, which might also be expressed ھم کو جايا چاھِئي 'we must go.' Sometimes, it may be used personally; as, تُم کو کْيا چاھِئي which may mean 'what is proper for you,' or 'what do you require,' etc. We could in this way say تُمکو وھان جانا چاھِئي 'you must go there,' or 'to go there behoveth you.'

c. Verbs meaning 'to sell,' or implying 'gain,' have هاتھ 'hand,' connected with them; as تُمْني کِسْکي هاتھ بيچا هَي 'to whom have you sold it?' وُہ کام بہُت مِحْنت سي هاتھ آيا 'that business was accomplished with great difficulty;' in like manner, اُسْکا ايک پھُول تُحْفه هاتھ آيا 'he gained a flower as his prize.' In such expressions the word هاتھ is used in the sense of 'possession.'

d. Verbs which in English require 'with,' 'from,' or 'by' after them, govern the ablative, and those which require 'in,' 'within,' 'into,' the locative case; as in the following sentence: بِہتر یِہہ هَي کِہ اُسکِي دوستِي کي وسِيلي سي دُشمنون کِي هاتهہ سي چهُوٹون 'this is better, that by means of his friendship I should escape from the hand of my enemies;' in like manner وُہ اپني گهرمين جاکر دِل مين سوچني لگا 'going into his house, he began to think within himself.' Verbs of fear and caution require the ablative case; as, شايد وُہ تُم سي ڈرتا هَي 'perhaps he is afraid of you;' عاقِل حرامزادون سي خبردار رهتا هَي 'the sage keeps on his guard against reprobates.'

TENSES OF THE ROOT.

80. We have already given the general signification of each tense, in the various paradigms of the verb, pp. 44 to 59. We shall now, following the same order, briefly notice such peculiarities as some of them present. The reader will recollect that they are three in number —the aorist, future, and imperative, of which the aorist is the most important, on account of its extensive use and application.

a. The *Aorist* generally corresponds with the present subjunctive of the Latin, or what in English grammar goes under the name of 'present potential'; hence the conjunctions کہ and تاکہ 'that,' اگر and جو 'if,' اگرچِہ 'although,' جب تک 'until,' and مبادا 'lest,' generally require the use of this tense after them; as, اگر مَين چاهُون کِہ جب يک مَين آؤن وُہ ٹهہري تو تُجهي کيا 'if I desire that he should stay till I come, what is it to thee?' It further implies possibility or obligation; as in the sentences, آج جو کُچهہ هو سکي وُهي کرو 'whatever it may be possible to do to-day, that do;' همين اُميد هَي کِہ يِہہ کام سرانجام هووي 'our hope is that this business may be brought to a conclusion;'

جو بادشاہ ایلچي کِسي جگه بهیجي — چاهِئي که وُہ اپني قوم مین سبسي دانا اور زبان آور هو 'if a king sends an ambassador to any place, it is desirable that he should be the wisest and the most eloquent man of his tribe.' When the power of doing a thing is designed to be expressed, the verb سکنا 'to be able,' is used in all its parts, with the root (or sometimes the inflected infinitive) of the principal verb; as, وُہ جا نہین سکتا هَي or less frequently, وُہ جاني نہین سکتا هَي 'he cannot go.'

b. The aorist is very frequently employed to denote present time when general and unrestricted, hence it is used much in proverbial expressions, with which the language abounds; as, پاپي کا مال اکارته جائي 'the wealth of the wicked goes for nought.' It also expresses time future or past, conditionally; as, اگر پاوي گلي تیري تو بُلبُل گُلستان بهولي 'if the nightingale find thy abode, then will the rose-garden be forgotten;' or, 'if the nightingale found thy abode, then would the rose-garden be forgotten.' On the subject of this tense, Muhammad Ibráhím has given several sound remarks in his grammar, already alluded to; p. 59, etc. He gives it the name of 'future of the subjunctive or potential mood.' We have discarded the term *mood* altogether, as utterly inapplicable to the Hindústání language, and infinitely more perplexing than useful. Lastly, the aorist is sometimes accompanied by the present auxiliary tense هُون, etc., page 43, the precise effect of which it is difficult to determine; as, مَین کہُون هُون 'I may speak;' جسودا کہي هَي 'Jasodá is *or* may be saying.'

c. The Future presents few peculiarities, save that in respectful language it is often employed for the imperative, and occasionally for the aorist; as, صاحِب عنایت کرکي مُجهي ایک کِتاب دینگي 'have the kindness, Sir, to give me a book;' so, likewise,

مَين سمجھتا ھُون کِه جو کُچھ وي کہتي ھَين سو حسد سي ھوگا 'I am thinking that whatever they say may be from envy.' Our *Second Future* or *Future Perfect* is formed by the future of چُکنا 'to finish,' to the root of the verb; as, مين کہا چُکونگا 'I shall have eaten,' وُه کہا چُکيگا 'he will have eaten,' etc.

d. The *Imperative* is confined in its application, strictly speaking, to the second person, singular and plural. The honorific form addresses itself as to a third person by way of respect; as, چُپ رهو 'be silent;' اِدھر آؤ 'come hither;' ھمکو مُعاف کِيجِئي pardon me,' or 'may he pardon me.' It is not considered polite to use the second person singular of the imperative to any one, however low his condition. The adverb مت is applicable to the imperative mood alone, نه is applied to it in common with the other modes, نہين is never used with it; as, مت بھولِيو or بِھُولِيو مت 'don't forget;' اَيسا نکر 'don't do so.' The imperative mood is sometimes used idiomatically, as in the following expressions: ھو تو ھو 'perhaps it is,' or 'it may be;' آؤ تو آؤ 'come, if you mean to come.'

TENSES OF THE PRESENT PARTICIPLE.

81. Of these, the Indefinite claims most attention. The name and signification given to it in most grammars, is 'Present Indefinite Tense.' The epithet of *present* is misapplied, as the tense generally refers to the *past.*

a. Among the tenses of the present participle, the *Indefinite* holds the same rank that the aorist does in those derived from the root. Its most ordinary significations are, first, to denote *conditional past time,* in which case it is generally preceded by اگر or جو 'if,' and followed by تو 'then;' as in the sentences, اگر وُه آتا تو کُچھ نقّصان نه ھوتا 'if he had come, then there would have been no loss;' جو مین کہتا تو میري بات نه سُنتا 'if I had spoken, he would not have regarded what I said,' or 'if I should speak, he would not regard.' So in the 'Bágh o Bahár,' p. 71: بڑھیا بولِي کِه اگر هماري دِن کُچھ بهلي آتي - تو حاتِم کو کہین هم دیکھ پاتي - اَور اُسکو پکڑکر نوفل کي پاس لیجاتي - تو وُه پانچ سَو اشرفِي دیتا - اور هم آرام سي کهاتي - اِس دُکھ دهندهي سي چھوٹ جاتي 'If our days were at all lucky, then we should have somewhere found Ḥátim, and having seized him, we should have carried him to Nauful, then he would have given five hundred ashrafís,' *etc.* The conjunction is frequently omitted in the former or latter part of the sentence, and sometimes in both; as, اگر مَین جاتا اُسي خُوب مارتا or مین جاتا تو اُسي خُوب مارتا 'had I gone, I should have beaten him soundly;' in like manner, مَین هوتا گهوڑا چھوٹني نه پاتا 'had I been present, the horse should not have been allowed to escape.'

b. In the second place, the indefinite is employed to denote continuative past time, or to express an act or event that was habitual; as the reader may observe in the following passage: جب جُوارِي جِیتتا تب ایَسا غافِل هوجاتا کِه کوئِي اُسکِي کپڑي اُتار لیتا تَوبهِي اُسي نه معلوم هوتا 'When the gamester used to win (*jittá*) he used to become (*ho-játá*) so careless, that any one might take off (*utár-letá*) his clothes; then even it would not be (*na hotá*) known to him.' In like manner, 'Bágh o Bahár,' p. 9: سارِي رات دروازي گهرون کي بند نه هوتي - اَور دُوکانین بازار کِي کهُلِي رهتِین - راهِي مُسافِر جنگل مَیدان مین سونا اُچھالتي چلي جاتي - کوئِي نه پُوچھتا 'All night the doors of the houses used not to be fastened, and the shops of the market used to remain open; the travellers used to go along,' etc.

c. The indefinite is occasionally used for the present by omitting the auxiliary; as, وه كيا كرتا 'what is he doing?' The student must be careful, however, *not* to fancy that this tense corresponds with our present indefinite, as some of our grammars inculcate. Its use as a present tense is the exception, not the rule.

d. The *Present Tense* is used both to express the precise point of time when the action takes place, and also to denote a continuous or habitual state of action; hence it corresponds with both our forms of the present tense; as, وه گهر جاتا هي 'he is (now) going home;' but in the sentence وه رات كو هميشه گهر جاتا هي it must be translated, 'he always goes home at night.' The present is frequently used for the future, when it is meant that the action will be done quickly; as, مين جلد كهانا لاتا هون 'I am bringing (shall bring) the dinner quickly.'

e. In vivid descriptions, when the narrator represents a past occurrence in the same manner as he or the person of whom he speaks originally saw it, and as if it were still apparent to the view, the present is frequently used; as in the following passage: جب اس درخت كي پاس پهنچا ديكها كه هر ايك ڈالي مين اسكي سيكڑون سر آدميون كي لٹكتي هين ـ اور اسكي نيچي ايك تالاب نهايت خوش قطعه ملتب هي ـ اور اسي كا پاني جنگل كي طرف چلا جاتا هي 'When he arrived at the tree, he saw that on every branch of it *are hanging* hundreds of human heads; and under it *is* a beautiful tank full of water, and the stream of it *is flowing* towards the desert.' In such instances the past tense may be used, but it is less animated and impressive; as وه اس درخت كي نزديك گيا تو كيا ديكهتا هي كه اسكي تلي ايك سل سنگ مرمر كي ڈهري هي 'he went near the tree, and what does he see but a marble slab *was* placed at the bottom of it.'

f. The *Imperfect* denotes a past action in progress, and corresponds with our own compound tense formed in a similar manner; as, وُہ لکھتا تھا 'he was writing.' In most of our English grammars, the Indefinite Past Tense, such as 'he wrote,' 'he spoke,' is very improperly called the Imperfect. It is needless to state that these expressions in Hindústání must be rendered by اُسنی لِکھا and اُسنی کہا that is, the simple past, of which we shall say more immediately.

g. The tense called the *Present Dubious* (page 51) is generally employed to denote a future action of uncertain occurrence; as, مَین مارتا ہوُون '(perhaps) I may beat,' or 'be beating;' or ہوُونگا so in 'Bágh o Bahár, p. 38: وُہ اپنی جِي مين كيا كہتا ہوگا 'What will he (or may he) saying in his own mind?'

TENSES OF THE PAST PARTICIPLE.

82. The main peculiarity in the use of these is, that when the verb is transitive, the nominative must be put in the case of the agent, as explained p. 103, etc.

The *Past Tense* corresponds with what is improperly called the imperfect in most English grammars; as, وُہ چلا گَیا 'he went away;' تُم نی لِکھا 'you wrote;' which expressions, though indefinite as to time, convey the idea of a complete or perfect action; hence the absurdity of calling it the imperfect tense. In addition to its common acceptation, it is sometimes used with a present, and sometimes with a future meaning; as in the following: جو وُہ مِلِي تو هماري جان رِهي نہِين تو گَئِي 'if she is found, then my life remains; if not, it is gone;' جو بويا سو كاٹا 'what he sows, that he reaps.' We have already stated that the present is sometimes used for the future to denote speed; the past is employed for the same purpose. Thus a man says to his servant, پانِي لاؤ

bring water,' and the answer will probably be لايا خُداوند 'I have brought it, Sir,' meaning, 'I will bring it immediately.' It is sometimes applied in an idiomatical manner, ; as, هُوا تو هُوا 'if it be so, why be it so.'

b. The verb 'to be' has, in Hindústání, two tenses expressive of the past, viz. تها 'was,' and هُوا 'was' (or 'became'), which may often be translated by the same word in English. In many cases these appear to be synonymous in their application ; the student, however, must pay particular attention to the following rule. تها is used in reference to simple existence at a distant time or particular place, while هُوا is applied to time or circumstances less remote, in the sense of 'became ;' as follows : اُس مُلك مين ايك پادشاه تها 'there was a king in that country ;' وُه حيران هُوا 'he was (became) confounded.' In short, تها denotes permanent existence, and هُوا that which *was*, or *became* existing, through circumstances generally stated in, or easily inferred from the context.

c. The *Perfect* answers to the Perfect tense in English, being used to denote an action newly past and finished ; as follows, ميرا بهائي پهنچا هي 'my brother has arrived ;' مين ني پهل كو كهايا هي 'I have eaten the fruit.' Sometimes it is used with adverbs of time, in a manner that cannot literally be rendered in English ; as مين كل وهان گيا هُون 'I have gone there yesterday,' for 'I went there yesterday.' In this case, the usage of the French 'je suis allé,' would have come nearer the Hindústání.

d. The *Pluperfect* in English will generally be expressed by the Pluperfect in Hindústání, representing a thing not only as past, but as prior to some other event ; as in the sentence, اُسكي پهنچني كي آگي مين ني خط لكها تها 'I had written the letter previous to his arrival.' But the converse of this rule does not hold, the pluperfect being frequently used in Hindústání where in English we employ the simple past; thus in Story 16, a learned Káyath orders his slave to get up during the night, and see if it rains. The slave, feeling himself very comfortable where he is, concludes, without getting up, that it does rain; and gives the following ingenious process of reasoning: بِلّي آئي تِهي ـ مَين ني اُسْكو ٹٹولا تها ـ بهيگِي تِهي 'the cat came in, I put my hand upon her, she was wet' (*ergo*, it rains); but the literal meaning is, 'the cat had come in, I had put my hand upon her, she had got wet.' The general rule is, that when one definite past even precedes another past event in point of time, the former is expressed in the pluperfect. It may happen that the latter of the two events is not expressed, but merely passing in the speaker's mind; as in the above example, where the slave might have added, as he no doubt meant, 'thence, I have ascertained that it is raining,' which would have completed the chain of reasoning.

e. The tense called the *Past Dubious* (p. 51), formed of the past participle and the aorist or future of هونا is used to express remote probability past or future; as in the following examples: مَين نه جانْتا هُون كِه وُه كهان گيا هوگا 'I know not where he may (or will) have gone;' پنْتهه مين تُم ني بهُت كشْٹ پايا هوگا 'on the way, you must have met with much difficulty.' The *Past Conditional* (p. 51.) is of very rare occurrence, and is understood to express the event in a more remote manner than the Indefinite (p. 45); thus, اگر مَين ني پِنْجڑا كهولا هوتا تو وُه اُڑ جاتا 'if I had opened the cage, then it would have flown.' A kind of expression like the *Paulo-post-futurum*, is expressed by چاهْنا 'to desire,' with the past participle of another verb; as, وُه مرا چاهْتا هَي 'he is about to die,' 'is dying,' or 'will soon die.' There are also other ways of expressing the same idea: thus, وُه مرْني كا هَي or وُه مرْني والا هَي or وُه مرْني پرهَي.

INFINITIVE.

83. The infinitive is used as a substantive to denote the state or action of the verb; it is frequently used for the imperative, and occasionally it is employed adjectively in connection with another substantive.

a. All *Infinitives* used as substantives or adjectives are subject to inflection like nouns of the third class; thus, اُسکا جانا مُناسِب هَي 'his departure is proper;' اِنْتِقام لينے کا يہي وقت هَي 'this is the very time for taking revenge;' وُہ گهر ديکهنے کو آيا or وُہ گهر ديکهنے کي واسطي آيا 'he has come to see the house.' The infinitive is often used as an imperative, and as such it may even have the negative *mat* before it; as, هرگِز قسم نکهانا 'swear not at all;' وهان مت جانا 'don't go there,' or 'you must not go there.' Sometimes it is used with the verb هونا, instead of the regular tenses of the verb which it represents; as follows, کِس مُلک سي آنا هُوا 'from what country are you come?' instead of کِس مُلک سي آئي هو. It is also used with the verb 'to be,' like the Latin gerund, to denote necessity or obligation; as, تُم کو وهان جانا هوگا 'you must go there;' so, likewise, آخِر ايک روز مرنا هَي ـ اَور سب کُچه چهوڑ جانا هَي 'one must die (*moriendum est*) some day at last, and must give up every thing.'

b. Sometimes the infinitive, together with its complement (that is, the noun which it governs, along with its circumstances), may form the subject or predicate of a proposition; as follows, پادشاهون کي حُضُور مين بي سبب دانت کهولني ادبسي باهر هَين 'to laugh (*lit.* to display the teeth) in the presence of kings is unmannerly.' In the following sentence from the 'Khirad Afroz,' both the subject and the predicate are of this description: لڑکون کو کِمينونکي صُحبت مين رکهنا خراب کرنا هَي 'to keep children in the society of the vile, is to effect their ruin.' When an infinitive thus used has a feminine noun for its complement, it generally agrees adjectively with the substantive (like the Latin participle in *dus*) by changing نا into نِي or نِين; thus, مَين نے تُمهارِي زبان بولنِي نہين سِيكهِي 'I have not learned to speak your language;' نشتر پر اُنگلِي رکھنِي مُشکل هَي 'it is hard to put one's finger on a lancet.' So, in the 'Bágh o Báhár,' p. 32: اي صاحِب ! اگر تُم کو اَيسِي هِي نا آشنائِي کرنِي تهِي — تو پہلي دوستِي اِتنِي گرمِي سي کرنِي کيا ضرُور تهِي ? 'O Sir, if it was your intention thus to act the stranger, then where was the necessity of previously tendering your friendship with such ardour?' Here the infinitive *karní* agrees with *ná-áshná,í* and *dostí* in the feminine gender; so, p. 35, تکلِيف مِہمان کو دينِي خُوب نہين 'to give trouble to one's guest is not proper.' Sometimes (though rarely) the infinitive does not agree with the feminine noun which it governs; as may be seen in the following sentence: دُنيا کي واسطي بہُت مِحنت کرنا فِي الواقِع زِيادہ دَوڑنا هَي ناچِير پر 'to toil much for this world is in fact much-ado about nothing.' If the infinitive, with the feminine noun which it governs, be not the subject or predicate of a sentence, this concord does not hold between the infinitive and the word which it governs; as ايک بُوڑها اَور اُسکِي بُوڑهِيا لکڑِيان توڑنِي کي واسطي آئي — اَور لکڑِيان چُننِي لگي 'an old man and his wife came to cut wood (sticks), and began to gather sticks.' Here the infinitives *torná* and *chunná* do not agree with *lakriyán*, because they are neither subject nor predicate to a sentence. We have been rather diffuse in explaining this peculiarity of the infinitive, because the rule respecting it, as given in most grammars, is, to say the least of it, unsound. It runs thus: "The termination نِي is used with certain verbs or with post-positions;

نِي (*ni*), نِين (*nín*), or نِيان (*niyán*), when a feminine noun singular or plural is the object of the verb; and نَ in all other cases!" We have just shewn from the best authority that *ne* is used when there is neither 'a certain verb' nor 'post-position' in the case, and that *ni* is not necessarily used at all times when a 'feminine noun is the object of the verb.'

c. The inflected infinitive with *ká* (*ke* or *ki*) is also used adjectively in a sense somewhat like the Latin participles in *turus*; as, يِه هوني كا نهين 'this cannot be;' اب مَين عجم نِہين جاني كا 'now I do not mean to go to Persia' (*non sum iturus*); so, مَين نِہين ماني كا 'I am not the man to believe, *or* submit.' Lastly, the inflected infinitive is used with لگنا when it means 'to begin;' with دينا 'to grant leave;' and with پانا 'to get leave;' as, وُه كہني لگا 'he began to say;' هم كو جاني دو 'allow us to go;' وي آني پاتي هَين 'they are allowed to come.' The verb جانا 'to go,' may also govern the inflected infinitive of another verb (*ko* being understood); as, وي كهيلني گئي 'they went to play.' The verb سكنا 'to be able,' generally governs the root of another verb, but it is often used with the inflected infinitive, particularly when accompanied by a negative particle; as, مَين چل سكونگا 'I shall be able to move;' وُه چلني نه سكتا تها 'he was not able to move;' مَين بولني نِہين سكتا 'I cannot say.' Lastly, the verb *honá*, denoting obligation, may govern the inflected infinitive; as, تُمكو جاني هوگا 'you must go;' تُمكو لِكهني هوگا 'you must write.'

PARTICIPLES.

84. The present and past participles, when used participially and not forming a tense, generally add هُوَا (p. 46), and agree, like adjectives, with the noun which they qualify. In many instances they are used adverbially

in the masculine inflection, or, more strictly speaking, they are verbal nouns in an oblique case.

a. The following examples will illustrate what we have just stated regarding the participles when accompanied by *hú,á*; هي كوئي برج مين جو چلتي هوئي گوپال كو ركهي 'is there any one in Braj who will stop the departing Gopál?' So likewise, موئي هوئي شير كي هڈيان 'the bones of a dead tiger;' and, اسني ايک نقاري كو كسي درخت مين لٹكا هوا ديكها 'he saw a kettledrum suspended in a tree.' Sometimes the past participle is used like a mere adjective; as, ايک پهولا پهلا باغ تها 'there was a flowery and fruitful garden' (not 'flowered and fructified'); but the words *phúlá* and *phalá* here may be real adjectives (not participles) derived from *phúl*, 'a flower,' and *phal*, 'fruit,' by adding *á*, which is agreeable to analogy. In expressions like the following, they are used adverbially; as, سبح هوتي 'when it was morning;' شام هوتي 'when it was evening;' ميري رهتي 'while I remain;' جنكي ديكهي 'at the sight of whom;' بنا سمجهي 'without understanding;' ديتي وقت 'at the time of giving.' The present participle is doubled, to express the continuation or frequency of the act; as, همارا كام هوتي هوتي نه هوا 'our work being and being, was not,' *i.e.* 'continuing to be done, was not completed.'

b. From the present participle is formed the compound verb called *statistical* (p. 65), by using the masculine inflection of the participle together with some verb of motion; as, وه گاتي آتي هي 'she comes singing.' The present participle in this case is employed precisely like the ablative of the Latin gerund. Dr. Gilchrist has suggested that *ki ḥálat men* should be considered to be understood: thus, *wuh gáté ki ḥálat men átí hai*, 'she comes in the state or condition of (a person) singing;' but a moment's consideration will shew that this theory is more ingenious than sound. For instance, وُہ گاتي (كِي حالت مين) آتا هَي 'he comes (in the state of) one singing,' is all very well, but, on the other hand, when the nominative is feminine, as, وُہ گاتي (كِي حالت مين) آتي هَي 'she comes (in the state of) one singing,' the expression is absurd; because *she* is a female, and the *one singing* is a male; and we leave the authors of the theory to account for the curious fact of *her* coming *in the state of* (*a male*) *singing*, at that particular juncture. We believe that in these instances the present participle is a verbal noun in the locative case, similar to those Sanskrit verbals in *ti*, etc. (corresponding to the *tio* of the Latin), which denote the abstract action or condition of the verb. In fact we could add many instances where the participle is clearly used like a mere substantive, as سوتي سي 'from sleep,' evidently the same as سوني سي.

c. From the past participle are formed the compound verbs called frequentative and desiderative, by adding *karná* and *cháhná* respectively to the simple masculine form of the participle. The only peculiarity about these is, that the verbs مرنا 'to die,' and جانا 'to go,' employ the regular forms of the participle *mará* and *jáyá*, in preference to the usual forms *mú,á* and *gayá*; as, *wuh mará cháhtá hai*, 'he is about to die,' or 'will die,' or 'wishes to die;' so, *wuh jáyá kartá thá*, 'he was in the habit of going.' The past participle with *hú,á* in the inflected state is sometimes used like the conjunctive participle, or, indeed, it may be a compound form of the latter, for ought we can say; thus, ايک جوگِي دَهُونِي لگاني هُوئي بَيتها هَي 'a Jogí having applied the smoke (by way of penance) is seated;' so likewise, وي رنگ برنگ كِي پوشاكين پہني هُوئي ناچتي تهين 'they having put on various coloured garments, were dancing.' Sometimes the past participle of a neuter verb is used adjectively (that is, agreeing with the nominative), along with another verb; as, چلا جانا; thus, وي چلي جاتي هَينْ 'they go along;' so, ايکٔ لومْڑي پڑي پهِرْتي تهِي 'a fox was roaming about.'

d. The conjunctive participle, by connecting the similar numbers of a sentence, saves the use of verbs and conjunctions; it commonly refers to the agent, sometimes to the object of the verb; as, آج وهانْ جاکر هماري كِتاب ليكر پهِر آؤ 'having gone there to-day, and having taken my book, return;' and again, اِس كام مينْ جلْدِي كر كي مُجهي يِه پشيمانِي هُوئِي هَي 'this regret has come upon me (through) making haste in this business.' The student will recollect that this participle has several forms, the first of them the same as the root; the second, the same as the masculine inflection of the past participle, or the second and third persons singular of the aorist; but the context generally suffices to prevent any ambiguity.

e. The masculine inflection of the present participle with the addition of the particle هِي *hí*, forms what may be called the adverbial participle. Its signification is very nearly the same as that of the conjunctive participle above described; the adverbial form conveying perhaps the idea of more speed or precision; as, يِه بات سُنْتي هِي '(immediately) on hearing this statement. This participle may be applied in three ways, all of them tending to prove what we have stated above, that it is merely a verbal noun. Thus we may say, يِه بات سُنْتي هِي where *yih bát* is the first form of the accusative; we may also say, اِس بات كو سُنْتي هِي where *is bát-ko* is the second form of the accusative; lastly, we may say, اِس بات كي سُنْتي هِي 'on the hearing of this statement.' Here, we see *sunte* in the first two expressions acting the part of a transitive verb, and in the last that of a substantive.

85. We have little more now to add on the syntax of the Hindústání language, which, we believe, we have discussed more fully, and we would fain hope, more intelligibly, than has yet been done. The following few remarks may be still added, as belonging to no particular department of the subject.

a. Sometimes a verb plural is used without a nominative case, some such word as 'they' or 'people' being understood; as in the following examples: يُوں كہتي هَيں 'thus they say;' and ايک تلوار سي سيكڑوں كو مارتي هَيں 'men kill thousands with one sword.' In negative sentences, the verb 'to be' is generally understood; as, ظُلم تيرِي شان كي لائِق نہيں 'oppression (is) not becoming your dignity.' The particle كہ *ki* is frequently used after verbs of speaking, asking, etc., in the sense of 'thus,' 'as follows,' etc.; as, اُس ني كہا كِہ مَيں ني نہ كيا 'he said he had not done it;' lit. 'he said thus, I have not done it.' This is very like the use of the particle ὅτι as it frequently occurs in the Greek text of the New Testament. In a sentence consisting of two or more clauses, it is not necessary to repeat the auxiliary verb in each; as بيمارِي قَيد بدن كِي هَي — اَور غم قَيد رُوح كِي 'sickness is the thraldom of the body, and sorrow that of the spirit.'

b. We may here state in conclusion, that throughout this long section on Syntax, it has been our principal aim to illustrate those peculiarities in which the Hindústání language differs from our own. Such rules and principles as completely accord with those of the languages supposed to be familiar to the reader, we have either passed over unnoticed, or handled very briefly. It may further be stated that there remains a difficult department of the language which must be overcome by practice, viz., the use of idiomatical expressions. These do not constitute the subject of grammar, and a knowledge of them is to be acquired by reading the best authors, and by free intercourse with the natives of the country.

SECTION VI.

THE NÁGARÍ OR DEVANÁGARÍ ALPHABET.

86. This is the character generally used by the Hindús. It is read and written from left to right, like our own. The alphabet, as used for the Hindústání, consists of eleven vowel sounds, and thirty-three consonants, all arranged as follows:—

Vowels.

अ	आ	इ	ई	उ	ऊ	ऋ	ए	ऐ	ओ	औ
ă	*á*	*ĭ*	*í*	*ŭ*	*ú*	*rĭ*	*é*	*ai*	*ó*	*au*

Consonants.

क	ख	ग	घ	ङ	च	छ	ज	झ	ञ	ट
k	*kh*	*g*	*gh*	*ṅ*	*ch*	*chh*	*j*	*jh*	*ñ*	*ṭ*
ठ	ड	ढ	ण	त	थ	द	ध	न	प	फ
ṭh	*ḍ*	*ḍh*	*ṇ*	*t*	*th*	*d*	*dh*	*n*	*p*	*ph*
ब	भ	म	य	र	ल	व	श	ष	स	ह
b	*bh*	*m*	*y*	*r*	*l*	*w, v*	*sh*	*ṣh*	*s*	*h*

a. To the above letters may be added the symbol ं, called *anuswára*, which represents the nasal *ṅ* (page 6), and the *visarga* ः, which corresponds with the final weak *s* (p. 6) of the Persian character. We would at the same time draw the student's attention to *two* compound characters, of which the elements are so disguised as to have the semblance of single letters; viz. क्ष *ksh*, compounded of क and ष, sounded like our *x* in *fluxion*, or *ct* in *faction*; and ज्ञ *jñ*, sounded like our *gn* in *bagnio*, or the French *gn* in *ligne, champagne,* etc. The mark । is used in poetry to indicate the first member of a *sloka* or couplet; and at the end of a *sloka* it is generally doubled ॥.

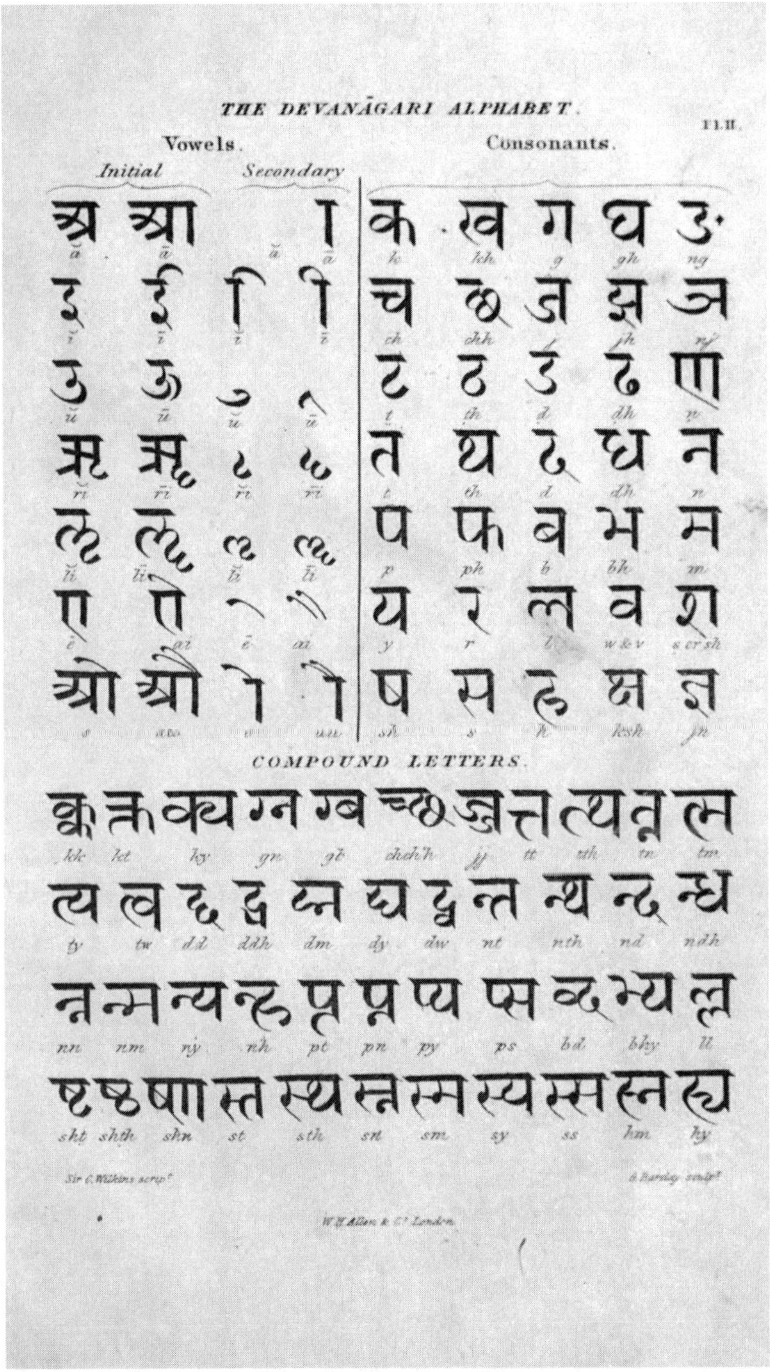
THE DEVANĀGARI ALPHABET.
Pl. II.
Vowels.
Initial
Secondary
Consonants.
COMPOUND LETTERS.
Sir C. Wilkins script.
G. Barclay sculpt.
W. H. Allen & Co. London.

In prose the same marks serve to denote stops. In many books lately published in India, in the Devanágarí character, the English stops have been very properly and successfully introduced.

b. In naming the consonants, the short vowel *ă* (the *fatḥa* of the Persi-Arabic alphabet, p. 8) is inherent in each; thus *kă, khă, gă,* etc.: and in reading, this vowel is to be supplied after every letter (except the final letter of a word), provided it be not accompanied by any other symbol; thus, कनक *kănăk,* 'gold,' नगर *nagar,* 'a city.' If a word terminates with a compound consonant, the short *ă* may be frequently supplied at the end, as in पुत्र *putra,* 'a son.' Whenever a consonant in the middle of a word is not to be uttered with the short *ă,* the consonant is marked underneath with the symbol (्) called *viráma* or 'rest' (the same as the *jazm* of the Persi-Arabic, p. 10), as बोल्ना بولنا 'to speak;' or the *ln* may be combined into one compound character, as ल्न; but in works circulated among the natives this nicety is not attended to.

c. The first of the vowels, अ *ă,* is never written except it begin a word or syllable. With regard to the remaining vowels, they have each two forms: that given above, which may be called their primary form, is used only when they begin a word or syllable; but when they follow a consonant, they assume a totally different shape, which may be called *secondary forms*; thus, ा *á,* ि *i,* ी *í,* ु *u,* ू *ú,* ृ *ri,* े *e,* ै *ai,* ो *o,* ौ *au,* as may be seen in the following exemplification of them with the letter ग *ga*: thus,

ग,	गा,	गि,	गी,	गु,	गू,	गृ,	गे,	गै,	गो,	गौ.
ga,	*gá,*	*gi,*	*gí,*	*gu,*	*gú,*	*gri,*	*ge,*	*gai,*	*go,*	*gau.*

And the same rule applies to the rest of the consonants.

d. It will be seen that the secondary form of इ, viz, ि, is written before its consonant ग, though sounded after it; and the student will do well to bear in mind this apparent anomaly. The ा and ि take their place after the consonant; the ु ू and ृ are fixed to the letter beneath; the े and ै above; and the ो and ौ are merely the ा surmounted by the े and ै. The vowels ु and ू in combination with the letter र *r*, are written रु *ru*, and रू or रू *rú*; and the vowel ृ joined to ह *h*, is written हृ *hṛi*.

87. The strict rule in Devanágarí writing is, that when two or more consonants come together, without the intervention of a vowel, such consonants unite into one compound group; thus, in the word मत्स्य *matsya*, 'a fish,' the त स and य are blended as it were into one character. For the formation of the compound letters no general rule holds, except that the last of the group remains entire, and the rest are more or less contracted by omitting the perpendicular stroke, and sometimes by changing their primitive form.

a. The letter र, being of frequent occurrence in compounds, is subject to two special rules of its own; 1st. It is written over a letter, or group of letters, in the form of a crescent (र्) when it is to be sounded first, as in the words तर्क *tarka*, 'reasoning,' and पार्श्व *párshwa*, 'a side'; 2nd. When the र follows another letter, or group of letters, it is represented by an oblique stroke (्र) underneath, as in सूत्र *sútra*, 'rule,' and चन्द्र *chandra*, 'the moon.'

b. In books recently printed at Calcutta, such as the *Prem Ságar*, the *Baitál Pachísí*, the *Adventures of Ḥátim Ṭá,í*, etc., all in the Devanágarí character, very few compound letters occur; and as a general rule they are very little used in any of the spoken languages of India. being chiefly confined to manuscripts and printed works in the Sanskrit language. The following, however, occur in our Selections, and a perusal of these will suggest the method by which others may be formed. Compounds of which the letter र forms the first or last element, are purposely omitted, that letter, as we have just seen, having special rules applicable to itself.

क्क	क्त	क्य	ग्न	ग्ब	च्छ	ज्ज	त्त	त्थ	
kk	*kt*	*ky*	*gn*	*gb*	*chchh*	*jj*	*tt*	*tth*	
त्न	त्म	त्य	त्व	द्द	द्ध	द्म	द्य	द्व	न्त
tn	*tm*	*ty*	*tw*	*dd*	*ddh*	*dm*	*dy*	*dw*	*nt*
न्थ	न्द	न्ध	न्न	न्म	न्य	न्ह	प्त	प्न	प्य
nth	*nd*	*ndh*	*nn*	*nm*	*ny*	*nh*	*pt*	*pn*	*py*
प्स	ब्द	भ्य	ल्ल	ष्ट	ष्ठ	ष्ण	स्त	स्थ	स्न
ps	*bd*	*bhy*	*ll*	*shṭ*	*shṭh*	*shn*	*st*	*sth*	*sn*
स्म	स्य	स्स	ह्म	ह्य					
sm	*sy*	*ss*	*hm*	*hy*					

c. Compounds of three letters are very rare, and when they do occur, it will be found that they generally consist of one of the semivowels य र ल or व combined with a compound of two letters, thus: क्त्व *ktw*, न्त्र *ntr*, प्त्य *pty*, स्त्य *sty*. As for compounds of four letters, they are merely matters of curiosity, as ल्प्स्म *lpsm*, त्स्न्य *tsny*.

88. The best dictionaries of the Hindústání language are printed in the Persian character; hence it will be necessary for the student to know exactly how he may convert the Devanágarí letters into the former. This he will be able to do efficiently by a reference to the following tables:—

I. *Initial Vowels.*

अ	आ	इ	ई	उ	ऊ	ऋ	ए	ऐ	ओ	औ
ا	آ	اِ	اِيـ	اُ	اُو	رِ	ايـ	اَيـ	او	اَو

II. *Consonants.*

क	ख	ग	घ	ङ	च	छ	ज	झ	ञ	ट
ک	کھ	گ	گھ	ن	چ	چھ	ج	جھ	ن	ٹ
ठ	**ड**	**ढ**	**ण**	**त**	**थ**	**द**	**ध**	**न**	**प**	**फ**
ٹھ	ڈ	ڈھ	ن	ت	تھ	د	دھ	ن	پ	پھ
ब	**भ**	**म**	**य**	**र**	**ल**	**व**	**श**	**ष**	**स**	**ह**
ب	بھ	م	ي	ر	ل	و	ش	کھ or ش	س	ہ

III. *Secondary Vowels.*

बद	बाद	बिद	बीद	बुद	बूद
بد	باد	بِد	بِید	بُد	بُود
बृद	**बेद**	**बैद**	**बोद**	**बौद**	**बः**
بْرِد	بید	بَید	بود	بَود	بہ

a. In the preceding table it will be observed that the ten aspirated letters of the Devanágarí alphabet are uniformly represented by the corresponding unaspirated letter, together with the round or *butterfly* form of the letter ھ, ہ *h*; thus, घर *ghar*, 'a house,' گھر; धर *dhar*, 'a place,' دھر. The real *h* ह of the Devanágarí is represented in the middle of the word by ہ; as, कहा 'he said,' کہا: if, however, the letter preceding the ھ be د, ر, or و, then the form ھ must be used, and the preceding letter marked with the appropriate vowel; as, दहान *dahán*, 'the mouth,' دَھان. The cerebral letters ट and ड are represented by ٹ and ڈ, or ٹ and ڈ. Sometimes the ड and ढ have the sound of a cerebral *ṛ* and *ṛh* respectively; in which case they are generally marked with a dot beneath, thus ड़ and ढ़, and and with ڑ or ڑ in the Persian character; as, बड़ा *baṛá*, 'great,' بڑا, The various nasals of the Devanágarí are represented by the Persian ن, which will be found sufficient for all useful purposes.

b. The letter य is sometimes represented by ج : the letter श generally by ش, sometimes by س; and the letter ष is more frequently کھ than ش. The compound क्ष is generally represented by چھ or کھ, seldom by کش, its proper sound. The compound ज्ञ is represented by گي; as, आज्ञा *ágyá* (*ájná*), آگیا; its real sound, as already stated, is that of *gn* in the French words *champagne*, *ligne*, etc.

89. It appears, then, that the Devanágarí alphabet may be represented with tolerable exactness in the Persian character; but the converse does not hold, as the Persi-Arabic alphabet has fourteen letters which have no exact counterpart in the Devanágarí. The plan adopted in this case is to represent the letters in question with such Nágarí letters as approximate them in sound, which in some printed books are distinguished with a dot underneath; thus,

ط	ض	ص	ژ	ز	ذ	خ	ح	ث
त़	ज़	स़	ज़	ज़	ज़	ख़	ह़	स़

ق	ف	غ	ع	ظ
क़	फ़	ग़	अ़ *etc.*	ज़

a. In a few printed books, attempts have been made to invent distinct letters for the various forms of the Persian and Arabic *z*, which, it will be observed, are all represented by ज़; but in reality the subject is not worth the labour. In the first place, the Hindús, who alone use the Devanágarí character, are sparing in the use of Persian or Arabic words, to one or other of which the various forms of the letter *z* belong; and, secondly, such words as they have in the course of centuries adopted have become naturalized, or, if the critic will have it, corrupted, so as to suit the elements of the Nágarí:

thus, حاضِرِي is written and sounded हाजिरी *hájirí*. In a new edition, in the Devanágarí character, of the 'Adventures of Ḥátim Ṭá,í,' which we have lately received from India, almost all dots and double letters are discarded, as a useless incumbrance.

b. The letter ع is generally represented in Nágarí by employing the vowel with which it is connected, in the initial form, with a dot under it; as, بَعْد बअ़द *ba'd*; علم इ़ल्म *'ilm*; عُمْر उ़म्र *'umr*. This method is sufficient for practical use; but it is by no means satisfactory, as may be seen in the monosyllable बअ़द, which in Persian and Arabic is sounded *ba'd* (the *a* uttered from the bottom of the throat); but, according to the rules of the Devanágarí alphabet, it makes *bă'ăd*, unless we use the *viráma* (्) under the अ़, as बअ़्द, which would amount to something like an absurdity.

c. When, in a word, two vowels follow each other, the rule is, to write the second vowel in the initial form; for though not at the beginning of a word, it is the beginning of a syllable; thus, हुआ *hú'á*; होओ *ho'o*. This is precisely the same in principle as the use of the mark *hamza* (p. 17) in the Persi-Arabic alphabet.

d. The best mode of learning the Devanágarí character is to write out several times the whole of the single letters in Plate II. The various elements of each letter will be found in Plate I. fronting the title page; the small dot accompanying each shews where the pen starts from in their formation. When the student has made himself tolerably familiar with the letters, he may commence with the first story, which is the same as the third story of the Extracts in the Persian character. In like manner he will find that the Devanágarí Stories, from 2 to 7 inclusive, are old acquaintances. Stories 8, 9, and 10 also occur in the other Extracts, but some of the words differ, viz., those of Persian or Arabic origin are displaced in the Devanágarí for words purely Indian and Sanskrit. The rest of the Extracts in this character are taken from the scarce and valuable 'Hindústání and Hindí Selections,' edited by Tárini Charan Mitr, head Munshí in the College of Fort William, Calcutta, 1827, in two vols. 4to. In their style and grammatical construction they offer no peculiarity differing from those of our Hindústání Extracts in the Persian character.

OF MANUSCRIPTS.

90. We briefly alluded, at page 21, to the three most prevalent handwritings in use among the Arabs, Persians, and Musalmáns of India. Of these, the Naskhí, being like the type used in this country, requires no explanation; and the Shikasta, from its extreme irregularity, scarcely admits of any. We shall therefore confine ourselves at present to the description of the *Ta'lík*, of which we have given fourteen plates of engraved specimens at the end of this work.

a. Plate I. Division 1st presents all the simple elements of this character, the small cross mark shewing the commencement of each. The 2nd elementary form, here marked ب, with one dot subscribed, so as to be equivalent to *be*, may, by a mere change of its dots, become پ ت ث (*p, t, s*). The third form, now a ج *j*, becomes in the same manner چ خ ح (*ch, kh, h*). The 4th makes two letters, د ذ. The 5th, ر ز ژ and ڑ. The 6th is represented as consisting of two forms; one an indented, the other a protracted line, may in either shape form the *sin* and *shin* (*s* and *sh*), as the only distinction between them is that the *sin* (*s*) wants, and the *shin* (*sh*) has, three dots superscribed, whether short or protracted. The 7th form, ص and ض. The 8th, ط and ظ (*t, z*). The 9th, ع and غ. The next letters are ف ق ک ل م ن و and ه. Then follow the initial, medial, and final forms of the ه ﮨ ﻪ or *he* linked together.

Lastly, the لا ء ي (*lá, hamza,* and *ye*), the latter under two varieties of form, the last of which is now conventionally used by the natives to denote the *yáe majhúl* (p. 13).

b. Division 2nd exhibits the second elementary form (viz. that of ب پ ت ٹ ث), and likewise that of ن and ي, as they appear initially, when combined with each of the others following them. Division 3rd shews the ج (i.e. ج چ ح or خ), prefixed in the same manner to each of the others. Division 4th (Pl. II.), the س ش. Division 5th, the ص ض. Division 6th, the ط ظ. Division 7th (Pl. III.), the ع غ. Division 8th, ف and ق. Division 9th, the ک گ, and by leaving off the top part we shall in most instances have the initial ل. Division 10th (Pl. IV.), the م. Division 11th, the ه combined initially with the rest of the elementary forms. The tail of the *he* is given only in *há, hd, hk, hl,* and *hlá,* but omitted in all the rest, according to the practice of Oriental writers. Hence the initial form of this letter is often too apt to be mistaken for the *mím.* The 12th Division contains the combination of the characters as arranged in alphabetical notation, noticed in p. 20, forming the fanciful words, '*Abjad, hawaz, ḥuṭṭí, kaliman, sa'faṣ, ḳarashat, s̤akhaz̤, z̤az̤agh,*' and the last line may be read thus, indicating the name of the chirographer: *Al'abd ul muz̤nib, al faḳír 'ubaid ulláhi ḥusainí shírín raḳam ghaffara z̤unúbahu.*

c. Plates V. to XIV. inclusive, consist of a series of words in alphabetical order containing combinations of three or more letters. The student should endeavour to transcribe these into the Roman character, and after some time retranscribe them, as an exercise, into their original state. Thus, the first line of Plate V. forms the combinations *bkht, bhjt, bhsht, pnj, blkh,* and *blnd,* and so on with regard to the rest. Coming now to complete words, we may premise, as a general remark, that when these contain of the letters ي ن ث ت پ ب in the middle of a combination, it is usual to give the middle one a bold dash upwards, terminating in a sharp point vertically, like the *n* in تنبو *tnbw* (Plate V. line 8), or like the *y* in سيب *syb* (Plate VII. line 1).

d. Concluding remarks.—In manuscripts the short vowels and other marks seldom make their appearance; and even the diacritical dots are often either altogether omitted or irregularly placed. It may be useful to observe, then, that when from the ambiguous position of a dot, it may apply to more letters than one, it should of course be assigned rather to the letter, which is not complete without a point, than to one which may dispense with it. Thus the third combination Plate I. No. 2, should be read *bḥ*, and the eighth *nṣ*, though the dot be over the last letter as if it intended to be a ض. But in many cases the sense alone can determine *the point*. Thus the last word of No. 2 may be either *be* or *pe*; and the dot over the ninth word of No. 3 is so equivocally placed between that and the word above it, that it may be read either حض خض or جف, according as the dot is conceived to belong to one or the other, above or below. The grand key, however, to the reading of manuscripts, is to *know the language*; at the same time many useful hints may be gleaned from Ouseley's 'Persian Miscellanies,' 4to. London, 1795; Stewart's 'Persian Letters,' 4to. London, 1825; and 'Essai de Calligraphie Orientale,' in the Appendix to Herbin's 'Dévcloppments des Principes de la Langue Arabe,' 4to. Paris, 1803. See also a work entitled 'Oriental Penmanship; an Essay for facilitating the Reading and Writing of the Ta'lík Character,' by the author of this Grammar. London: Wm. H. Allen & Co. 1849.

MUHAMMADAN CALENDAR.

91. The Musalmáns reckon by lunar time, their æra called the *Hijra*, commencing from the day on which Muḥammad departed, or rather *retreated*, from Mecca to

Medina; which, according to the best accounts, took place on Friday, the 16th of July (18th, new style), A.D. 622. Their year consists of 12 lunations, amounting to 354 days and 9 hours, very nearly; and hence their New-year's Day will happen every year about eleven days earlier than in the preceding year.

a. To find the Christian year corresponding to that of the Hijra, apply the following rule:—From the given number of Musalmán years, deduct *three per cent.*, and to the remainder add the number 621.54, the sum is the period of the Christian æra at which the given current Musalmán year ends. For example, we mentioned (p. 20), that the death of the poet Ahlí happened, A.H. 942; from this number deduct three per cent. or 28.26, and the remainder is 913.74. To this last add 621.54, and the sum = 1535.28, which shows that the Musalmán year 942 ended in the spring of 1536. This very simple rule is founded on the fact that 100 lunar years are very nearly equal to 97 solar years, there being only about eight days of difference. A more accurate proportion would be 101 lunar to 98 solar years, but this would lead to a less convenient rule for practical use.

b. When great accuracy is required, and when the year, month, and day of the Muḥammadan æra are given, the precise period of the Christian æra may be found very nearly, as follows:—*Rule.* Express the Musalmán date in years and decimals of a year; multiply by .97; to the product add 621.54, and the sum will be the period of the Christian æra. This rule is exact to within a few days, and if in the Musalmán date the day of the week be given, as is generally the case, the *very day* is easily determined.

c. The Muḥammadan or lunar months are made to consist of thirty and twenty-nine days alternately, but in a period of thirty years, it is found necessary to intercalate the last month eleven times so as to be reckoned thirty days instead of twenty-nine. The months retain their Arabic names in all Muḥammadan countries, as follows:—

LUNAR MONTHS.

		DAYS.			DAYS.
مُحرّم	*muharram*	30	رجب	*rajab*	30
صفر	*safar*	29	شعْبان	*sha'bán*	29
رِبيع آلاوّل	*rabí ul-awwal*	30	رمضان	*ramazán*	30
رِبيعُ آلثانِي	*rabí'us-sání*	30	شَوّال	*shawwál*	29
رِبيعُ آلآخِر	*rabí' ul-ákhir*		ذي آلقَعْده	*zi,l ka'da*	30
جُمادَ آلاوّل	*jumád-al-awwal*	30	ذي قعْده	*zi ka'da*	
جُمادَ آلثانِي	*jumád-as-sání*	29	ذي آلحِجه	*zi,l hijja*	29
جُمادَ آلآخِر	*jumád-al-ákhir*		ذي حِجه	*zi hijja*	

d. We here subjoin the days of the week; on the left hand are the names in use among the Musalmáns of India, next those of the Hindús; and on the right, the Persian names, which last are much used in the dates of letters, etc.

DAYS OF THE WEEK.

MUSALMÁN.	HINDÚ.	ENG.	PERSIAN.
اِتْوار *itwár.*	رِبیبار *rabí-bár.*	Sun.	یکشنْبه
سومْوار *somwár* or پِیر *pír.*	سومْبار *som-bár.*	Mon.	دُوشنْبه
منْگل *mangal.*	منْگلبار *mangal-bár*	Tues.	سِه شنْبه
بُدْه *budh.*	بُدْهبار *budh-bár.*	Wed.	چهارشنْبه
جُمْعه رات *jum'a rát.*	بْرِهَسْپتِبار *brihaspati-bár.*	Thur.	پنْجشنْبه
جُمْعه *jum'a.*	سُکْربار *sukra-bár.*	Fri.	آدِینه
سنِیچر *saníchar.*	سنِیبار *saní-bár.*	Sat.	شنْبه *or* هفْته

92. The Hindús reckon by *solar* years, and *luni-solar* months. Their principal æra is that of the *Kali-Yug*, of which the year 4956 expired about the 11th of April, A.D. 1855, at which period their new year generally commences.

a. The Hindú year is divided into twelve equal portions, which may be called solar months; but all festivals and dates are reckoned, not by these simple months, but by the duration of the moon which terminates in each. Hence, although the month *baisákh* begins *de jure* about the 11th of April, it may have commenced *de facto* from one day to twenty-eight days sooner. When two new moons occur during one solar month, which happens once in three years, there is an intercalary month, and the month so intercalated receives the name of the one which preceded it, that is, of the solar month within which the two new moons may happen.

b. Beside the æra of the *Kali-Yug*, the Hindús in the northern half of India reckon from the time of a renowned prince, by name Vikramáditya, who lived (or died) about 57 years before the commencement of our æra. Another common æra is that of a prince named Sálaváhana, which commences 78 years after the birth of Christ. The former of these æras is called the Samvat, and the latter the Sáká æra. Several other æras are in use in certain parts of the country, for a full account of which the reader may consult a profound work devoted entirely to the subject, entitled 'Kála Sankalita,' 4to. Madras, 1825.

THE HINDÚ SOLAR MONTHS.

بَیساکھ	April.	بھادوں	August.	پُوس	December.
جیٹّھ	May.	کُوار or آسِن	September.	ماگھ	January.
اساڑھ	June.	کاتِک or کارتِک	October.	پھاگن or پھالگن	February.
ساوَن or سراوَن	July.	اگھن	November.	چَیت	March.

मनोहर कहानियां

सुगम बाली में

---

१ किसी मोची का घर जाड़े के मौसम में जल्ने लगा. एक ग़रीब पड़ोसी वहां आकर सेंक्ने लगा. यिह हालत देख्के एक ठठोल ने कहा, क्या ख़ूब! किसीका घर जले कोई तापे.

२ एक कमीने और भले आदमी से इफ़्लास में दोस्ती हुई. कमीनः दौलत्मन्द होते ही नजीब्ज़ादे से आंखें लगा चुराने. तब वुह ख़फ़ा होकर बोला, यिह सच है, कमीने की दोस्ती जैसी बालू की भीत.

३ अक्बर ने बीर्बल से पूछा, कि लड़ाई के वक़्त क्या काम आता है? बीर्बल ने अर्ज़ किया, कि जहान पनाह! औसान. बाद्शाह ने कहा, हथ्यार और ज़ोर क्यूं नहीं कह्ता? बीर्बल ने कहा, जहान पनाह! अगर औसान ख़ता हो जावे, तो हथ्यार और ज़ोर किस काम आवे?

४ एक ऊंट और गधे से निहायत दोस्ती थी. इत्तिफ़ाक़न् दोनों को सफ़र दर्पेश हुआ. दर्मियान राह के एक नदी

मिली. पहले ऊंट पानी में पैठा. उसके पेट तक पानी हुआ. कहने लगा, ऐ यार! इधर आओ, पानी थोड़ा है. गधा बोला, सच है, तेरे शिकम तक है, तुझे थोड़ा मअ़लूम होता है; लेकिन मेरी पीठ तक होगा, मैं डूब जाऊंगा.

५ एक शख़्स बादशाह के ऐन क़िलए के नीचे लूटा गया. उस्ने बादशाह की खिद्मत में अ़र्ज़ की, कि जहान पनाह! मुझे क़ज़्ज़ाक़ों ने हुज़ूर के क़िलए की दीवार के नीचे लूट लिया. बादशाह ने फ़र्माया कि तू हुश्यार क्यूं न रहा? बोला कि ग़ुलाम को मअ़लूम न था कि हज़रत के ज़ेर झरोखे मुसाफ़िर लूटे जाते हैं. बादशाह ने कहा, क्या तूने यिह मसल नहीं सुनी? चिराग़ के नीचे अन्धेरा.

६ एक कायथ और उस का ग़ुलाम दोनों एक घर में सोते थे. लाला ने कहा, राम चेरा! देख ता पानी बरस्ता है या खुल गया. उस ने कहा, बरस्ता है. पूछा तू किस तरह जान्ता है? तैं तो पड़ा सोता है. कहा बिल्ली आई थी, उस को मैं ने टटोला था, भीगी थी. कहा, चिराग़ बुझा दे. कहा, मुंह ढांप के सो रहो, अन्धेरा हो जाएगा. फिर कहा, दर्वाज़: बन्द कर दे. कहा, भया जी! दो काम हम्ने किये, एक काम तुम करो. ग़रज़ ऐसा सुस्त था, आख़िर न उठा; पड़ा पड़ा जवाब देता रहा.

७ एक मुसल्मान बीमार था. ग़ुलाम से कहा, कि फ़ुलाने हकीम के पास जाकर दवा ला. उस्ने कहा, शायद हकीम

जी इसवक़ घर में नहोवें. कहा, होंगे, जा. तब उसने कहा अगर मुलाक़ात भी होवे, लेकिन दवा नदें. तद कहा हक़्क़ः हमारा लेजा, अलबत्तः देंगे. फिर कहा, कि जो उन्हों ने दवा भी दी, अगर फ़ाइदः नकरे. कहा, ऐ कम बख़्त! यहीं बैठा तन्हीदें बान्धा करेगा या जाएगा? कहा, साहिब! फ़र्ज़ किया कि अगर फ़ाइदः भी करे, तो हासिल क्या? आख़िर एक दिन मर्ना बर हक़ है; जैसा अब मरे तैसा तब मरे.

८ कोई मनुष कहीं को चिठी लिखता था; एक पर्देशी उस के पास आ बैठा, और उस के लिखे को देखने लगा. तो उस ने चिठी में लिखा, जो बहुत सी बातें लिखनी थीं, सो नहीं लिखी गईं क्यूं कि मेरे कने एक निपट चिबिल्ला बैठा है, और इस चिठी को देखता है. वुह बोला, अपने भेद की बात चीत जो लिखनी हो, सो लिखते क्यूं नहीं? मैं ने तो कुछ तुम्हारा लिखा हुआ नहीं देखा. तब लेखक ने उत्तर दिया, भला, जो तुम ने मेरा लिखा हुआ नहीं देखा; कहो तो, यिह क्यूंकर जाना जो मैं ने यूं लिखा है? इस बात से बहुत लजाया; और चुप हो रहा.

९ एक सिचक किसी गांव में कितने एक लोगों को सिचा देता था, इस में कोई गंवार भी वहां आ बैठा, और लगा उस का मुंह देख देख बेचैन हो रोने. इस को रोता देख सब ने जाना कि यिह कोई बड़ा कोमल सुभाव है जो इतना

रोता है. एक ने इस से पूछा, कि भाई! सच कह, तू जो इतना रोता है, तेरे मन में क्या आया है? सिचक को उंगली से बता बोला, कि इन मियां की डाढ़ी हिल्ती देख मुझे अपना मुआ हुआ प्यारा बक्रा स्मरन आया, कि जब न तब उस की भी इसी भांत डाढ़ी हिल्ती थी, इस लिये मैं रोता हूं. यिह सुन सब खिल्खिला उठे, और सिचक लज्जित हो चुप रहा.

१० एक राजा ने अपना लड़का किसी जोतकी को सौंपा, जो इसे जोतिक सिखाओ; जब उस में यिह पूरा हो, तो मेरे पास लाओ. पांडे ने बड़े प्यार और दुख से जितनी बातें उसकी थीं, सो उसे अच्छे ढब से सिखाईं. जब देखा वुह लड़का बड़ा गुनी हुआ, तब राजा के साम्हने जाकर कहा, महाराज! आप का बेटा अब जातिक में चौकस हुआ; जब चाहिये उसे जांच लीजिये. राजा ने यिह सुन्ते ही कहा, अबही बुलाओ. लड़का आया और हाथ जोड़के खड़ा रहा. राजा ने अप्ने हाथ की अंगूठी मुट्ठी में लेकर पूछा, कहो बेटा! हमारे हाथ में क्या है? उस ने कहा, कुछ गोल गोल सा है, जिस में छेद और पत्थर भी है. महाराज ने कहा, उसका नांव क्या है? बोला चक्की का पाट. तब राजा जोतकी के मुंह की ओर ताक्ने लगा. वुहीं वुह हाथ जोड़ कर बोला, महाबली! गुन का कुछ दोष नहीं, यिह मत की चूक है.

११ कोई पोस्ती जंगल में बैठा कटोरी में पोस्त घोल रहा था. दैवी किसी झाड़झूड़ से एक खरहा जो निकल्के दौड़ा, तो उस के धक्के से इस की कटोरी लुढ़क पड़ी. यिह रिसाय के बोला, कि तुझ से क्या कहें! भला, तेरे बाप ही से जा कर कहेंगे. इत्ना कह, कूंडी सोंटा कांख में दबा, नगर में जा, हर एक चोपाये को देख्ता चला; निदान एक गधे को जो उस के बरन के समान था, पाया. तो गधेवाले से जाकर कहा, कि तेरे इस पशु के बेटे ने मेरी पोस्त की कटोरी भरी हुई लुढ़ा दी. उस ने कहा, कि जिस्के बेटे ने लुढ़ाई है तिसी से जाके कहो. यह सुन, वह गधे के पास जा, उस की पीठ पर हाथ रख, चाहे कि कुछ कहे, वोंहीं उस ने फिर्कर एक ऐसी दुलत्ती मारी, कि यह बिचारा हाथ कर बैठ गया, और हंस्कर बोला, कि क्यौं न हो, जिस्का बाप ऐसा हो, तिस का लड़्का वैसा हुआ ही चाहे. इत्ना कह चला आया.

१२ दो जान्पह्चान मिल्कर भ्रमन को निक्ले, और चले चले नद्दी के तीर पर पहुंचे. तब एक ने दूसरे से कहा, कि भाई! तुम यहां खड़े रहो, तो मैं शीघ्र एक डुब्की मार लूं. इस ने कहा बहुत अच्छा. यह सुन वह बीस रूपये इसे सौंप्कर, कपड़े तीर सर रख, जों पानी में पैठा, तों इस ने चतुराई से वे रूपये किसी के हाथ अपने घर भेज दिये. उस ने निकल, कपड़े पहन, रूपये मांगे. यह बोला लेखा सुन

लो. उस ने कहा, अभी देते अबेर भी नहीं हुई, लेखा कैसा? निदान दोनों से बिबाद होने लगा, और सौ पचास लोग घिर आये. उन में से एक ने रूपयेवाले से कहा, कि अजी! क्यौं झगड़ते हो, लेखा किस लिये नहीं सुन लेते? हार मान उस ने कहा, अच्छा कह. वह बोला, जिस काल आप ने डुब्की मारी, मैं ने जाना डूब गये; पांच रूपये दे तुम्हारे घर संदेसा भेजा; और निकले तब भी और पांच रूपये आनंद के दान में दिये; रहे दश, सो मैं ने अपने घर भेजे हैं, विन की कुछ चिंता हो तो मुझ से टीप लिख्वा लो. यह धांधल्पने की बात सुन, वह बिचारा बोला, भला भाई! भर पाये.

१२ एक कच्कुए और कौवे से वड़ी प्रीत थी, काम पड़ने से एक एक का सहारा कर्ता. एक दिन किसी चिड़ीमार ने कौवे को पकड़ा, तब कच्कुए ने चिड़ीमार से कहा, कि तुझे इस के लेजाने से हाट में क्या मिलेगा? बोला, दो पैसे. कहा, जो तू इसे छोड़ दे, तो मैं तुझे एक मोती दूं. कहा अच्छा. उस ने डुब्की मार के मोती ला दिया; पर इस ने कौवे को न छोड़ा. तद कच्कुए ने कहा, कि मैं ने मोती तो तुझे ला दिया, अब इसे क्यौं नहीं छोड़ता; बोला, एक मोती और ला दे, तो छोड़ दूं, नहीं तो नहीं छोड़ूंगा. इस ने कहा, अच्छा. तू इसे छोड़ दे, मैं ला देता हूं. वह बोला, मैं तेरी बात को कैसे प्रतीत करूं? कहा इस ने, मैं झूठ नहीं

बोल्ता. इस बात के सुन्ते ही उस ने कौवे को छोड़ दिया, और इस ने दूसरा मोती ला दिया. फिर चिड़ीमार दूसरे मोती को छोटा देख बोला, कि यह मैं न लूंगा, इसी के समान का ला दे. इस ने कहा, यों तो नहीं, पर जो तू यह मोती मुझे दे, तो मैं इस के समान का वहीं से देख लाऊं. मारे लालच के इस ने मोती दिया, वह ले डुब्की मार, बैठ रहा. एक पहर के पीछे इस ने घब्राके विसे पुकारा. तब उस ने आकर रिसियाय के कहा, कि तू बड़ा मूढ़ है जो मुझे पुकार्ता है; क्या तैं ने यह कहावत नहीं सुनी? जो कुछ खुदा करे सो हो, लेना एक न देना दो. यह सुन चिड़ीमार निरास हो अप्ने घर गया.

१४ एक दिन अक्बर बाद्शाह ने बीर्बल से कोई बात कह्के उस का उत्तर पूछा. बीर्बल ने वह उत्तर दिया, कि जो बाद्शाह के मन में ठह्रा था. सुन्कर शाह ने कहा, कि यही बात मेरे भी जी में आई है. बीर्बल बोला, कि महाराज! यह वही बात है, जो सौ सियाने एक मत. शाह ने कहा कि, यह कहावत भी प्रगट है, जो सिर सिर अक़्ल, गुर गुर बिद्या. फिर बीर्बल ने कहा कि, महाराज! जो मन में आवे तो इस बात को जांच लीजे. कहा बहुत अच्छा. इत्नी बात के सुन्ते ही बीर्बल ने नगर में से सौ बुद्धिवान बुला भेजे, और दो पहर रात के समय बाद्शाह के सोंहीं उन्हें एक सूना कुंड बताकर कहा, महाराज की आज्ञा है कि इसी

बिरियां हर एक लोग एक एक घड़ा दूध का भर्‌कर इस कुंड में ला डाले. बाद्‌शाह की आज्ञा को सुन्‌ते ही हर एक ने अप्‌ने जी में यह बात समझ्‌के, कि जहां निनानवे घड़े दूध के होंगे, तहां मेरा एक घड़ा पानी का क्या जाना जायगा? पानी ही ला डाला. बीर्‌बल ने शाह को दिखाया; शाह ने उन सब से कहा, तुम ने क्या समझ्‌के मेरी आज्ञा को न माना? सच कहो, नहीं तो भला न होगा. तिन में से हर किसी ने हाथ बांध बांध कर कहा, कि महाराज! चाहो मारिये, चाहो छोड़िये, हमारे जी में यह बात आई, कि जहां निनानवे घड़े दूध के होंगे, वहां एक घड़ा पानी का क्या जाना जायगा? यह बात सब के मुख से सुन्‌कर बाद्‌शाह ने बीर्‌बल से कहा, जो कानों सुन्‌ते थे सो आंखों देखा, कि सौ सियाने एक मता.

१५ अक्‌बर बाद्‌शाह की यह रीति थी, कि सदा फ़कीर का भेष ले, रात को नगर की गली गली नाके नाके में फिर्‌ते, और जिस दरिद्री कंगाल दुखी को देख्‌ते, उस का दुख दूर कर्‌ते. एक दिन जों निक्‌ले तों देख्‌ते क्या हैं, कि कोई साहूकार की बेटी पार के ऊपर गोख में खड़ी रो रो बिसूर रही है. ये बोले, माई! टुक्‌ड़ा भेजियो. वह रोटी देने आई; इन्हों ने उस से पूछा, तू क्यों रोती है? उत्तर दिया मेरा स्वामी बारह बरस से जहाज़ ले बनज को निक्‌ला है, उस का कुछ समाचार नहीं पाया, इस दुख से रोती हूं.

इत्ना सुन, रोटी ले, असीस दे, आगे बढ़े, तो देखा कि कोई रंडी रो रो चक्की पीस रही है. उसी भांति उस से भी पूछा. उन्ने कहा, मेरा स्वामी चोरी को गया है, उसे तीन दिन हुए, न जानूं जीता है कै मारा गया, इस दुख से रोती हूं. यह सुन वहां से भी चल निक्ले. फिर देखा, कि एक स्त्री नवयौवना खिड़की में बैठी डाढ़ें मार मार रोती है. उस से पूछा, तू क्यों रोती है? उन्ने कहा, मेरा स्वामी अल्प वयस्क है. इस बात के सुन्के ही बाद्शाह उदास हो घर आये, और दूस्रे दिन राज्मंदिर में बैठ, बीर्बल की ओर देख बोले, बीर्बल! वे तीनों बिल्लायं. बीर्बल ने कुछ उत्तर न दिया. फिर बाद्शाह ने कहा, बीर्बल! वे तीनों बिल्लायं. बोला, हां महाराज! इत्नी बात के सुन्ते ही, बाद्शाह ने लीली पीली आंखें कर कहा, बीर्बल इस का बखान कर, नहीं तो अभी मार डाल्ता हूं. तू ने क्या समझ्के मेरी बात का उत्तर न दिया? बोला, एक समंदर बनज करे, और नित उठ चोरी जायं; बालक ही से नेह लगावे, वे तीनों बिल्लायं. इस बात के सुन्ते ही प्रसन्न हो बाद्शाह ने बीर्बल को निहाल कर दिया.

१६ शाहजहां बाद्शाह ने दीवानिख़ास से ले गढ़ के पौर तक एक रस्सा बंधवा दिया था, और उस में घंटालियां गुंथवा, छोर उस का बीच बाज़ार में डलवा दिया था, इस लिये कि जो कोई बादी आवे, सो उस रस्से को खैंचे,

घंटालियां बाजें, और वादी की पुकार महाराज के निकट बिन बीचबिचाव के पहुंचे. एक दिन किसी भिस्ती का बैल भरी पखाल समेत उस रस्से के पास आनकर खड़ा हुआ, भिस्ती किसी के यहां मशक डालने गया था; बैल ने रस्से से सिर खुजलाया; उस के सींग का झटका जो लगा, एकी दांव सब घंटालियां बाज उठीं; सुनते ही बादशाह ने कहा, देखो, कौन है? लोगों ने झट समाचार दिया, धर्म्मावतार! और तो कोई नहीं, एक भिस्ती का बैल है. आज्ञा की, कि उसे उस के स्वामी समेत ले आओ. लोग वोंहीं ले गये. बादशाह ने आज्ञा की, कि इस की पखाल का पानी तोलो कि कितना है? तोलकर निवेदन किया, कि पृथ्वीनाथ! साढ़े पांच मन है. सुनते ही बादशाह ने आज्ञा की, कि आज से साढ़े तीन मन पानी से अधिक नगर में कोई पखाल न बनावे. उसी घड़ी डौंडी फिर गई, तभी से साढ़े तीन मन पानी से अधिक पखाल नहीं बनती.

१७ लाड़ कपूर एक दिन अकबर बादशाह के वोंहीं अच्छा गाये; शाह ने रीझकर हाथी दिया, ये ले आये. बरस एक पीछे इन दोनों भाइयों के जी में आया कि आज हाथी का आहार चलकर देखें कितना खाता है, और किस प्रकार खाता है? निदान आहार के समय मूंढा बिछा बिछा हाथी के पास जा बैठे, और उसका खाना देख निपट चकित और सोच में हो आपस में कहने लगे, कि भाई जी! बादशाह

ने यह हमारे पीछे कोई बड़ी बिपत लगा दी, न इसे बेंच सकें; न किसी को दे सकें; जो यह कई दिन यहां रहा, तो इसके खाने के आगे हमारा गाना बजाना सब मिट्टी में मिल जायगा. इतना कह, कुछ मन में समझ, ढोलक तंबूरा उसके गले में डाल छोड़ दिया. उसने नगर में जा धूम की. और नगर के लोगों ने जा बादशाह के यहां पुकारा की. शाह ने कहा, देखो किस का हाथी है? किसी ने आ कहा, महाराज! लाड़ कपूर का. आज्ञा की कि उन्हें बुलाओ. कहने के साथ ही वे आन उपस्थित हुए. देखते ही क्रोध कर महाराज ने कहा. कि क्यों बे! तुम ने हाथी क्यों छोड़ दिया? उन्होंने हाथ बांधकर कहा, महाराज! हम को जो विद्या आती थी सो बरस दिन में सब सिखला, ढोलक तंबूरा उस के हाथ दिया, इस लिये कि बादशाही नगर है, इस में जाकर कमावे, और कुछ तिस में से आप खा हमें खिलावे. इस रहस के सुनते ही प्रसन्न हो बादशाह ने उनका अपराध क्षमा किया, और हाथी के लिये एक गांव दिया.

१८ कोई कायथ सदा अपने बेटे को समझाता, और यह कहता, कि बाबा! संसार बुरी ठौर है, कर तो डर, न कर तो भी डर. उस का बेटा सुनकर यह उत्तर देता, लाला जी! बुरी बुरे के लिये है, कर तो डर, न कर तो न डर. निदान जब न तब उन दोनों में यही बातचीत होती. एक दिन उस ने अपना वह घोड़ा असवारी को मंगवाया, कि जिस

पर कभी न चढ़ा था. घोड़े के आते ही, बाप ने बेटे से कहा, बाबा! इस पर तुम चढ़ो, हम देखें. बेटे ने भी यही कहा. निदान बहुत सी कहा सुनी के पीछे उस का बाप ही असवार हुआ, और बेटा पीछे पीछे देखता चला. इस में कई एक जनों ने देखकर कहा, यह क्या अभागी है? कि गोर में पांव लटका चुका, और तो भी इस की चोप नहीं गई; जुबा बेटा पीछे जूती चटकाता आता है, और आप घोड़े पर चढ़ा जाता है. यह सुन वह उतर पड़ा, और बेटे को चढ़ा, आप पीछे पीछे देखता चला. फिर कई लोग देखके बोले, कि देखो, यह क्या निकम्मा और कपूत है, जो आप आरूढ़ हो बाप को जलेब में दौड़ाता है. यह सुन, आगे बढ़, वे दोनों चढ़ लिये. तब कोई बोल उठा, कि ये क्या निलज्ज हैं जो एक घोड़े पर दो लद लिये हैं. यों सुन, वे दोनों उतर पड़े, और साईस ने घोड़ा डुरिया लिया, ये पीछे पीछे देखते चले; तब इन्हें देख एक ने एक से कहा, कि भाई! देखो, हराम का माल मुफ़्त जाता है, और किसी के काम नहीं आता. इस बात के सुनते ही कायथ ने बेटे से कहा, क्यों बाबा! लोगों के मुख से बचने का कोई और उपाय हो तो करो, मुझ से तो अब कुछ नहीं बन आती. निरुत्तर हो बेटा बोला, लाला जी! तुम सच कहते थे, संसार बुरी ठौर है, कर तो डर, न कर तो भी डर. इस का कुछ उपाय नहीं.

१८ किसी ठौर पर कोई मुल्ला बैठा लड़के पढ़ाता था,

कि एक लड़के के बाप ने आकर उसे उलहना दिया, मियां साहिब! मेरे बेटे को आप ने कुछ न सिखाया पढ़ाया; देखो, अबतक छोकरों के साथ वह खेलता फिरता है, और मेरा कहा नहीं मानता. इतनी बात के सुनते ही मियां जी रोसकर बोला, कि हां जी, नेकी बरबाद गुनह लाज़िम. मैं ने एक बरस परिश्रम कर, लिखा पढ़ा गधे से मनुष बनाया, और तुम ने यह बात कही, अब मुझे तुम से कुछ लेने पाने की आस न रही. यह निरास की बात सुनकर लड़के का बाप तो मियां जी को बहुत सा भरोसा देके चला गया; पर एक धोबी और धोबिन बड़े धनी, जिन्हों ने मियां जी के मुंह यह बात गैल में खड़े होके सुनी थी, कि मैं ने तुम्हारे लड़के को बरस दिन में लिखा पढ़ा गधे से मनुष किया, वे दोनों स्त्री पुरुष आ उपस्थित हुए, और हाथ जोड़कर बोले, कि मियां जी! जितने रुपये चाहिये लीजे, और मेरे भी गधे को मनुष बना दीजे. मुल्ला ने उन दोनों की बात सुनके मन में बिचारा कि ये हिये के अंधे, मत के हीन, गांठ के पूरे, मेरे भाग से आन मिले हैं, इन से रुपये क्यों नहीं लेता? यह समझ, इन्ने उन से कहा, सहस्र रुपये दो, और गधे को बांध जाओ. इस बात के सुनते ही, वे झट तोड़ा दे गधा बांध गये; और एक बरस पीछे फिर आन उपस्थित हुए. उन के देखते ही मियां जी ने कहा, कि दो दिन पहले आते तो उसे पाते; अब तो वह जाके जौनपुर का क़ाज़ी हुआ. उन्हों ने पूछा,

कि अब हम उसे क्योंकर पावें? मियां जी ने कहा, कि तुम उस के बांधने की रस्सी और दाना खाने का नंदोला ले जाके सोंहीं खड़े हो दिखलाओ; जब वह पहचानके तुम्हें पास बुलावे, तब तुम निराले ले जाके सब वृत्तांत कहियो, अपना ब्यौरा सुनकर वह तुम्हें बहुतेरा डरावेगा, पर तुम न डरियो, और कहियो, जो तुम हमारी बात न मानो, तो चलकर मियां जी से पूछ लो. निदान वे दोनों जौनपुर गये, और उसी भांति करने लगे; तब क़ाज़ी ने इन दोनों को पास बुलाकर पूछा, कि तुम यह क्या करते हो? बोले, निराले चलो तो इस का वृत्तांत कहें. क़ाज़ी उन्हें निराले ले गये; फिर उन्हों ने सब वृत्तांत कह सुनाया. क़ाज़ी समझा, किसी ने इन्हें बहकाया है, इस से इन की बात बिन माने किसी भांति मेरा पीछा न छोड़ेंगे. यों समझ, क़ाज़ी ने कहा, जो तुम ने कहा सो सब सच्च; पर अब तुम हम से क्या चाहते हो? ये बोले, हम अपुत्रक हैं, हमारा धन संपत का मीरा होके मरने से मिट्टी दीजो, यही हम चाहते हैं. निदान मारे लाज के क़ाज़ी ने उन की बात मान ली इस लिये कि कोई और न सुने.

२० अकबर बादशाह के साम्हने एक दिन मियां तानसेन ने सूरदास का यह बिसनपद गाया; जसुदा बार बार यह भाषे, है कोई ब्रज में हितू हमारी चलत गोपालहि राखे. बादशाह ने इस के अर्थ पूछे; मियां ने कहा, जसुदा घड़ी

घड़ी यह कहे है, है कोई ब्रज में मित्र हमारा जो चलते हुए गोपाल को रखे? मियां तो गाय समझाय चले गये; इस में आये बीरबल; महाराज ने उन ने भी उस का अर्थ पूछा; बीरबल बोले, धर्मावतार! बार कहते हैं पौर को, सो जसुदा पौर पौर यह कहती है कि है कोई ब्रज में मित्र हमारा जो गोपाल को न जाने दे? इतने में राजा टोड़लमल आये; महाराज ने उस से भी अर्थ पूछा; कहा पृथ्वीनाथ! जसुदा कृष्ण की मा, बार कहते हैं पानी को, और द्वार को; सो पानी का द्वार हुआ घाट; इस से अर्थ यह हुआ, कि जसुदा घाट घाट यह कहती है, कि है कोई ब्रज में मित्र हमारा कि गोपाल को चलने से फेर रखे? इस बीच आये मुल्ला फ़ैज़ी; बादशाह ने उन से भी विस का अर्थ पूछा; उत्तर दिया, कि बार ब मअ़नी आब ओ दर; यहां आब से मुराद है आंसू, और दर से मुराद है आंख; इस से मअ़ने ये निकले, कि जसुदा रोकर यह बात कहती है, कि है कोई ब्रज में दोस्त हमारा जो गोपाल को न जाने दे? इस बीच आये नव्वाब ख़ानख़ानान; बादशाह ने उन से भी उस का अर्थ पूछा; तब नव्वाब ने कहा, कि धर्मावतार! इस बिसनपद का अर्थ किसी और ने भी कहा है? इस बात के सुनते ही, जिस जिस ने जो जो अर्थ कहे थे, महाराज ने कह सुनाये. तब नव्वाब ने कहा, महाराज! ये तो उस बिसनपद के अर्थ नहीं, पर हां, हर किसी ने अपने मन का अनुभाव बखान

किया. बादशाह ने पूछा, सो क्या? बोला, वह बिचारा कलावंत जैसे एक नीम तीम शब्दों को घड़ी घड़ी कहता है, उस के मन में यही ध्यान बंधा, कि जसुदा घड़ी घड़ी कहती है. और बीरबल जात का ब्राह्मन, पौर पौर का फिरनेवाला; उस के भी मन में यही ध्यान बंधा, कि जसुदा पौर पौर कहती है. और टोड़लमल मुतसद्दी, उस के ध्यान में यह बूझ पड़ा, कि जसुदा घाट घाट कहती है. और फ़ैज़ी कवि, बिन रोने के और अर्थ न सूझा, इस से उस के ध्यान में आया, कि जसुदा रो रो कहती है. यह बात सुनकर बादशाह ने कहा, भला अब तुम कहो, उस का क्या अर्थ है. निबेदन किया, कि पृथ्वीनाथ! बार कहते हैं बाल को, सो जसुदा का बाल बाल यह कहता है, कि है कोई ब्रज में मित्र हमारा जो गोपाल को न जाने दे. अर्थ के सुनते ही, बादशाह ने प्रसन्न हो सब को प्रसंशा की, और ब्रज भाषा के बिस्तार को बहुत सराहा.

احمق *aḥmaḳ*, very foolish, a fool. *a*

احوال *aḥwál*, m. condition, circumstances, events. *a*

اختراع *ikhtirá'*, m. contrivance, invention. *a*

اختيار *ikhtiyár*, m. choice, power. *a*

آخر *ákhir*, last, at last, the end. *a*

آخرت *ákhirat*, f. futurity, a future state. *a*

آخون *ákhún*, m. teacher, preceptor. *p*

ادا *adá*, performance; payment; blandishment. *a*

اداس *udás*, grieved, dejected. *s*

ادب *adab*, m. institute; politeness, manners; plur. *ádáb*, ceremonies, etc. *a*

آدمي *ádmí*, m. f. a descendant of Adam, a human being (man or woman), people. *a*

آدها *ádhá*, half, *s*

ادهر *udhar*, thither. *h*

ادهر *idhar*, hither. *h*

ادهك *adhik*, more, exceeding. *s*

ادهيانا *adhyáná* or *adhyá-lená*, a. to halve. *h*

اراده *iráda*, m. desire, purpose. *a*

آرام *árám*, m. comfort, health, repose. *p*

ارته *arth*, m. substance, purport. *s*

آرزو *árzú*, f. wish, desire, want. *p*

آروڑه *árúṛh*, mounted, riding. *s*

اڑانا *uṛáná*, a. to dissipate, squander; to cause to fly. *s*

اڑنا *uṛná*, n. to fly, to soar up. *s*

آزاد *ázád*, free, solitary; a hermit. *p*

ازبسک *az-bas-ki*, inasmuch as. *p*

آزردگي *ázurdagí*, f. affliction; displeasure, vexation. *p*

آزرده *ázurda*, afflicted, vexed. *p*

آزمايش s. f. *ázmá,ish*, trial. *p*

اژدها *azhdahá*, m. a dragon. *p*

اس *us*, that; *is*, this; inflections of the pronouns *wuh* and *yih*; *is-meṅ*, during this, in the meantime. *h*

آس *ás*, f. hope, desire, reliance. *s*

آسان *ásán*, easy; *ásání*, facility. *p*

اسباب *asbáb*, m. causes; goods and chattels. *a*

استاد *ustád*, m. a teacher, master. *p*

استفسار *istifsár*, m. searching for information, inquiry. *a*

آسرا *ásrá*, m. refuge. *s*

اسراف *isráf*, m. prodigality, ruin. *a*

اسطرح *is-ṭarah*, in this manner; *us-ṭarah*, in that manner, *h a*

اسليي *is-liye*, on this account. *h*

آسمان *ásmán*, m. the sky, the firmament, heaven. *p*

اسوار *aswár*, riding, mounted; *aswárí*, act of riding. *s*

اسواسطي *iswáste*, for this reason; *uswáste*, for that reason.

اسيس *asis* (or *ásis*), f. a benediction. *s*

اشاره *ishára*, m. a hint, a signal. *a*

اشرار *ashrár*, miscreants, scoundrels. *a*

اشراف *ashráf*, nobles, grandees; *ashráf-zádí*, daughter of a grandee. *a*

VOCABULARY.

[N.B.—The letter m. signifies masculine, f. feminine, a. active, n. neuter. It has not been deemed necessary to give the names of the different parts of speech, except when a word belongs to more than one division. In the Hindústání words and phrases, *k.* stands for *karná*; *h.* for *honá*; *d.* for *dená*; *j.* for *jáná*; and *l.* for *lená*. The letters *a*, *p*, *s*, and *h*, at the end of each definition, denote respectively the Arabic, Persian, Sanskrit, or Indian origin of the word explained.]

ا

اب *ab*, now, presently; *ab tak*, till now; *ab-ká*, of now, of the present time. *s*

آب *áb*, m. water, lustre. *p*

ابتدا *ibtidá*, f. beginning. *a*

ابهاگي *abhágí*, ill-starred, wicked. *s*

ابهي *abhí*, just now, immediately. *s*

ابير *aber*, m. time, delay. *h*

آپ *áp*, self, selves; your honour. *s*

اپترک *aputrak*, childless. *s*

اپرادھ *aparádh*, m. fault, transgression. *s*

آپس *ápas*, our-, your-, or them-, selves, one another; *ápas-men*, among themselves, etc. *s*

اپستهت *upasthit*, arrived, present. *s*

اپنا *apná*, belonging to self, own. *s*

آ پهنچنا *á pahunchná*, n. to arrive at. *h*

اتارنا *utárná*, a. to cause to descend, strip off. *s*

اتر *uttar*, m. an answer; the north. *s*

اترنا *utarná*, n. to descend, to alight. *s*

اتفاقاً *ittifáḳan*, accidentally. *a*

اتنا *itná*, so much, so many. *s*

آٹھ *áṭh*, eight. *s*.

اٹھانا *uṭháná*, a. to lift or raise up, to take away. *s*

اٹھنا *uṭhná*, n. to rise up, to be abolished, to go away; *uṭh-jáná*, n. to depart. *s*

اثناي *asnáe*, in the midst, in the course of. *a*

اثر *asar*, m. impression, effect. *a*

آج *áj*, to-day. *s*

اجازت *ijázat*, f. permission, orders. *a*

اجي *ají*, an interjection to call or bespeak attention, as: Sir, hark you! *h*

اچها *achchhá*, good, excellent, well. *s*

احمد آباد *Aḥmad-ábád*, the capital of Gujerát. *p*

نہین * اَور دُوسْرا اُس مُنْہ زور خچر کي برابر هَي ـ جو لگام نہین مانْتا *

۸ ایکْ کمِیني اَور بهلي آدْمِي سي اِفْلاس مین دوسْتِي هُوئي * کمِینه دَولْتمَنْد هوتي هِي نجِیب‌زادي سي آنْکهین لگا چُراني * تب وُہ خفا هوکر ـ بولا ـ یِہ سچ هَي کمِیني کِي دوسْتِي جَیسِي بالُو کِي بهِیت *

۹ ایکْ شخْص ني افْلاطُون سي پُوچها ـ کِہ تُم ني بهُت برْسون درْیا کا سفر کِیا * درْیا مین کیا کیا عجائِب دیکهي ؟ افْلاطُون ني جَواب دِیا ـ کِہ یِهِي عجُوبه دیکها ـ کِہ مَین درْیا سي کِناري کو سلامت پہُنْچا *

۱۰ اکْبر ني بِیرْبل سي پُوچها ـ کِہ لڑائِي کي وقْت کیا کام آتا هَي ؟ بِیرْبل ني عرْض کِیا ـ کِہ جهان‌پناه ! اَوسان * بادْشاه ني کها ـ هتْهیار اَور زور کیُون نہِین کہْتا ؟ بِیرْبل ني کها ـ جهان‌پناه ! اگر اَوسان خطا هو جاوي ـ تو هتْهیار اَور زور کِس کام آوي ؟

۱۱ ایکْ هِرن پِیاسا هوکر پانِي کي چشْمي پاس آیا ـ کِہ اُس سي پانِي پِئي * وُہ چشْمه بڑي غار مین تها * جب پانِي پِیکر چاها کِہ اُوپر چڑْهي ـ چڑْه نه سکا * ایکْ لومْڑِي ني دیکْهکر کها ـ اَي بهائي ! تُو ني بهُت بُرا کام کِیا ـ کْیُونْکِہ اُترْني سي پہْلي چڑْهني کا رسْته دیکه نه لِیا *

۱۲ ایک شیر اَور ایک مرد ني اپني تصوِیر ایک گھر مین دیکھي * مرد ني شیر سي کها - دیکھتا هَي اِنسان کي شجاعت کو؟ کَیسا شیر کو اپنا تابِع کِیا هَي * شیر ني جَواب دِیا که مُصَوِّر آدمي تها - اگر اِسکا مُصَوِّر شیر هوتا تو اَیسا نه هوتا *

۱۳ ایک درویش ني ایک بخِیل سي کچھ سُوال کِیا * بخِیل ني کها اگر تو ایک بات میري قبول کري - تو جو کچھ کهیگا سو کرونگا * فقِیر ني پُوچها وه کیا بات هَي؟ اُس ني کها مجھ سي کبھي کچھ مت مانگ * اُسکي سِوا جو کچھ تو کهیگا سو مانونگا *

۱۴ نقل هَي که ایک حکیم بِیمار هُوا * بهت لوگ اُس کي عِیادت کو آئي - اَور دیر تلک بَیٹھي رهي * حکِیم اُن سي بهت ناخوش هُوا * ایک ني اُن مین سي یه دریافت کِیا اَور کها - که حکِیم صاحِب! کچھ همین نصِیحت کرو * حکِیم ني کها که اگر کِسي کي عِیادت کو جائِیي - تو دیر تک نه بَیٹھئي *

۱۵ ایک شخص کِسي بخِیل سي دوستي رکھتا تها * ایک دِن اُس سي کها - مَین سفر کو جاتا هون - تو اپني انگوٹھي مجھي دي - تو مَین اپني پاس رکھون * جب اُسکو دیکھونگا تجھکو یاد کرونگا * بخِیل ني جَواب دِیا - جو مجھي یاد رکها چاهتي هو * تو اپني اُنگلي کو خالي دیکھ کر یاد کرنا که فُلاني شخص سي انگوٹھي مانگي تهي - اُس ني نه دِي *

١٦ ایکٹ کایتھ اَور اُس کا غُلام دونون ایکٹ گھر مین سوتي تھي * لالا ني کہا - رام چیرا ! دیکْھ تو پانِي برسْتا ھَي یا کھُل گَیا ؟ اُس ني کہا - برسْتا ھَي * پُوچھا - تُو کِس طرح جانْتا ھَي - تَین تو پڑا سوتا ھَي * کہا - بِلّي آئي تِھي - اُس کو مَین ني ٹٹولا تھا - بھِیگِي تِھي * کہا - چِراغ بُجْھا دي * کہا - مُنْھ ڈھانْپ کي سو رھو - انْدھیرا ھو جائیگا * پھِر کہا - دروازہ بنْد کر دي * کہا - بیَّا جِي ! دو کام ھمْني کِئي - ایکٹ کام تُم کرو * غرض اَیسا حُجّتِي اَور سُسْت تھا - آخِر نہ اُٹّھا - پڑا پڑا جَواب دیتا رھا *

١٧ ایکٹ ني ایکٹ سي یِہ شرْط کِي تِھي - کِہ اگر مَین بازِي نہ جِیتُون - تو سیر بھر گوشْت میري بدن سي تراش لو * اَیسا ھُؤا کِہ اُس ني بازِي نہ پائِي * حرِیف ني کہا شرْط ادا کر * اُس ني نہ مانا * دونون قاضِي کي پاس نالِشي گَئي * قاضِي ني مُدّعِي سي فرْمایا مُعاف کر * اُس ني اِنْکار کِیا * قاضِي ني برْھم ھوکي کہا کِہ نراش لي - پر جو ایکٹ سیر سي ایکٹ رتِي زِیادہ کاٹیگا تو سزا پاویگا *

١٨ ایکٹ شخْص بادْشاہ کي عَینِ قِلْعي کي نِیچي لُوٹا گَیا * اُسْني بادْشاہ کِي خِدْمت مین عرْض کِي کِہ - جہان پناہ ! مُجْھي قِصاقون ني حُضُور کي قِلْعي کِي دِیوار کي نِیچي لُوٹ لِیا * بادْشاہ ني فرْمایا کِہ تُو ھشْیار کیون نرھا ؟ بولا کہ غُلام کو معْلُوم نتھا کہ حضْرت کي زیر جھروکھي

مُسافِر لُوٹتي جاتي هَين * بادشاه ني کها کیا تُوني یِه مثل نهِین سُنِي ؟ چِراغ کي نِیچي اَندهیرا *

١٩ کِسِي کو بادشاه کي یهان سي بڑا کام مِلا * یِه خُوش خبرِي سُن کر اُس کا ایک دوست مُبارکبادِي دیني کو ایک دِن اُس کي گهر آیا * اُس ني اَپني دوست سي اَنجان هوکر پُوچها تُم کَون هو؟ اَور یهان کیُون آئي هو؟ وُه غرِیب نِهایت خفِیف هُؤا اَور کهني لگا - کیا مُجهي تُم نهِین پهچانتي هو؟ مَین تُمهارا قدِیم دوست هُون * سُنا تها کِه اندهي هو گئي هو - اِس لِئي تُمهارِي خبر کو آیا هُون *

٢٠ ایک بڑا سَوداگر تها - اُس کي دو بیٹي تهي * تهوڑي دِنون مین وُه سَوداگر مر گیا * تب باپ کي دَولت دونون ني بانٹ لِي * ایک ني دو تِین مهِیني مین اَپنِي سب دَولت اُڑا دِي - بُري آدمِیون کِي صلاح سي * دُوسرِي ني سَوداگرِي اِختیار کِي - بهلي آدمِي کي کهني سي * ایک فقِیر هُوا - دُوسرا دَولتمند * پس جو کوئي بهلي آدمِي کِي بات مانیگا اُس کا بهلا هوگا * اور جو کوئِي بُري کِي بات مانیگا اُس کا بُرا هوگا - جَیسا اُن دونون کا هُوا *

٢١ ایک شخص سِوائِي ایک گهوڑي کي اَور کُچه نهین رکهتا تها * اُسني اُس گهوڑي کو اِصطبل مین باندها - پر اِسطرح کِه اگاڑِي کِي طرف پِچهاڑِي کِي * اَور شهر مین منادِي دِي - کِه عجب تماش

دیکھو - کِه دُم کِي جگهه گهوڑي کا سِر هَي * شهْر کي لوگ جمْع هُوئي * وُه شخْص کُچهه نقْد لیتا - تب آدْمِیون کو اِصْطبل مین جانی دیتا * جو کوئِي طَویلي سي پهِرْتا شرْم سي کُچهه نه کهْتا * وُه مُفْلِس تها - اُس بهاني سي اپْنا کام کر لِیا *

۲۲ ایکٔ بخِیل مسْجِد کِي طرف واسْطي نماز کي چلا جاتا تها * اثْنائي راه مینْ اُس کو یاد آیا - کِه چِراغ گهر کا بُجْهاکر نهین آیا هُون * وَهان سي پهِرا - اَور درْوازي پر آ لَونْڈِي سي پُکارْکر کها - چِراغ کو گُل کر - اَور درْوازه مت کهول - کِه گهسیگا * لَونْڈِي ني کها - اَي صاحِب ! اِتْنِي راه جو آئي گئي جُوتا نه گهِسا هوگا ؟ بولا اَي عقْلْمنْد لَونْڈِي انْدیشه مت کر - کِه مَین ننْگي پاؤن آیا هُون - اَور بغل مین جُوتي کو لایا هُون *

۲۳ ایکٔ مُسلْمان بِیمار تها * غُلام سي کها - کِه فُلاني حکِیم کي پاس جاکر دَوا لا * اُسْني کها - شاید حکِیم جِي اِسْوقْت گهر مین نهووین * کها * هونْگي - جا * تب اُسْني کها - اگر مُلاقات بهِي هووي لیکِن دَوا ندین ؟ تد کها - رُقْعه همارا لیجا - الْبتّه دینگي * پهِر کها - کِه جو اُنْهون ني دَوا بهِي دِي اگر فائِده نکري ؟ کها - اَي کم بخْت ! یهین بَیْٹها تمهِیدین بانْدها کریگا یا جائیگا ؟ کها - صاحِب ! فرْض کِیا کِه اگر فائِده بهِي کري - تو حاصِل کیا ؟ آخِر ایکْدِن مرْنا بر حق هَي * جَیسا اب مري تَیسا تب مری *

۲۴ دو آشنا اپنی شہر سی تباہ ہوکر کِسی مُلک مین گئی * ایک اُن مین سی پڑھ سکتا تھا ـ سو لڑکی پڑھانی لگا ـ اَور دُوسرا جو ہُنر جانتا تھا ـ سو اپنا پیشہ کرنی لگا * اِتِفاقًا وی دونون بِیمار پڑی * جو پڑھا تھا سو اُس حالت مین پڑھاتا تھا ـ اَور پیسی پَیدا کرتا تھا * اَور جو ہُنرمند تھا ـ سو ماری مُفلِسی کی مرتا تھا * کیُونکِہ وُہ تو لیٹی لیٹی ہِی پڑھا سکتا تھا ـ اور اِسکا کام بی ہاتھ پانو کی ہِلائی ہو نسکتا تھا * پس لازِم ہَی کِہ پڑھنا سِیکھِی کِہ یِہ سب سی بِہتر ہَی *

۲۵ ایک شخص کی گھر مین رُوپئی کا توڑا گُم ہُوا تھا * اُسنی قاضِی کو خبر دِی * قاضِی نی گھر کی سب آدمِیون کو طلب کِیا ـ اَور ایک ایک لکڑِی طُول مین برابر سب کی حوالی کِی ـ اَور کہا کہ چور کِی لکڑِی ایک اُنگل بڑھ جائیگی ـ تِس پِیچھی سبکو رُخصت کِیا * جِس نی چورِی کِی تھِی ـ خَوف سی ایک اُنگل لکڑِی کاٹ ڈالِی * دُوسری روز قاضِی نی سبکِی لکڑِیان دیکھِین ـ چور کو پہچانا * اُس سی رُوپئی لِئی اَور سزا دِی *

۲۶ دو عَورتین ایک لڑکی کی واسطی آپس مین جھگڑا کرتِی تھِین ـ اَور گواہ نہِین رکھتِین * دونون قاضِی کی پاس گئِین ـ اَور اِنصاف چاہا * قاضِی نی جلّاد کو بُلا کی فرمایا ـ کِہ اِس لڑکی کی دو ٹُکڑی کر ایک ایک دونون کو دی * ایک عَورت یِہ بات سُنتی ہِی چُپ رہِی ـ دُوسرِی نی فریاد شُرُوع کِی ـ کِہ خُدا کی واسطی میری لڑکی

کي دو ٹکڑي مت کر۔ اگر اَيسا اِنصاف هَي تو مَين لڑکا نہين
چاہتي هُون * قاضِي کو يقِين هُؤا کِه لڑکي کِي ما يِہِي هَي * لڑکي
کو اُسي سپُرد کِيا ۔ اَور دُوسرِي کو کوڑي مار کي نِکال دِيا *

٢٧ ايک شخص هر روز چهه روٹيان خرِيد کرتا تها * ايک دوست
ني اُس سي پُوچها کِه چهه روٹِي سي کيا کرتا هَي ؟ اُسني کها ۔ ايک
رکهتا هُون ۔ ايک ڈال ديتا هُون ۔ دو پهير ديتا هُون ۔ دو قرض ديتا
هُون * دوست ني کها مَين يِه مُعمّا نہين سمجها ۔ صاف کہه * اُسني
جَواب دِيا ۔ ايک روٹِي جو رکهتا هُون ۔ اُسکا يِه مطلب کِه مَين
کهاتا هُون * ايک روٹِي ميرِي ساس کهاتِي هَي ۔ وُه ڈال ديني مين
داخِل هَي * دو جو واپس کرتا هُون ۔ اُس سي يِه مُراد کِه ماباپ،
کهاتي هَين * دو روٹِي جو بيٹي کهاتي هَين ۔ وُه قرض ديتا هُون *

٢٨ ايک دِن سِکندر ني اپني مجلِس مين کها ۔ کِه جِسني
جو کُچه مُجه سي مانگا سو پايا۔ کوئي محرُوم نہين گيا * ايک شخص
ني عرض کِيا ۔ کِه اَي خُداوند ! مُجهي ايک دِرم درکار هَي عِنايت
کر * سِکندر ني فرمايا پادشاهون سي چهوٹِي چِيز کِي درخواست
کرنا بي‌ادبِي هَي * اُسني اِلتماس کِيا ۔ کِه جو بادشاه کو ايک دِرم
کي ديني سي شرم آتِي هَي ۔ تو ايک مُلک مُجهي بخشِئي * سِکندر
، کها تُو ني دو سوال يبجا کِئي ۔ پہلا ميري مرتبي سي کم ۔ دُوسرا
پنِي قدر سي زياده * وُه لاجَواب اَور شرمنده هُؤا *

2

۲۹ کوئي شخص کہین کو خطّ لِکھتا تھا ۔ ایک بیگانہ اُس کي نزدیک آ بَیٹھا ۔ اَور اُس کي خطّ کو دیکھني لگا * تب اُس ني خطّ مین لِکھا ۔ که بہت سِي راز کِي باتین لِکھنِي تھین ۔ سو نہین لِکھِي گَئین ۔ اِس واسطي کِه میري نزدِیک ایک بڑا بیوُقوف بَیٹھا هَي * اَور اِس خطّ کو دیکھتا هَي * وُه بولا اپني رازکِي حقِیقت جو لِکھنِي هو ۔ سو کِس واسطي نه لِکھتي ؟ مَین ني تو تُمهاري خطّ کو مُطلق نه دیکھا * تب کاتِب ني جَواب دِیا ۔ خَیر اگر تُم ني میرا خطّ نه دیکھا ۔ کہو تو کِس طرح معلُوم کِیا کِه مَین ني یُون لِکھا هَي ؟ اِس بات سي وُه بہت شرمِنده هُوا اَور دم کھا رها *

۳۰ دو مُصَوِّر ني آپس مین کها کِه هم دونون تصوِیر کھَینچین ۔ دیکھین کَون اچھِي کھَینچتا هَي * ایک ني انگُور کي خوشي کِي شبِیه کھَینچِي ۔ اَور دروازي پر لٹکا دِي * چڑیان اُسپر چھونچ مارني لگِین * دیکھني والي بہت خُوش هُوئي * ایک دِن لوگ دُوسري مُصَوِّر کي گھر گَئي ۔ پُوچھا کِه تُمني کهان تصوِیر کھَینچِي هَي ؟ اُسني کها کِه اِس پردي کي پِیچھي * پہلي مُصَوِّر ني پردي پر هاتھ رکھا ۔ سمجھا کِه پرده نہین ۔ دِیوار مین پردي کا نقش کھَینچا هَي * تب دُوسري مُصَوِّر ني کها ۔ تُمهاري کام سي چڑِیون ني فریب کھایا ۔ اَور میرِي نقاشِي سي تُمني *

۳۱ نقل هَي کِه ایک کِشتِي مین دو شخص سَوار هُوئي ۔ ایک

اُن مین منطِقي تها ـ دُوسرا پَیراک * منطِقي ني پَیراک سي پُوچها * کهو یار تُمني کُچه عِلم منطِق کا بهِي سِیکها هي کِه نهِین؟ وُه بولا کِه مَین ني اب تک منطِق کا نام بهِي نهِین سُنا ـ سِیکهني کا تو ذِکر کیا هي؟ سُنکر افسوس لگا کرني ـ کِه تُمني اپني آدهي عُمر جهالت کي دریا مین ڈُبائِي * اِتني مین طُوفان نمُودار هُوا * پَیراک ني تهتهولِي سي منطِقي کو کها ـ کهو صاحِب کُچه پَیرنا بهِي آپ کو آتا هي کِه نهِین؟ یِهه بولا سِواي منطِق کي مَین ني کُچه نه سِیکها هي * تب اُسني حَیف کهاکر کها کِه تُمني اپني سارِي عُمر برباد کِي *

۳۲ ایک درویش کِسي بنئي کِي دُوکان پر گیا ـ اَور سَودي کي لئي شِتابِي کرني لگا * بقّال ني گالِي دِي * درویش ني ایک جُوتي اُسکي سِر پر مارِي * اُسني کُتوال سي نالِش کِي * کُتوال ني فقِیر سي پُوچها ـ کِه بنئي کو کِسواسطي مارا؟ فقِیر ني کها ـ کِه اُسني دُشنام دِي تهِي * کُتوال بولا کِه تُجه سي بڑِي تقصِیر هُوئِي ـ پر فقِیر هَي ـ اِس لئي سِیاست نهِین کرتا هُون * جا آٹه آني فریادِي کو دي ـ تیري قُصُور کِي سزا یِهِي هَي * درویش ني ایک رُوپیا جیب سي نِکال کُتوال کي هاته مین دِیا ـ اَور ایک پاپوش کُتوال کي سِر پر مارکر یِهه کها ـ کِه اگر اَیسا اِنصاف هي ـ تو آٹه آٹه آني تُم دونون بانٹ لو *

۳۳ ایک روز کِسي مسخري سي بڑِي تقصِیر هُوئِي * بادشاه ني اُس کِي گردن مارني کا حُکم کِیا ـ اَور فرمایا ـ میري رُوبرُو گردن مارو * جلّاد

ني تلوار نکالي - اور مسخره تلوار کي نيچي گهبراتا تها - اور سر کو ادهر ادهر کرتا - اس واسطي که بادشاه کي خو پر اعتماد نه رکهتا تها - اور تلون مزاجي اس کي جانتا تها * مصاحبون مين سي ايک ني کها - اي نامرد کيا گهبراتا هي ؟ - مردانه وار ره - که آدمي ايک روز جهان مين آتا هي - اور دوسري روز جاتا هي * يهه کيا بي جگري هي ؟ مسخره بولا - اگر تو مرد هي - اور تيرا بڑا کليجه هي - تو آ - ميري جگهه بيٹهه - مين اٹهون اور تيري جوان مردي ديکهون * بادشاه بي اختيار هنسا - اور اس کي گناه سي درگذرا *

٣٤ ايک دانشمند کسي شهر مين وارد هوا - سنا که يهان ايک بڑا سخي هي - سب مسافرون کو کهانا کهلاتا هي * دانشمند پهٹي پراني کپڑون سي اسکي گهر گيا * اسني کچهه التفات نه کيا - بلکه بات بهي نه پوچهي * دانشمند شرمنده هو کي پهر آيا * دوسري دن پاکيزه کپڑي کرائي منگوا پهن کي اسکي گهر گيا * اسني ديکهتي هي لنبي تعظيم کي - اپني پاس بٹهايا اور لذيذ کهانا منگوايا * جب دسترخوان پر بيٹها - دانشمند لقمي اپني کپڑي مين رکهني لگا * تب اسني پوچها که يهه کيا حرکت هي ؟ دانشمند ني جواب ديا که کل پراني کپڑي پهني هوي آيا تها - ذره طعام نهين پايا * آج معلوم هوا که يهه نفيس کهانا اس کپڑي کي سبب سي ملا هي * صاحب خانه بهت شرمايا اور کچه نه کها *

۳۵ کِسِي وقت مین ایک شیر بِیمار پڑا * سب درندي اُسکِي عِیادت کو آني - مگر لومڑِي نه آئِي * بھیڑِئِي ني اُسکِي چُغلِي کِي * یِہ خبر لومڑِي کو پہُنچ گئِي * شیر ني بھیڑِئِي سي کہا کِه جب لومڑِي آوي تب مُجھي خبر کرنا * جسوقت که وہ آئِي بھیڑئِي ني اِشاره کر دِیا * شیر ني پُوچھا اِتني دِن تک تُو کہان تھِي ؟ اُسني کہا - دَوا کِي تلاش مین * پھِر اُسني کہا - کیا دَوا لائِي ؟ کہا بھیڑِئِي کِي ساق کا مُہره آپ کِي دَوا هَي * شیرني اُسیوقت چنگُل بھیڑئِي کو مارا - اَور ھڈِي اُسکِي نِکال کر کھا گیا * لومڑِي رُخصت ھُوئِي اَور بھیڑِیا پِیچھي سي لوھُو مین تربتر نِکلا * لومڑِي ني کہا جب بادشاھون کي پاس بَیٹھِئي - تو اُس بات کو کِه مُنہ سي کیا نِکلتا هَي خِیال رکھنا ضرُور چاھِئي *

۳۶ نقل هَي که ایک شخص کِسِي طبِیب پاس آیا * پیٹ کِي درد سي بي قرار هوکر زمِین پر لوٹتي اَور بیتابِي سي ناله کرتِي ھُوئِي دَوا مانگني لگا * طبِیب ني اُسکِي همراھِیون سي پُوچھا - اِسني آج کیا کھایا هَي ؟ کہا جلِي روٹِي کا ٹُکڑا * اُسني فرمایا جو دَوا آنکھ کِي بصارت کو زِیاده کرتِي هَي سو لائو تاکه اِس بِیمار کِي آنکھون مین لگاؤُون * وہ چِلّایا کِه اَي طبِیب ! یِہ کَون سا مقام خُوش طَبعِي اَور هزل کا هَي ؟ مَین پیٹ کِي درد سي چِلّاتا ھُون - اَور تُو آنکھون کِي دَوا بتاتا هَي * آنکھ کِي دَوا دردِ شِکم سي کیا علاقه رکھتِي هَي ؟ طبِیب ني

کہا مَین چاہتا ہُون کِہ تیرِي آنکھین روشن ہون۔ تاکِہ سِیاہ اَور سُفَیہ مین تفاوُت کر سکي۔ پِھر کبھِي جلِي ہُوئِي روٹِي نکھاوي * پس تیرِي آنکھون کِي دَوا پیٹ کي عِلاج سي واجِبتر ہَي *

۳۷ ایکٔ مرتبي ایکٔ کي گھر مین بڑِي آگ لگِي۔ چارون طرف لُوکا اُڑنِي لگي * گھروالي دو بھائِي تھي۔ اَور اُنکي ما باپ نِہایت ضعِیف۔ کِہ ہِلنِي کِي طاقت نہِین رکھتي تھي۔ اَور اُس آگ سي بچ نہِین سکتي۔ بلکِہ خَوف سي کانپتي تھي * وي دو بھائِي اُس مُصِیبت مین حَیران۔ ایکٔ ني اِرادہ کِیا کِہ گھر سي اسباب باہِر نِکالي * تب اُنھون ني آپسمین یِہ کہا۔ کِہ کہان پاوینگي ہم اَیسِي بیشُمار دَولت جِس سي ہمني زِندگانِي پائِي ؟ آؤ۔ اسباب چھوڑ کي اُنکو نِکال لاوین * یِہ بات کہکي ایکٔ ني باپ کو کانڈھي پر چڑھا لِیا۔ اَور دُوسرِي ني ما کو۔ اَور اُس آگ سي بچا کر اُنکو ایکٔ جگہ مین بَیٹھا دِیا۔ اَور کِسِي چِیز کا خِیال نہ کِیا۔ سب اسباب جل گَیا *

۳۸ ایکٔ واعِظ کِسِي گانو مین کِتنِي ایکٔ آدمِیون کو وعظ کرتا تھا * اِس مین کوئِي گنوار بھِي وھان آ بَیٹھا۔ اَور لگا اُس کا مُنہ دیکھ دیکھ بیقرار ہو رونِي * اِس کو روتا دیکھ۔ سب ني جانا۔ کِہ یِہ کوئِي بڑا مومدِل ہَي جو اِتنا روتا ہَي * ایکٔ ني اِس سي پُوچھا کہ بھائِي ! سچ کہہ تُو جو اِتنا روتا ہَي تیرِي دِل مین کیا آیا ہَي ؟

واعِظ کو اُنگلي سي بتا بولا - کِه اِن مِیان کِي ڈاڑھي ہِلتي دیکھ مُجھي اپنا مُؤا ہُؤا پیارا بکرا یاد آیا - کِه جب نه تب اُس کِي بھي اِسي طرح ڈاڑھي ہِلتي تھي - اِس لِئي مَین روتا ہُون * یِہ سُن سب کھِل‌کھِلا اُٹھي - اَور واعظ شرمِنده ہو دم کھا رہا *

۳۹ کِسي بادشاه ني اپنا فرزند ایک مُعلِم کو سَونپا - کِه اِسکو عِلمِ نُجُوم سِکھاؤ - جب اُسمین لاثاني ہو - تو اِسي حُضُور مین لاؤ * آخُون بڑي شفقت اَور مِحنت سي جِتني مراتِب اُس عِلم مین تھي - خاطِر خواه جتائي * جب دیکھا کِه لڑکي کو اُس عِلم مین خُوب مهارت ہو چُکي - تب حُضُور مین آکر عرض کِي - کِه جهان‌پناه! شہزاده اب نُجُومِ مین لائِق و فائِق ہُؤا - جب مرضئ مُبارک مین آوي - تب اُسکا اِمتِحان لِیجِئي * فرمایا کِه اِسي وقت حاضِر کرو * حُکم کي ساتھ ہِي لڑکا آ پہُنچا - اَور بادشاه کِي خِدمت مین آداب بجا لایا * حضرت ني اپني دستِ مُبارک کِي انگُوٹھي مُٹھي مین لیکر فرمایا - بُوجھو تو! ہماري مُٹھي مین کیا ہَي؟ لڑکي ني عرض کِي کِه پِیر مُرشِد! کُچھ گول گول سا ہَي - اُس مین سُوراخ اَور پتھر بھِي نظر آتا ہَي * حضرت ني کہا - اُسکا نام کیا ہَي؟ لڑکا بولا - چکّي کا پاٹ * تب عالم‌پناه مُعلِم کي چِہري کِي طرف دیکھني لگي - اُسني عرض کِي کِه خُداوند! عِلم کا نقص نہِین - یِہ عقل کي کوتاہِي ہَي *

۴۰ دو مُسافِر ایکؔ سرای مین جا اُتری * صُبح هوتی هِی چل کهڑی هُؤی * ایکؔ نی دُوسْری سی پُوچها کِه تُم نی اپْنی اُونٹ پر کَون سِی جِنْس لادِی هَی ؟ کها ایکؔ آکْهی مین گیهُون اَور دُوسْری مین ریت ـ تاکِه دونون کا بوجْه برابر رهی * کها ریت کو ڈال دی ـ اَور گیهُون کو دونون طرف ادْهیا لی شُتر سُبکؔبار هوگا اَور تُم هُشْیار * اُس نی کها ـ اَی دوسْت ! تُمْهاری یهان اِتْنی دانائِی پر کِتْنی دَولت هَی ؟ بولا یِهی فقط میرِی جان جو دیکْهتی هو ـ اِس کی سِوا اَور کُچه اپْنی قبْضی مین نهِین رکْهتا هُون * کها تُم آگی جاؤ ـ مَین پِچْهی رهُون ـ نهِین تو مین آگی جاؤُن ـ تُم پِچْهی آؤ * خُدا نه کری تُمهاری اِفْلاس کی هَوا مُجهی لگی * مَین باز آیا اَیسی دانائِی سی ـ میرِی نادانِی هِی بِهْتر هَی *

۴۱ ایکؔ بہْرا گُدڑیا جنْگل مین اپْنی بهیڑین چراتا تها * قضاکار اُسْکی ایکؔ بهلِی بهیڑ کهوئی گئی * تب اُس نی ایکؔ لنْگڑی بهیڑ کی طرف دیکه کر کها ـ کِه جو وُه بهیڑ مِلی ـ تو اِسی مَین کِسی کو خُدا کِی راه پر دُونْگا * اِتْنا کہْتی هِی بهیڑ مِلِی ـ تد وُه لنْگڑی بهیڑ کا کان پکڑ کِسی کو دینی لی چلا * اِس مین سونْهِین سی ایکؔ اَور بہْرا آیا * اِس نی وِس سی کها ـ کِه یِه بهیڑ تُو لی * وُه بولا ـ خُدا کِی قسم ! مَین نی اِسْکی ٹانگؔ نهِین توڑِی * غرض یِهی کہْتی کہْتی دونون قاضِی کی یهان گئی * قاضِی بِهِی بہْرا تها ـ اَور اپْنی گهر مین کِسی سی خفا هو

بَیٹھا تھا * اِنھین دُور سي آتي دیکھ - اُن ني اپْني جِي مین جانا - کہ شاید یي اُسِي کا پَیغام لِئي آتي ھَین * یِہ سمجھ اِتْنا کہ اپْني گھ بھِیتر بھاگ گیا - کِہ اُس بدْذات کِي بات مَین کبھِي نہ سُنُونْگا *

۴۲ ایک بادْشاہ وزِیر کي ساتھ سَیر کو گیا تھا * گیہُون کي درخْت آدْمِي کي قدّ سي لنبي دیکھ کي مُتعجّب ھُؤا اَور بولا - کِہ ایسي بُلنْد درخْت گیہُون کي کبھِي نہِین دیکھي * وزِیر ني عرْض کِیا کِہ میري وطن مین ھاتھِي کي ڈِیل برابر ھوتي ھَین * بادْشاہ مُسْکُرایا - وزِیر ني جانا کِہ بادْشاہ ني میري قَول کو دُروغ سمْجھا - اُسِي سي ھنْسا * آخِر گھر پہُنْچْتي ھِي اُسْني وطن کي لوگون کو لِکھا - کِہ تھوڑي درخْت گیہُون کي بِھجْوا دو * خطّ پہُنْچْني تک فصْل آخِر ھو گئِي * ایک سال کي بعْد گیہُون کي درخْت وھان سي آئي * وزِیر بادْشاہ کي حُضُور مین لي گَیا * بادْشاہ ني سب اِسْتِفْسار کِیا * اُسْني عرْض کِي - کِہ پار سال مَین ني کہا تھا - کِہ گیہُون کي درخْت ھاتھِي کي برابر لنْبي ھوتي ھَین - تب جہان پناہ ھنْسي تھي - اپْني بات کِي تصْدِیق کي لِئي لایا ھُون * بادْشاہ ني فرْمایا کِہ اب مَین ني باور کِیا - پر ھرْگز کِسِي سي اَیسِي بات مت کہہ جو ایک برس گُذرْني کي بعْد اِعْتِبار کِي جاوي *

۴۳ کہْتي ھَین کِہ سُلْطان محْمُود غزْنوِي اَیاز کو بہُت دوسْت رکھْتا تھا * حسد کي سبب سب اَمِیرون ني بادْشاہ سي کہا - کِہ اَیاز ھر روز اکیلا جَواھِرخاني مین جاتا ھَي - معْلُوم ھوتا ھَي کِہ کُچھ

چوراتا هَي - نہيِن تو جَواهِرخاني مين اُسکا کيا کام هَي ؟ بادشاه ني فرمايا کِه جب اپني آنکھ سي ديکھُون - تب باور کرُون * دُوسري دِن لوگون ني سُلطان کو خبر دِي - کِه اَيَاز جَواهِرخاني مين گيا - محمُود ني فورًا جھروکھي سي جھانکا - ديکھا کِه اَيَاز ني ايک صندُوق کھول کي پُرانا مَيلا کپڑا پہنا هَي * بادشاه مکان کي اندر گيا - اَيَاز سي پُوچھا کِه اَيسي کپڑي کيون پہني ؟ اُسني عرض کِي - کِه جب مَين حُضُور کِي بندگي مين نه تھا اَيسي کپڑي پہنتا تھا - اب خُداوند کِي عِنايَت سي نفِيس پوشاک مُيَسّر هي - اِس لِئي پُرانا جامه هر روز پہنتا هُون - کِه اپني قدِيم حالت فراموش نه کرُون - اَور بادشاه کِي نِعمت کِي قدر سمجھُون * سُلطان کو يِه بات پسند آئِي - اُسکو چھاتِي سي لگايا - اَور اُسکا مرتبه بڑھايا *

۴۴ دو آدمِي باهم هوکر نکلي - کِه کِسي دُور ديس مين جا رهِيي * تھوڑي دِنون کي بِيچ ايک مُلک مين جا پہُنچي * ايک ني دريافت کيا کِه دِل جمعِي اَور خُوبِي کي ساتھ جو يهان رهِيي - تو ضرور هَي کِه پہلي يهان کي رهني والون کِي بھاکھا سِيکھِيي * غرض اُسني سِيکھِي * دُوسرا اِتنا مغرُور تھا کِه عَوَامُ النّاس کِي زبان کو حِقارت سي نه سِيکھا - صِرف درباري اَور عالِمون کِي زبان تحصِيل کِي * قضاکار بعد کَئِي برس کي دونون کِسِي بستِي مين آئي * وهان کِي بھاکھا اَور اُس مُلک کِي ايک تھِي - پر وهان کي رهني والون ني هنگامه مچاکر غير مُلک کي

حاکِم کو قتّل کرڈالا تھا * وي دونون مسافِر جُدي جُدي مکانون مين بازار کي بِيچ تهي * کِه اُنْہين خُونِيون ني اُنْهين پکڑا - اَور الگ ليجاکر هر ايک سي پُوچْهني لگي - کِه تُمهارا يہان کيا کام هَي ؟ جِس ني مُحاوره وهان کا سِيکها تها - خُوبِي سي جَواب دِيا * اُس کو اُنْهون ني سلامت چهوڑا * اَور دُوسْرا مُسافِر جِس ني صِرْف حاکِمون هِي کِي زبان سي جَواب دِيا - اُس انْبوه ني جلْکر خفگِي سي سِر اُسْکا کاٹ ڈالا *

۴۵ کہْتي هَين کِه ايکْ مرْتبي لُقْمان کي صاحِب ني اُسي کہا - کِه فُلاني کهيت مين جَو بو * لُقْمان ني اُس زمِين مين چينا بويا * لُقْمان کا مالِک اُس جگہه مين گَيا اُور هرِي کهيتِي ديکه لُقْمان سي بولا - که مَين ني تُجه سي کہا تها اِس کهيت مين جَو بو - کِسْواسْطي تُو ني چينا بويا ؟ لُقْمان ني جَواب دِيا - اِس اُمّيد پر مَين ني چينا بويا کِه جَو پهليگا * مالِک ني کہا - يِہه کيا بينْڈِي سمجه هَي ؟ کہِين اَيسا هوتا هَي ؟ لُقْمان ني فرْمايا کِه تُم هميشه دُنْيا کي کهيت مين گُناهونْکا بِيج بوتي هو - اَور گُمان رکْهتي هو کِه قِيامت کي دِن ثَواب کا پهل پاؤگي * اِس سبب سي مَين ني بِهي خِيال کِيا - کِه اِس چِيني سي جَو پَيدا هونگي * اِس بات سي شرْمنْده هو اُسْکي صاحِب ني لُقْمان کو آزاد کِيا * بي باتين بِهي لُقْمان کِي فرْمائِي هُوئِي هَين - کِه نادان هرْچنْد خُوبْصُورت هو اُسْکي ساته صُحْبت نه رکها

چاہئي - کِسواسطي کِه تلوار اگرچِه ديکھني مين سُڈَول هَي - پر کام اُسکا بُرا هي * جو کوئي اچّهي خو رکھتا هَي - بيگاني اُسکي دوست هوتي - اَور بدخو والي کي يگاني دُشمن هوجاتي هَين * جو جيسا بوئيگا سو وَيسا هِي پاويگا *

۴٦ ايک شخص ني بہت سا مال ايک صرّاف کو سُپرد کِيا * اَور آپ سفر کو گَيا * جب پهِر آيا صرّاف سي تقاضا کِيا - اُسني قسم کهائي کِه تُو ني مُجهي نہين سَونپا هَي * مُدّعِي ني قاضِي کو اِطلاع کِي * قاضِي ني تأمُّل کرکي کہا - کِه کِسُو سي مت کہيو کِه فُلانا صرّاف ميرا مال نہين ديتا - مَين تيري مال کي لِئي ايک تدبِير کرُونگا * دُوسري دِن قاضِي ني اُس صرّاف کو بُلا کي يِه کہا - کِه ميري پاس بہت کام هَي - اکيلا نہين کر سکتا هُون - چاهتا هُون کِه تُجهي اپنا نائِب کرُون - کِسواسطي کِه تُو بڑا ايمان‌دار هَي * صرّاف ني قبُول کِيا اَور بہت خُوش هُوا * جب وُه اپني گهر گَيا - تب قاضِي ني مُدّعِي سي کہا - کِه اب مال کِي درخواست صرّاف سي کرو - اَلبتّه ديگا * وُه شخص صرّاف کي گهر گَيا * صرّاف ني اُسکو ديکهتي هِي بُلايا - کِه اجِي اِدهر آؤ - بهلي آئي - مَين تُمہارا مال بهول گَيا تها - اگلي رات مُجهي ياد آيا * خُلاصه يِه هَي - کِه مال اُسکا پهير دِيا - اَور نِيابت کِي طمع سي قاضِي کي پاس گَيا * قاضِي ني فرمايا کِه آج مَين

ني پادشاه كي دربار مين سُنا كه پادشاه تجهكو بڑا كام دِيا چاهتا هي * خُدا كا شُكر كر۔ تو رُتبهٔ اعلىٰ پاويگا ۔ مَين دُوسرا نائِب تلاش كرونگا * آخِر قاضِي ني اِس بهاني سي اُسكو رُخصت كِيا *

۴۷ دو لڑكي نَو جَوان ايك هِي ساته عِلم سِيكهني لگي * اُن مين سي ايك لڑكا بهت اچها نيك بخت تها ۔ اُستاد جو سبق اُسي پڑها ديتا سو ياد كر ليتا ۔ اَور اپني كِتاب اپني گهر مين پڑها كِيا كرتا * دُوسرا غافِل بڑا شرِير تها ۔ جو اپني هم عُمر كي مِحنت پر هنسا كرتا تها ۔ اَور هميشه يِه بات اپني هم مكتب سي كها كرتا تها ۔ كِه تُو گدها هَي * وُه اُسي اكثر يِه جَواب دِيا كرتا ۔ كِه يار! تهوڑي دِنون مين ديكها چاهِئي كيا هو * آخِر اِمتحان كا روز آ پهنچا ۔ اُن دونون كو عِلم كي دريا مين پَيرني پڑا * دانا لڑكي ني اُس احمق كو بهت پِيچهي جهالت كي گِرداب مين شرم سي ڈُوبتي هُوئي چهوڑا ۔ اَور پُكارني لگا ۔ اَي يار! جو تُمهاري خِيال مين بي وُقُوف نظر آتي هَين ۔ سو اكثرون كي نزديك عقلمند هو نِكلينگي ۔ اَور جو اَيسي وقت تُمني سِيكها تو تُمهاري كام نهِين آني كا ۔ لاحاصِل هَي * اگر اپني هم جولِي پر اب هم بهي ٹهٹهي مارين ۔ تو هماري بازِي هوتي ۔ مُوافِق اُس مثل كي ۔ كِه جو جِيتي سو هنسي * لِيكِن داناؤن كي نزدِيك نِهايت بعِيد هَي كيا دوستي كيا دُشمنِي سي اَيسِي حالت مين افسوس كِي جگه تضحِيك كرنا * اب مَين اپني بات كو مَوقُوف كرونگا اِس نصِيحت اَور كهاوت

سي ـ که هونا ایک خُوبي کا دیر کر بِہتر هَي نه هوني سي ـ اَور جِتني جلدِي هو سکي بُري کام کو چهوڑ کر بهلي کِي طرف آنا اچها هَي *

۴۸ ایک بادشاه ني ناگهان اپني خِدمت گار کو پُکارا * جب آواز کِسي کِي نه پائي ـ تب دروازه کهول کر باهِر گیا * ایک چهوٹي لڑکي کو جو اُسکا نوکر تها دیکها * اُسکي پاس گیا کِه اِسکو جگا دیوي * کیا دیکهتا هَي ؟ کِه ایک لِکها هُوا کاغذ اُسکِي جیب مین پڑا هَي * بادشاه مُتعجِب هُوا کِه دیکهون اِس کاغذ مین کیا لِکها هَي * اُس کاغذ کو جیب سي نِکال کر دیکها ـ که اُسکِي ما کا خطّ هَي ـ اَور یِهه بات لِکهِي هَي * کِه برخوردار میري ! تُمني بڑِي تصدیع اُٹها کر اپني تنخواه سي تهوڑِي رُوپئي همکو بهیجي * نِهایت سعادت مندِي جو فرزندونکو لائِق هَي تم بجا لائي ـ خُدا تُمکو اِسکا عِوض دیگا * بادشاه اُسکو اپني کمري مین لي گیا ـ اَور ایک کاغذ مین کئِي اشرفیان لپیٹ کر اُسکِي جیب مین رکهه دِین ـ اور اُسي چِلّا کي پُکارا کِه اُٹهه بیٹها * بادشاه ني کها ـ تُم کیا اَیسي بي خبر هو جاتي هو؟ لڑکا کُچهه جَواب نه دیسکا ـ اَور جب اُسني اپني جیب مین هاتهه ڈالا ـ تو خطّ مین لپیٹِي هُوئِي اشرفِیان پاکر نِهایت حَیران هُوا ـ اَور خَوف سي بادشاه کي پاؤن پر گِر پڑا ـ اَور اشرفِیان دیکهکر روني لگا * بادشاه ني کها ـ تُم کیون روتي هو؟ لڑکي ني کمال عاجِزِي سي جَواب دِیا ـ کِه اَي بادشاه !

کِسي آدمِي ني ميرِي هلاکت کي لِئي يِہ کام کِيا هَي * مَين نہِين جانتا کہ يِي کَيسِي اشرفِيان هَين * بادشاہ ني تسلِّي ديکر کہا ۔ اَي عزِيز! خُدا ني يِہ اشرفِيان تُجهي دِي هَين ۔ عِوَض اُس نيکِي کي کہِ تُو ني کِي هَي * اِن اشرفِيون کو اپني ما پاس بهيج ۔ اَور مَين تيرِي ما کِي خبرگِيرِي کرُونگا ۔ يِہ بات اُسکو لکھ بهيج *

۴۹ ايک بادشاہ ني اپني وزِير اَور مِيربخشِي سي صلاحًا پُوچها ۔ مال اَور لشکر کي جمع کرني مين ميرِي عقل کُچھ کام نہِين کرتِي * اگر مال جمع کرُون تو لشکر نہِين رهتا ۔ اَور جو فَوج رکهُون تو دَولت نہِين رهتِي * وزِير ني عرض کِي ۔ خُداوند! دَولت جمع کِيجئي ۔ جو فَوج نہ رهيگِي تو کُچھ نُقصان نہِين ۔ کيُونکہ جب ضرُور هوگي رکھ لِيجئيگا * جو ميرِي بات کا آپکو اِعتبار نہو ۔ تو اِسکي يِہ دلِيل هَي ۔ کہ ايک برتن مين تهوڑا شہد رکهوا دِيجئي ۔ ابهِي هزارون مکهِيان گِرد اِسکي آ جمع هونگِين * جونہِين شہد کا باسن رکهوا دِيا ۔ لاکهون مکهِيان بات کہتي هِي اُسکي گِرد آ لِپٹِيان * تب اُسني کہا کہ ديکهئي حضرت جو فِدوِي ني عرض کِي تهِي ۔ سو آپ ني ديکها * پهر مِير بخشِي ني کہا ۔ اگر ميرِي عرض سُنئي تو فَوج رکهئي ۔ جو وقت پر کام آوي اُسوقت مال هرگِز کُچھ فائِدہ نہ کريگا * اگر آپکو يقِين نہ هو تو ميرِي بات کو اِمتحان کر لِيجئي * ايک هانڈِي مين شہد رات کو اِس جگہ رکهوا دِيجئي ۔ جو مکهِيان

اُسپر آ لگین ـ تو میري بات جھوٹھ ـ اَور جو نہین تو سچ ھَي * اِسکي کہنی پر رات کو شہد کا باسن جو رکھوایا ـ تو ایک مکھِي بھِي نه آئِي * خُلاصه اِسکا یِہ ھَي ـ جب اَپنِي فَوج اَپني قبضي سي گئِي ـ پھِر روزِ سِیاه مین مال بھِي خرچ کِیجئي تو وَیسي مُیَسّر نہوگِي *

۵۰ ایک دانِشمند هزار رُپَئي ایک عطار کو سُپُرد کرکي سفر کو گَیا * ایک مُدت کي بعد پھِر آیا ـ اَور رُپَئي عطارسي مانگي * عطار ني کہا تُو جھوٹھا ھَي * آخِر گُفتگو بڑھِي ـ بہُت لوگ جمع ھو گئي * سبھون ني دانِشمند کو جھُوٹھا ٹھہرایا اَور کہا ـ کِه یِه عطار بڑا دِیانت‌دار ھَي ـ اُسني کبھِي خِیانت نہِین کِیه * اگر تُو اُس سي اُلجھیگا ـ تو سزا پاویگا * دانِشمند چُپ رها ـ اَورسوال اُس مطلب کا بادشاه کو گُذرانا * بادشاه ني اُسکو فرمایا کِه تِین روز اُسکِي دُوکان پاس بَیٹھ ـ اُس سي کُچھ نه کہه * چَوتھي دِن مَین اُس طرف آؤنگا اَور تُجھي سلام کرُونگا ـ سلام کي جَواب کي سِوا مُجھ سي کُچھ نه کہِیو * جب مَین وهان سي چلا جاؤن ـ عطارسي رُپَئي مانگِیو ـ اَور جو کُچھ وُه کہي مُجھکو اِطلاع کرِیو * دانِشمند ني وَیسا هِي کِیا * چَوتھي روز بادشاه کِي سَوارِي اُدھرگئِي ـ دیکھتي هِي بادشاه ني دانِشمند کو سلام کِیا * اُسني سلام کا جَواب دِیا * بادشاه ني کہا ـ کِه اَي بھائِي ! کبھُو میري پاس نہین آتا ھَي ـ اَور مُجھ سي کُچھ اَپنا حال نہین کہتا * دانِشمند ني ذرا سِر هِلایا اَور کُچھ نه کہا *

عطّار دیکھتا تھا اَور ڈرتا * جب بادشاہ کِي سَوارِي نِکل گئي ـ عطّار نِي دانِشمند سي کہا ـ کِه جِسوقت تُمنِي مُجھي رُپئي سونپي تھي ـ مَین کہان تھا؟ کوئِي اَور بھِي میرِي نزدِیک تھا؟ پھِر کہو شاید مَین بھُول گیا ہُون * دانِشمند نِي پھِر سب ماجرا بَیان کِیا * عطّار نِي کہا ـ کِه تُو سچ کہتا ہَي ـ اب مُجھي یاد آیا * حاصِلِ کلام یِہ ہَي * کِه اُسنِي ہزار رُپئي دانِشمند کو دِئي اَور بہُت عُذر کِیا *

EXTRACTS FROM THE 'KHIRAD AFROZ.'

۱ نقل ہَي که ایک مردِ پارسا کِسي سَوداگر کي ہمسائي مین رہتا تھا ـ اَور اُسکِي بدَولت پارسا کِي اَوقات خُوشِي اَور کامرانِي مین گُذرتِي تھِي * سَوداگر ہمیشه شہد اَور گھِي کِي تِجارت کِیا کرتا ـ اَور ہر روز اُس مین سي تھوڑا پارسا کي یہان بھیجتا ـ اَور وُہ اُس مین سي کُچھ خرچ کرتا اَور باقِي گھڑون مین رکھتا جاتا * ایکدِن گھڑون کو بھرا دیکھہ کر سوچا که اگر یِہ دس سیر ہو دس دِرم کو بیچُونگا ـ اَور اپنا سر انجام کرُونگا ـ اَور اُس زر سي پانچ بکرِیان مول لُونگا * وي چھ چھ مہِینِي مین جنینگِي ـ اَور ہر ایک کي دو دو بچّي ہونگي * ہر سال بِیس بچّي ہونگِي ـ دس برس مین اُنکي بچّون سي کَئي گلّي ہو جائینگِي * اُن مین سي بعضونکو بیچُونگا ـ اَور اُس سي اَوقات بسرِي کرُونگا * اَور ایک رنڈِي کِسِي بڑِي گھرانِي کِي ڈھُونڈھکر اُس سي

بیاہ کرُونگا * نَو مہینِي کي بعد ایک لڑکا پَیدا ہوگا * تب اُسکو تَربِیت کرُونگا اَور عِلم و ادب سِکھاؤُنگا ۔ اگر کبھِي بي‌ادبِي کریگا تو اِسِي عصا سي جو میري ہاتھ مین ہَي اُسي ادب دُونگا * غرض اِس خِیال مین بي‌ادب لڑکي‌کو اپني سامھني حاضِر جان کر عصا اُٹھا شہد اَور گھِي کي گھڑون پر مارا * وي طاق پر دھري تھي اَور آپ نِیچي اُسکي مُقابِل بیٹھا تھا ۔ جونْہِین عصا اُن پر لگا وي ٹُوٹ گئي * تمام شہد اَور گھِي اُسکي سِر اَور مُنہہ اَور ڈارھِي اَور کپڑون پر پڑا ۔ اَور وي سب خِیال ایکبارگِي جاتي رہي *

۲ نقل ہَي کہ کوئِي شِکارِي ایک دِن کِسِي جنگل مین چلا جاتا تھا * ایک لومڑِي نِہایت خُوب‌صُورت خُوش‌آیند نظر آئِي * شِکارِي کو پشم اُسکِي بہُت خُوش آیِي * خِیال کر لِیا کہ گویا بڑِي قِیمت مین اُسي بِکتا ہَي * لومڑِي کي پِیچھي چلا اَور بِل سي اُسکي مُطّلِع ہُوا * اُسِي کي نزدِیک راہ مین ایک کُوا کھود کر کُوڑِي سي چھِپا دِیا اَور ایک مُردار اُسکي اُوپر رکھ آپ گھات مین جا بَیٹھا * لومڑِي کو اُس مُردي کِي بو کھینچ کھَینچ کُوئي پر لائِي پر سوچ مین تھِي کہ اگرچِہ طُعمي کِي بو دِماغ کو مُعطّر کرتِي ہَي لیکِن بلا کِي بو بھِي دُوراندیشِي کي مغز مین پہُنچتِي ہَي * اگرچِہ ہو سکتا ہَي کہ کوئِي مُوا جانور ہو ۔ پر یِہ بھِي مُمکِن ہَي کہ اِسکي نِیچي دام لگایا ہو ۔ اَور دانا جس کام مین اِحْتمال زِیان کا ہو وہ نہِین کرتِي ہین *

آخِر لومڑِي دُوراندیشِي کِي مدد سي مُردي کا خِیال چھوڑ سلامت رہِي * اِس مین ایک بھوکھا چیتا پہاڑ پر سي اُترا اَور اُسکِي بو پر اپنِي تئین کُوئي کي اندر گِرایا * شکارِي نِي جب آہٹ دام کِي اَور جانور کُوئي کي اندر گِرنِي کِي سُنِي کمالِ حِرص کي مارِي اپنِي تئین معاً کُوئي کي اندر گِرایا * چِیتي نِي اس خِیال پر کِہ وُہ شِکارِي مُجھي اِس مُردي کي کھانِي سي باز رکھیگا جست کِي اَور صَیّاد کي پیٹ کو پھاڑ ڈالا * غرض وُہ لالچِي شِکارِي حِرص کِي شامت سي دام مین پھنسا اَور قانِع لومڑِي نِي ہلاکت سي مَخلصِي پائِي *

۳ نقل ہَي کِہ ایک درویشِ دانا جِسکا طرِیقہ قِناعت تھا بازار مین گیا * ایک حلوائِي نِي جو فقِیر کِي چاشنِي سي کُچھ بہرہ رکھتا تھا اُس عزِیز سي اِلتِماس کِي کہ ایکدم میرِي دُوکان مین ٹھہر تا آپکِي نصِیحت آمیز باتون سي مَین فائدہ مند ہون * وُہ مردِ خُداشناس دِل نوازِي سي وھان بیٹھا * حلوائِي نِي ایک طشت شہد سي بھرکر درویش کي آگي رکھا * مکّھِیان جو طَور اُن کا ھَي کِہ مِٹھائِي پر جمع ہوتِي ہَین ایکبارگِي اُسپر گِرِین * بعضِي کِنارِي پر بیٹھین اَور بعضِي درمِیان مین * حلوائِي نِي چونڑِي ہِلائِي تا مکّھِیون کو ہانکِي ـ وِي جو کِنارِي تھِین سہج سي اُڑ گئِین ـ اَور وِي جو بِیچ مین تھِین جب اُنھون نِي چاہا کہ اُڑِین شہد اُنکي پرون مین لِپٹ گیا اَور دامِ ہلاکت مین پھنسِین * درویش اِس احوال کو دیکھکر خُوش ہُوا

ور خُدا کي شُکر مین مُستغرِق * جب بحال آیا حلوائي ني اُس سي سبب خُوشِي کا پُوچها * اُسني کها اَي بهائِي مَین اِس طشت کو دُنیا اَور شهد کو دُنیا کِي نِعمتین اَور مکهِیون کو شِکم پرور نعمت خوارون کِي مانند سمجها * اَور اُنهین جو طشت کي کِناري بَیٹهین تهِین مردانِ آزاد که تقدِیر کي حُکم سي دُنیا مین آئي پر اِسمین جِي نه لگائي - اَور تهوڑي پر قناعت کِي اَور دُنیا کو ناچِیز جانا * اَور جانِیو که جب چَونري مَوت کي هِلِي جِنهون ني اپني دِل کو تهوڑاسا اُسکي عِشق مین آلُوده کِیا هَي وي سهج مین اِس بلا کي دام سي چهُوٹینگي - اَور جِنهون ني تمام هِمّت اپنِي دُنیا مین صرف کِي هَي اَور اُس تلخ مِتهاس ني اُنکي مِزاج کو خُداکِي راه سي پهیرا هَي آخِر وي رُسوا هونگي *

۴ نقل هَي که اگلي زماني مین ایک ظالم تها که غرِیبون کِي لکڑِیان ظُلم سي مول لیتا - اَور جِتني مول کِي هوتِین اُس سي قِیمت بهُت کم دیتا - اَور آپ مهنگِي کر کي دَولتمندون کِي سرکار مین بیچتا * غُربا اُسکي ظُلم سي عاجِز هُوئي تهی اَور دَولتمند بهِي تنگ آئي تهي * ایک دِن اُسني ایک مُحتاج بي بس کِي لکڑِیان ظُلم سي مول لِین - اَور آدهِي قِیمت دِي * وهُ مظلُوم خُداکِي درگاه مین آه و ناله کرني لگا * اِس مین کِسي صاحب دِل ني اِس احوال سي مُطّلِع هو کر اُس ظالِم کو نصِیحت کِي اَور کها - ظُلم کرنا اَور کِسیکا حق مار رکهنا دُون هِمّتي اَور بي مُرُوّتي هَي - اِسکي سِوا ناخُوشِي

خُداکِي بھِي هوتِي هَي - علاوه يِهہ که اِسِي دُنيا مين سَيکڑون رُسوائِي
سي بدِي کِي سزا اُسي مِلتِي هَي - خُصُوص اِن بيچارون پر ظُلم
کرني سي جو سِواي درگاه خُدا کي کوئِي آسرا نہِين رکھتي هَين *
اَيسِي بد سُلُوکِي نکر که اِس حال سی شِتابی بلا مين گِرفتار هوگا *
وُه ظالِم جو شرابِ غفلت کا نشا اپني دِماغ مين رکھتا تھا اُسکِي
راست‌گوئِي اَور نيک‌اندېشِي سي برهم هوکر بولا که اِن باتون سي
مُجھي دردِ سر ندي - اَور اِن افسانون سي رنجِيده نکر اَور خفا هوکر
اپني گھر گَيا * ازبسکه مآلِ کار ظالِمون کا اچّھا نہِين هَي - قضاء
الہِي سي اُسِي رات لکڑِيون کي ڈھير مين آگ لگِي - اَور وهان سي
گھر تلک پہُنچِي - جو کُچھ اسباب تھا جلکر خاک هوگيا * فجرکي
وقت اپني دوستون مين بَيٹھکر افسوس مال کا کرتا تھا - اَور کہتا تھا
يِهہ آگ کہان سي لگِی ؟ وُه درويش جِسني اگلي روز نصِيحت کِي
تھِي وهان آيا اَور کہا - اَي ظالِم اب تلک تُو ني نہِين معلُوم کِيا هَي
که يِهہ آگ مظلُومون کي دِل‌کي دھُوئين کِي هَي * اُسکي جو طالِع
ياور تھي اِس بات ني دِل مين اُسکي تاثِير کِي - شرمِنده هو کر کہني
لگا سچ هَي که بِيج ظُلم کا جو مَين ني بويا تھا اُسکا ثمرہ مُجھي مِلا *
آخِر اُس زبردستِي سي درگُذرا اَور ظُلم چھوڑ دِيا *

۵ نقل هَي که کِسي کِسان کا ايک پھُولا پھلا باغ تھا * گوشهٔ چمن
مين ايک جھاڑ گُلاب کا تھا نہالِ کامرانِي سي تازه - اَور درختِ

شادماني سي هرايک شاخ اُسکي زِيادہ ٭ هرصُبح پهُول کهِلتي اَور باغبان اُنهين ديکه کر خُوش هوتا ٭ ايک روز پهُولونکا تماشا ديکهني کو نِکلا تها ـ ايک بُلبُل کو ديکها که مُنهه کو گل کي صفحي پر رکهکي چهچهي ماررهِي تهي ـ اَور اُسکي رنگين پتّيون کو اپني تيز چونچ سي توڑتي تهي ٭ باغبان گل کي پريشاني ديکه بي صبر هُوا ـ اَور بُلبُل سي رنجيدہ هوکر فريب کا جال راہ مين بِچهايا ـ اَور حِيلي کي داني ڈال کر اُسي پکڑ پِنجري مين بند کيا ٭ اُس بيدِل بُلبُل ني طُوطي کي مانند زبان کهولي اور کها ـ اَي عزِيز مُجه آزُردہ خاطِر کو کيُون قيد کِيا تُوني ؟ جو ميري خُوش‌آوازِي تُجهي اِس بات پر لائي تو ميرا آشِيانه تيري هِي باغ مين هَي ٭ اگر کوئي اَور بات تيري خاطِر مين آئي هو اُس سي مُجهي اِطّلاع کر تو صبر کر کي چُپ رهُونگي ٭ کِسان ني کها نهِين جانتي هَي که تُوني ميرا کيا احوال کِيا ـ اَور گُلون پر جو وسِيله ميري زِندگي کا هي کيا خرابِي لائي ـ اَور مُجهي بسبب اُسکي کَيسا آزُردہ کيا ؟ بُلبُل بولي اِس بات سي درگُذر ـ اَور سوچ تو سهِي که مَين اِتني قُصُور سي جو ايک گُل کو پريشان کِيا پِنجري مين بند هُوئي ـ اَور تُو جو دِل کو رنجِيدہ کرتا هَي تيري حالت کيا هوگي ؟ اِس بات ني اُسکي دِل مين اثر کِيا بُلبُل کو آزاد کر دِيا ٭ بُلبُل اُسکا شُکر اد کرکي بولي ـ جب تُوني مُجه سي نيکي کي تو البتّه مَين بهِي اِسکي بدلي بهلائي کرُون ٭ معلُوم کر جِس درخت کي نِيچي تُو کهڑا هَي

یہان ایک آفتابہ اشرفیون سي بھرا ھُوا گڑا ھَي ـ نِکال کي اپني کام مین لا * کِسان ني جب وُہ جگہہ کھودي اَور بُلبُل کِي بات سچ ھُوئي کہا ـ اَي بُلبُل عجب ھَي کہ آفتابہ زمین کي نِیچي تُجھي نظر آیا ـ اَور دام خاک کي اُوپر تُوني نہ دیکھا * بُلبُل ني جواب دِیا تُو نہین جانتا ھَي جب قضا پہُنچي نہ دِیدۂ دانِش مین روشنِي رھي ـ نہ تدبِیر عقل کِي کُچھ فائِدہ کري *

٦ نقل ھَي کہ اگلي زماني مین کوئِي بادشاہ ایک بازکو بہُت پِیار کرتا تھا ـ اَور وُہ ھمیشہ بادشاہ کي ھاتھ پر بَیٹھا رھتا تھا * ایک روز باز کو ھاتھ پر بَیٹھا کر شِکار کو گَیا ـ اِتِّفاقاً ایک ھِرن سامھني نظر آیا * بادشاہ ني کمال شَوق سي اُسکي پِیچھي گھوڑا ڈالا اَور اُسکو پکڑا * مُلازِمِ درگاہ اگرچہ پِیچھي لگي چلي آتي تھي پر کوئِي بادشاہ تلک نہ پہُنچا تھا * اِس مین بادشاہ پِیاسا ھوکر ھر طرف پانِي کِي تلاش مین گھوڑا دَوڑاتا تھا * آخِر ایک دامنِ کوہ مین پہُنچکر دیکھا کہ پہاڑ پر سي پانِي ٹپکتا ھَي * ترکش مین سي پِیالہ نِکال نِیچي رکھا کہ قطري جو ٹپکتي ھَین اُس مین جمع ھون ـ اَور پِیالہ بھر جاوي * جب پِیالہ بھر چُکا چاھا کہ پِئي باز ني وونہین پر مارا ـ تمام پانِي گِر گَیا * بادشاہ ني اِس حرکت سي خفا ھوکر پھِر پِیالي کو اُسِي پتھر کي نِیچي رکھا * دیر کي بعد جب بھر چُکا چاھا کہ مُنہہ لگاوي ـ باز ني پھِر وھِي حرکت کِي ـ اَور اُس پانِي کو بھِي گِرا دِیا * بادشاہ

ني كمال تِشنگِي كي سبب بي تامُل باز كو زمِين پر پٹک دِيا اَور وُہ مر گيا • اِس مين رِكابدار آ پہُنچا - باز كو مُؤا اَور بادشاہ كو پِياسا پايا • فِي آلفور چھاگل شِكاربند سي كھول پِيالي كو خُوب دھو دھا كر چاها كه بادشاہ كو پانِي پِلاوي • اُسني فرمايا كه مُجھي اِس خالِص پانِي سي جو پہاڑ سي جھرتا هَي كمال رغبت هُوئِي هَي • تُو پہاڑ پر چڑھ اَور اِس چشمي سي پانِي كا پِياله بھر كر لي آ - كيُونكِه پھِر يِه تاب نہِين هَي كه جب تلك پِيالي مين قطرہ قطرہ جمع هو مَين اِنتِظار كرُون • رِكابدار جب چشمي كي كِناري پہُنچا ديكھتا كيا هَي كه ايك اژدها مُؤا هوا اُسكي كِناري پڑا هي - اَور زهر بھرا لُعاب اُسكا پانِي مين مِل كر قطرہ قطرہ پہاڑ پر سي ٹپكتا هَي • وُہ گھبراكر اُترا اَور يِه احوال عرض كر ايك پِياله ٹھنڈي پانِي كا چھاگل سي بھر كر بادشاہ كو دِيا • وُہ پِياله مُنھ سي لگا كر روني لگا - اَور رِكابدار كو باز كي ماجري سي آگاہ كركي اپني جلدِي اور اِضطرابي پر بہُت سي نفرين كِي - اَور جب تلك جِيا يِه داغِ حَيرت اُسكي دِل سي نگيا • فائدہ اِس قِصّي كا يِه هي - كه عقلمند اپني كام كو بغَير خُوب تأمُّل كِئي شُرُوع نہِين كرتي هَين •

۷ نقل هَي كه كوئي ٹٹ پُونجِيا سَوداگر سفر كو جاتا تها - سَو من لُوها كِسِي دوست كي گھر مين امانت ركها كه تنگ دستِي كي وقت مُوجِب فراغت كا هو • جب دُور دراز سفر كركي مُدّت كي بعد گھر

کو آیا اَور لوها مانگني دوست کي پاس گیا ـ وُہ بیچ کر تصرُّف مين لایا تها * کهني لگا اَي بهائِي تیري لوهي کو مَین ني گهر کي کوني مین رکها تها ـ اَور اِس بات سي مَین غافِل تها که اُس کوني مین چُوهي کا بِل هَي ـ جب تلک معلُوم هو چُوها فُرصت پاکر سب کا سب کها گیا * سَوداگر اِس بات کو جهُوٹھ سمجھ کر کوئِي تدبِیر سوچتا تها ـ اَور بظاهِر کهتا تها کیا بعِید هَي ؟ چُوهي کو تو لوهي سي کمال اُلفت هَي ـ اَور وُہ دانتون سي لوها چبا سکتا هَي * وُہ جهُوٹها اِس بات سي خُوش هُوا اَور دِل مین کها یِہ بڑا نادان هَي که میرِي باتون پر بهُول گیا اَور لوهي سي دست‌بردار هُوا ـ بِهتر هَي که اپني کام کِي مضبوطِي کي لِئي اُسکِي آج کي روز ضِیافت کرُون * تب اُسکو گهر مین لیگیا اَور دعوت کِي تیّارِي کرني لگا * سَوداگر ني کها آج مُجهي ضُرُور کام هَي کل آؤُنگا * غرض اُسکي گهر سي چلا اَور اُسکي چهوٹي لڑکي کو چُرا اپني گهر لیجاکر چهِپا رکها * فجر وعدي پر دوست کي گهر آیا اَور اُسکو پریشان دیکهکر پُوچها اَي بهائِي تُم کیُون گهبرایي هُوُي هو؟ کها کل سي بیٹا میرا جو نُورِ چشم اَور سُرُورِ دِل تها غائِب هُوا هَي ـ بهُتیرا ڈهُونڈها کُچھ پتا نپایا * بولا کل جو مَین تُمهارِي گهر سي نِکلا اُسِي شکل کي ایک لڑکي کو جو تُم بتاتي هو مَین ني دیکها که ایک چُوهي‌مار اُٹهائي اُڑا چلا جاتا هَي * تب وُہ چلّایا که اَي بیوُقُوف نا مُمکِن بات کیُون زبان پر لاتا هَي ؟ مُوش‌گِیر لڑکي کو کیُونکر لي اُڑیگا ؟ سَوداگر ني هنسکر کها اِس سي کُچھ تعجُّب نکر کیُونکه جِس شهر کا

چُوها سَو من لوها کهاتا هَي وهان کا چُوهيمار بِهي ايک لڑکي کو اُٹها سکتا هَي * اُسني حقِيقت دريافت کِي اَور کها کُچه انديشه نکر چُوهي ني تيرا لوها نهِين کهايا هَي * جَواب دِيا که تُو بِهي پريشان نهو که مُوشگِير تيري لڑکي کو نهِين لي گَيا هَي - ميرا لوها مُجهي دي اَور اپنا لڑکا تُو لي *

۸ نقل هَي که حضرت سُلَيمان کِي حُکُومت کي اَيّام مين (که وُه تمام جانداروں کي کيا آدمِي کيا سِواي اُنکي بادشاه تها) اُسکي حُضُور ايک دانا عالمِ غَيب سي پِياله آبِ حَيات کا بهر کر لايا اَور عرض کِي که اِلهام سي مُجه پريُون کهُلا هَي که اگر آپ اِس پِيالي کو نه پِيوين جلد اِس جهان سي رُخصت هووين - اَور جو پِيوين تو عُمردراز هو * اب يِه پِياله آبِ حَيات سي بهر کر لايا هُون - جِي چاهي پِيجِئي اَور قِيامت تلک زِيست کِيجِئي - يا نه پِيجِئي اَور مُلکِ عدم کو کُوچ فرمائِي * حضرت سُلَيمان دِل مين اپني سوچا اِس کام مين عقلمندون سي مشورت کِيا چاهِئي * حسبُ الحُکم اُس کي دانا اَور دُوراندِيش هر گُروه کي کيا اِنسان کيا حَيوان سب حاضِر هُوئي - اُس مخفِي بهيد کو اُن سي ظاهِر کِيا * تب هر ايک ني زِندگِي کي لِئي دِل پسند باتين کهِين * حاصِل اُنکا يِه هَي - که نقدِ عُمر وُه دَولت هَي که بمدد عقل کي اُس سي خُوبِيان بهم پهُنچائِيي - اَور رِضا خُداکِي حاصِل کِيجِئي * غرض سب کِي راي يِهي ٹههرِي که حضرت پِياله آبِ حَيات کا پِيوين * سُلَيمان فرمايا که ميري مُلک کي داناؤن

سي كوئي اَيسا هَي جو اِس مشْورت مين حاضِر نہين هَي ؟ سبهون ني عرض كِي كِه فُلانه بگلا نہين هَي * حضرت ني گهوڙي كو اُسكي بُلاني كي لِئي بهيجا - اُسني ايك گوشي مين قِناعت كركي خلق سي مِلنا ترك كِيا تها گهوڙي كِي بات نمانِي اَور باهِر نه نِكلا * دُوسرِي بار كُتّي كو بهيجا كه اُسي لي آ - بگلا اُسكي كهني سي حضرت كِي بارگاه مين حاضِر هُوا - حضرت ني فرمايا كه تُجهي ايك مشْورت كي واسطي بُلايا هَي - تب آبِ حَيات پِيني كا ذِكر درمِيان لايا * اُسني كها آبِ حَيات آپ هِي اكيلي پِيوينگي يا دوستون خَيرخواهون كو بهِي پِلاوينگي ؟ حضرت ني فرمايا كه صرف ميري لِئي آيا هَي اَورون كي ديني كِي اِجازت نہين هَي كيُونكر دُون ؟ اُسني عرض كِي اَي جهان پناه همدم اَور دوستون سي جُدا هوكر زِندگِي كرنِي كيا كَيفِيَت ركهتي هَي ؟ آپكو خُدا ني دُنيا مين سردار كِيا هَي بغَير مددگارون كي كوئِي كام سرانجام نهوگا * حضرت ني اُس سچّي دُوراندِيش كِي بات پر آفرين كِي اَور آبِ حَيات پهير دِيا *

٩ نقل هَي كه اگلي زماني مين ايك بادشاه ني دست ظُلم كا دراز كِيا تها - اَور قدم عدالت كِي راه سي باهِر ركها تها * رات دِن لوگ ظُلم سي اُسكي خُدا كِي درگاه مين نالان تهي - اَور اُسي لعنت كرتي تهي * ايك دِن بادشاه شِكار كو گيا اَور به سبب اِسكي كه فضلِ اِلهِي شامِلِ حال تها ايسي ايك مَيدان مين جهان بي تعلُّقِي كا

عالم تها اُسکو اِلهام هُوا - بادشاهِي نه عِبارت هَي اِس سي که دروازه عَيش و کامراني کا اپني اُوپر کهولي بلکه پادشاهِي پاسبانِي هَي که اَورون کي رنج کو اُتهاکر خلائِق کِي نِگاهبانِي کري - اَور ظالِمون کي دستِ ظُلم کو مظلُومون کي دامن سي کوتاه کري * جب شکارگاه سي بارگاه کِي طرف چلا اَور مَيدان سي شهر مين پهُنچا خِلقت کو بُلاکر فرمايا که اَي گُروه اب تک ميرا دِيدهٔ دِل حق بِيني سي بند تها - آج اِلهام سي مَين ني دريافت کِيا اَور خوابِ غفلت سي جاگا * اُمّيدوار هُون که آج کي دِن سي کِسي ظالِم کا دستِ ظُلم رعِيّت پر نه پهُنچي اَور کِسي جفاکار کا پانْو کِسي غرِيب کي گهر کي گِرد نه جاوي * حاجِبون کو فرمايا که يِه خُوش‌خبرِي شهر کي چهوٹي بڑون کو پهُنچا دو * اِس منادِي سي رعِيّت کِي جان مين جان هُوئِي - اَور گُل مُراد کي اُنکي اُمّيدوارِي کي باغ مين کهِلي * القِصّه مظلُوم نوازِي و ظُلم‌گُدازِي اُسکِي کمال مرتبي پر هُوئِي - اَور عدالت اُسکِي اَيسِي پهَيلِي که بکرِي کا بچّه شيرنِي کي تهن سي دُودهه پِيتا اَور تدرو باز کي ساتهه بازِيان کرتا * اِسواسطي لقب اُسکا شاه‌داد هُوا * درگاه کي محرمِ رازون مين سي کِسي ني پُوچها که اگلي آئين کو چهوڑ طرِيق عدالت کِي شُرُوع کرني کا سبب کيا هَي ؟ بادشاه ني ماجرا بَيان کِيا اَور کها که سبب اِس غفلت سي بيدار هوني کا اَور هُشيارِي کا يِه هَي - که ايک روز شِکارگاه مين هر طرف گهوڑا دَوڑاتا تها اَور نظر کرتا تها - اِکايک

دیکھا مَین نی که ایک کُتّا کِسي لومڑِي کي پِیچھي دَوڑتا هَي اَور
دانتون سي هڈّي اُسکي پاؤن کِي چابتا هَي ـ بیچارِي لومڑِي لنگڑي
پاؤن سي غار مین بهاگ گَئي اَور کُتّا پھِرا * وهِین ایک پِیادي ني
پتّھر کُتّي کو مارا که پاؤن اُسکا ٹُوٹ گیا * پِیاده هنوز کَئِي قدم نه گیا
تها که ایک گھوڑِي ني لات جو پاؤن پر اُسکي مارِي تو اُسکِي بهِي ٹانگ
ٹُوٹ گَئِي * وُه گھوڑا بهِي دُور نه گیا تها که پانو اُسکا سُوراخ مین آگیا
اَور ٹُوٹ گَیا * تب مَین مستِي سي هوش مین آیا اَور دِل سي اپني
کها دیکھا تُو ني اِن سبهون ني کیا کیا کام کَئِي اَور کیا کیا پائي ؟ خبردار
هو که تُجھي دِکھلاتِي هَین که جو کوئِي وُه کام کري که لائِق اُسکي نهِین
وُه اَیسا کُچھ دیکھي جو نه دیکھا هو * آخِر مَین غفلت سي باز آیا
اَور تَوفِیق کا دروازه مُجھ پر کھُلا *

EXTRACT FROM THE 'ÁRÁ,ISH-I MAḤFIL.'

هِندُوستان کي بَیلون مین گُجراتِي بَیل سب طرح سي اچّھا هَي *
هر چند کِه ناگورا بهِي اَور بَیلون سي بمرتبه بِهتر هَي ـ لیکِن اُسکو
نهِین لگتا * صُورت شکل اُس کِي نِهایَت خُوب ـ ڈِیل ڈَول نِپٹ
خُوش اُسلُوب ـ قدّ و قامت مین بهِي بُلند ـ بادشاه وزِیر و فقِیر هر
کِسي کِي پسند * قدم اَیسا چلي کِه رهوار تُرکِي نه پهُنچ سکي ـ
دَوڑي اِتنا کِه چالاک تازِي پِیچھي ره جائي * یُون سُنا هَي کِه سابِق

بعضي اشرار عيار احمد آباد گجرات مين وهان كي بيلون كو گاڑيون مين جوت سوار هو رهزني كو جنگل مين آتي تهي - اور مال متاع مسافرون سوداگرون كا لوٹ ليجاتي تهي * هر چند سوار گهوڑي اُن كي پيچهي ڈالتي - ليكن اُن كي گرد بهي نپاتي * اور يهه بهي مشهور هي - كه گاڑي خاص اختراع اهلِ هند كا هي * بيٹهني والي اُس كي گرمي سردي آندهي مينهه مين نهايت آرام پاتي هين * فراغت سي چار آدمي گپ شپ كرتي هوئي بيٹهي چلي جاتي هين - اور سفر مين كيفيت حضر كي اُٹهاتي هين * ليكن اُس كي پهيي دو هوتي هين - چهتري دار هو يا منڈي * اگر ڈهانچا اُس كا كچهه چهتاپي كي ساتهه هلكا هو تو منجهولي كهلايگي - اور بهت چهوٹا اور سبك هوگا تو گيني - اُس كي بيل بهي حد چهوٹي هوتي هين - اُنهين گيني كهتي هين - قسم هين اُنكي عليحده هي *

اور چار پهيون كي رتهه وه اِس سي كهين بهتر هي - به نسبت اُسكي اونچي نيچي سي كم گرتي هي - هچكولا بهي اُس مين تهوڑا لگتا هي * امير امرا كي سواري كي قابل هوتي هي * في الواقع بعضي تو ايسي هي خوش ڈول سبك نقاشيدار هوتي هي كه ديكهني والي نقشِ ديوار بن جاتي هين * اور ساز بهي اُس پر باناتي سادي يا كارچوبي و غيره نپت صفائي اور چمك كي ساتهه * اگر سورج اُسوقت زمين پر هووي - تو اپني رتهه سي اُتر اُس مين آ بيٹهي * اور راجه اندر بهي

دیکھي تو اپني تخت پر پھر پاؤن نرکھي * پر ساتھ اِن خُوبِیون کي بھِي اُمرا اُس مین براي تفننِ طبع کبھو کبھو سوار هوتي هَین * اور بعضي بڑي آدمِي مِیرزا منش هر چند کِه چڑھتي کم هَین - لیکِن هر موسم کا ساز اُنکِي سوارِي کِي رتھ پر هوتا هَي * چُنانچه گرمِیون مین خس کا - اَور برسات مین موم جامیکا - جاڑون مین باناتِي * پر اکثر اُس مین مہاجن صرّاف جَوهرِي مُتصدّي سَوار هوتي هَین - یا عَورات هِندُو مُسلمان کِي * اَور بعضِي اَوباش بیگمین یا بانکِي کسبِیان اپنِي رتھون پر نہایَت جھمجھماتي ساز سجوا - بیلون کي گلون مین گھنگھرو سِینگون پر سونِي رُوپي کِي سِنگوٹیان - اَور ساُونگیون مین ٹالِیان جھانجھ - جُوون مین زنگ لگوا بندھوا رکھوا - سَوار هوکر بڑي تھسّي سي میلي ٹھیلي مین پھرتیان هَین - یا باغون کِي سَیرین کرتِیان هَین * واقعِي اُنکِي آمد سي تماشائِیون کي هوش و حَواس جاتي هَین - گویا جھن جھن کرتي هُوئي پرِیون کي تخت چلِي آتي هَین *

بَیت * جہان هوتا هَي یُون اُنکا گُذارا - کِسي رهتِي هَي وهان تاب نظارا ؟ کہان هوتا هَي حاصِل لُطفِ دِیدار ؟ هر ایک بن جائي هَي بس نقشِ دِیوار * جو اِس مین اُٹھ گیا پردہ هَوا سي - جھمکڑا ایک نظر آیا ادا سي * جو وُہ بِجلِي کي بھِي یُون سامني آئي - تڑپھ کر اُسکي آگي لوٹ هِي جائي *

اَور صاحِبِ عِصمت بِیبِیون کِي رتھون پر گھٹا ٹوپ پڑي هُوئي -

چاندنیان کسین هوئین - کیا دخل که ایک مو برابر اُن مین رخنا یا سوراخ هووي؟ چنانچه نواب خاندوران و مظفرخان مرحوم کي ناموس کي رتهون پر بیشتر موتي میلي چاندنیان هوتین تهین * علی هذا القیاس میانون پر بهي - باوجود اسکي که ایک بهائي میر بخشي تها - اور دوسرا هفت هزاري * في الواقع تقاضا غیرت کا یهي هي - کیونکه جس کا میانه رته ایک جهمکڑي کي ساته نکلي - مقرر تماشائیون بازاریون کي جي مین آوي که اس مین کوئي چمک چاندني رشک پري جلوه گر هوگي * پس زناني سواري کي رته یا میاني کا پرتکلف هونا بعضي بعضي ثقه امیرون کي نزدیک بهي سخت معیوب هي * اصل یه هي که سواري اسکي في الحقیقت اچهي هي - طور طرز اپني اپني پسند پر موقوف هي * پر هچکولي بهت بري * اور سوائي اس کي بهي بهت سي سواریان صاحب سلیقه لوگون ني اور کاریگرون ني بنوائین اور بنائین * چنانچه ملوک و سلاطین کي واسطي تخت و نالکي - امیرون کي لئي جهالردار پالکي - اور شهزادیون وزیرزادیون و امیرزادیون کي واسطي مهاڈول چونڈول سکهپال میاني - اور غریبون کي عورتون کي لئي ڈولي * تا کوئي نجیب زادي اشراف زادي پیاده پا نه نکلي - اور اس کي قد و قامت کو کوئي نا محرم نه دیکهي *

مُنْتخباتِ مُختلِفه

زبانِ ریختہ مین

۱ سُسْتِي سي زِيان هَي * جلْدِي کا پهل ندامت هَي * قِناعت آرام کِي کُنْجِي هَي * مِحْنت سي بڑائِي هَي * پرْهیز اچّهِي دَوا هَي * عاقِل کو اِشاره بس هَي * خُدا کا خوف دانِش کِي اصْل هَي * گُونْگِي زبان بِهْتر هَي جهُوتهِي زبان سي * عِلْم کِي آفت بهُولِ هَي * اِنْصاف سي خلْق کو آرام هَي *

۲ تهوڑا کهانا بہُت بِیمارِي سي بچاتا هَي * طلب کر عِلْم کو طِفْلِي سي جَوانِي تک * بِیمارِي قَید بدن کِي هَي * اور غم قَید رُوح کِي * دانِشْمنْد بي سبب کام نہین کرْتا هَي * جاهِل طلب کرْتا هَي مال کو - اَور عاقِل کمال کو * عِلْم کِي تحْصیل سي عقْل صاف هوتِي هَي * جب دو بلا مین پڑو - تو آسان کو اِخْتیار کرو * دُنْیا کِي خُوشِي مین غم ملا هَي - اَور اُس کِي شِیرِینِي سي سمّ *

۳ کِسِي موچِي کا گهر جاڑي کِي مَوسم مین جلْني لگا * ایک غرِیب پڑوسِي وهان آکر سینکّني لگا * یِہ حالت دیکھ کي ایک تهٹهول ني کها - کیا خُوب ! کِسِي کا گهر جلي - کوئِي تاپي *

۴ یي کُتّي کِه آپس مین شور کرتي هَین - اَور بھونکتي هَین - کَیسِي تکلیف هَي ؟ مگر وي لوگ جو آپس مین جھگڑا کرتي هَین - اَور گالیان دیتي هَین - اَور قضِیَه اَور فساد برپا کرتي هَین - کُتّون سي زِیادہ خراب هَین - کیُونکه وي لوگ واقِف هَین کِه یِهہ گُناہ هَي *

۵ هِندُوستان مین ایک بڑا درخت هَي - جِس سي بهُت کام نِکلتي هَین * اُس کي سایي کي نِیچي هر ایک آدمي آرام پاتا هَي * اَور پتّي بجاءِ دَوا کي کام آتي هَین * اَور اُس کِي لات سي ناوین بنتي هَین - اَور شاخون سي مستُول * اُس کي پتّي بهُت بڑي هَین - جب اِکٹھي هو جاتي هَین - تو پال بنایا جاتا هَي *

۶ ایک اُونٹ اَور گدھي سي نِهایت دوستِي تھِي * اِتِّفاقاً دونون کو سفر درپیش هُوا * درمِیان راہ کي ایک ندِي مِلِي * پهلي اُونٹ پانِي مین پَیٹھا - اُس کي پیٹ تک پانِي هُوا * کهني لگا - اَي یار! اِدھر آءو - پانِي تھوڑا هَي * گدھا بولا - سچ هَي - تیري شِکم تک هَي - تُجھي تھوڑا معلُوم هوتا هَي - لیکن میرِي پیٹھ تک هوگا - مَین ڈُوب جاءُونگا *

۷ جو دانا لڑکا هَي - وُہ اپنِي کِتاب اپني گھر مین بي‌کھي پڑھتا هَي * اَور نادان لڑکا اپنِي کِتاب کو کھیل کي واسطي طاق پر ڈال رکھتا هَي - اگرچِه اُس کي ما باپ اُس بد چال سي هزار منع کرین * پهلا لڑکا اُس اِصیل گھوڑي کِي طرح هَي - که جِس کي واسطي کوڑا ضرُور

اشرفي *ashrafi*, f. a gold coin so called. The Calcutta ashrafi is worth a guinea and a half. *a*

آشنا *áshná*, an acquaintance, lover, friend. *p*

آشيانه *áshiyána*, m. a nest. *p*

اصطبل *iṣṭabal*, m. a stable. *a*

اصل *aṣl*, f. root, origin, foundation, capital. *a*

اصيل *aṣíl*, noble (as to blood or origin). *a*

اطلاع *iṭṭilá'*, f. manifesting, declaring; investigation, knowledge. *a*

اضطرابي *iẓṭirábi*, f. vehemence, passionateness. *a*

اعتبار *i'tibár*, m. confidence, credit, respect; *i'tibár-k.* to believe, or confide in. *a*

اعتماد *i'timád*, m. reliance, trust, *a.*

اعلي *a'lá*, higher, highest. *a*

اعمال *a'mál*, (plur. of *'amal*) actions, conduct. *a*

آفات *áfát*, f. calamities, misfortunes, evils. *a*

آفت *áfat*, f. calamity. *a*

آفتاب *áftáb*, m. the sun, sunshine. *p*

آفتابه *áftába*, m. an ewer. *p*

آفرين *áfrín*, f. praise, applause. *p*

افسانه *afsána*, m. tale, story. *p*

افسوس *afsos*, m. sorrow, regret, vexation, *interj.* ah! alas! *afsos-k.* or *afsos-kháná*, to lament. *p*

افلاس *iflás*, m. poverty, destitution. *a.*

افلاطون *Afláṭún*, m. Plato. *a*

اكايك *ikáyak*, on a sudden. *p*

اكبر *Akbar*, name of the best and greatest of the Mogul emperors. *a*

اكٹها *ikaṭṭhá*, united, together, *h*

اكثر *akṣar*, most, many, much; for the most part. *a*

آكها *ákhá*, m. a bag, sack. *h*

اكيلا *akelá*, a. alone. *s*

آگ *ág*, f. fire, *ág-d.* or *lagáná*, to set on fire; *ág-lagná*, to take fire. *s*

اگاڑي *agáṛi*, f. the fore part. *s*

آگاه *ágáh*, acquainted with, aware of. *p*.

اگر *agar*, if, when. *p*

اگرچه *agarchi*, although. *p*

اگلا *aglá*, prior, past, ancient. *s*

آگي *áge*, before, in front, formerly, forwards; in future. *s*

آگيا *ágyá*, f. an order, command. *s*

البته *albatta*, certainly, indeed. *a*

الپ *alp*, small, few; *alp-bayask*, of a tender age. *s*

التفات *iltifát*, f. courtesy, respect, notice. *a*

التماس *iltimás*, m. f. beseeching, petitioning. *a*

الجهنا *ulajhná*, n. to be entangled, to quarrel. *h*

الجهانا *uljháná*, a. to entangle. *h*

القصه *al-kiṣṣa*, in short. *a*

الگ *alag*, separate, apart. *s*

الفت *ulfat*, f. habit, familiarity. *a*

آلوده *álúda*, sullied, contaminated. *p*

الهام *ilhám*, divine inspiration. *a*

الہي *iláhí*, divine. *a*

امام *imám*, m. a leader in religion, a prelate, priest. *a*

امانت *amánat*, f. trust, deposit. *a*

امتحان *imtiḥán*, m. proof, trial, examination. *a*

آمد *ámad*, f. arrival, coming. *p*

امرا *umará* (pl.) nobles, grandees. *a*

اميد *umed* or *ummed*, f. hope; *ummed-wár*, hopeful. *p*

امير *amír*, m. a commander, a nobleman, a grandee, a lord; *amír-záda*, son of a grandee; *amír-zádí*, daughter of a grandee. *a p*

آميز *ámez*, (in comp.) mixed with, full of. *p*

ان *in*, (inflection), plur. of *yih*, this; *un*, plur. of *wuh*, that; (vide Gram.) *h*

آنا *áná*, n. to come; s. m. the sixteenth part of a rupee. *s*

انبوه *amboh*, m. a crowd, multitude, mob, concourse. *p*.

انبهو *anubhav*, m. imagination, idea. *s*

انتظار *intiẓár*, waiting, expectation. *a*

انجان *anján*, strange, unknown; *anján-h.* to act the stranger. *s*

اندر *andar*, within, inside, *p*; *Indar*, the god of Swarga or the higher regions. *s*

اندها *andhá*, blind, dark, *s*

اندهيرا *andherá*, dark. *s*

اندهيري *andherí*, f. darkness. *s*

انديشه *andesha*, m. thought, suspicion, anxiety. *p*

انسان *insán*, m. man, a human being, mankind. *a*

آنسو *ánsú*, m. a tear. *s*

انصاف *inṣáf*, m. equity, justice. *a*

انعام *in'ám*, m. a present, a gift, *a*

انكار *inkár*, m. refusal, denial. *a*

آنكه *áṅkh*, f. the eye. *s*

انگل *uṅgal*, m. a finger's breadth. *s*

انگلي *uṅglí*, f. a finger. *s*

انگوٹهي *aṅgúṭhí*, f. a ring worn on the finger. *s*

انگور *aṅgúr*, m. a grape. *p*

آنند *ánand*, m. joy, happiness. *s.*

انه and انهون *inh* and *inhoṅ*, same as ان *in*; *unh* and *unhoṅ*, same as *un*, (q.v.) *h*

آواز *áwáz*, f. noise, sound, voice. *p*

اوباش *aubásh*, dissolute, depraved. *a*

اوپر *úpar*, up, upwards, upon. *s*

اور *or*, f. direction, side. *h*

اور *aur*, (conj.) and, but; (adj.) more, other; *aur kuchh*, anything else. *h*

اوسان *ausán*, m. courage, presence of mind. *h*.

اوقات *auḳát* (pl. of *waḳt*), times (of devotion). *a*

اونٹ *úṅṭ*, m. a camel. *h*

اونچا *úṅchá*, high, height. *h*

آه *áh*, f. a sigh. *p*.

آهار *áhár*, m. food, subsistence. *s*

آهٹ *áhaṭ*, f. a sound, noise. *h*.

اهل *ahl*, m. people. *a*.

اي *ai*, O, Oh. *p h*

اياز *Ayyáz*, a man's name. *a*

ايام *aiyám* (pl. of *yaum*), days, seasons. *a*

ايسا *aisá*, such as this, so. *h*

ايک *ek*, one; (art.) *a*, *an*, frequently joined to its substantive, as ايکدن *ek-din*, one day. *s.*

ايکبارگي *ekbáragí*, all at once. *p*

ايمان *ímán*, m. faith, belief, religion, conscience. *a.*

ايماندار *ímán-dár*, faithful, honest; *ímán láná*, to believe. *p*

آئين *á,ín*, m. rule, law. *p*

ب

بابا *bábá*, father, son, sir. *h*

باپ *báp*, m. father. *h*

بات *bát*, f. a word, affair; *bát kahte hí*, on the speaking of a word, immediately; *bát-chít*, f. conversation, chit-chat. *h*

باد *bád*, f. wind. *p.*

بادشاه *bádsháh*, m. a king; *bádsháhí*, royal. *p.*

بادي *bádí*, m. a complainant, speaker. *s*

باجنا *bájná*, n. to sound, to ring. *s*

بار *bár*, m. load; fruit; time; door; water. *p h*

باره *bárah*, twelve. *h*

بارگاه *bárgáh*, f. a king's court. *p*

باز *báz*, back; *báz-áná*, to decline, reject; *baz-rakhná*, to keep from, to prevent; (s.m.) a hawk. *p.*

بازار *bázár*, m. a market; *bázárí*, one who attends a market. *p*

بازي *bází*, f. play, sport, a game. *p*

باسن *básan*, m. a basin, plate, dish, goblet, pot, etc. *h*

باغ *bágh*, m. a garden. *p*

باغبان *bághbán*, m. a gardener. *p*

بال *bál*, m hair. *s.* ear of corn. *h.* wing. *p*

بالا *bálá*, above, up, high. *p*

بالک *bálak*, m. a boy. *s*

بالو *bálú*, f. sand. *s*

باناتي *bánátí*, made of broad cloth, woollen. *h*

بانٹنا *bántná*, a. to share, to distribute, to divide; *bánṭ-l.* to divide and take. *s*

باندهنا *bándhná*, a. to bind, to shut up; to frame. *s*

بانکا *bánká*, foppish, impudent. *s*

باوجود *bá-wujúd*, notwithstanding *p a*

باور *báwar*, m. credit, faith; *báwar-k.* to believe. *p*

باهر *báhir* or *báhar*, without, outside. *s*

باهم *báham*, together. *p*

بباد *bibád*, m. quarrel, fight. *s*

بپت *bipat*, f. misfortune, calamity. *s*

بتانا *batáná*, a. to point out, to teach. *h*

بتي *battí*, f. a candle, lamp. *s.*

بٹھانا *biṭháná*, a. to cause to sit, to seat. *h*

بجالانا *ba-já láná*, a. to perform, carry into effect. *h*

بجانا *bajáná*, a to sound, to play on a musical instrument. *s*

بجاي *ba-jáe* or *ba-já*, in place, instead of. *p*

بجلي *bijlí*, f. lightning. *h.*

بجنا *bajná*, n. to be sounded, to sound. *s.*

بجهانا *bujhání*, a. to explain; to extinguish (a candle). *h*

بچارا *bichárá*, helpless, wretched. *p.*

بچانا *bacháná*, a. to save, protect. *h*

بچنا *bachná*, n. to be saved, to escape. *h*

بچه *bachcha*, m. an infant, a child, the young of any creature. *p.*

بچهانا *bichhána*, a. to spread. s.

بحال آنا *ba-hál áná*, to recover. *a.*

بخشش *bakhshish*, f. gift, grant, forgiveness. *p*

بخشنا *bakhashná*, or *bakhsh-d.* or *bakhshish-k.* a. to give, to bestow. *p*

بخشي *bakhshí*, m. a general, a commander in chief. *p*

بخل *bukhl*, m. avarice, stinginess, parsimony. *a*

بخيل *bakhíl*,a, a miser, niggard. *a*

بد *bad*, evil, bad; used in compounds, as *bad-zát*, a rascal; *bad-kho*, ill-disposed; *bad-ṣúrat*, ugly, ill-favoured. *p*

بدبخت *bad-bakht*, unfortunate, wicked. *p*

بد سلوکي *bad-sulúkí*, f. ill-usage. *p a*

بدن *badan*, m. the body. *p*

بدولت *ba-daulat*, by favour of. *a*

بدهوان *buddhiwán*, wise, intelligent. *s*

بدي *badí*, f. badness, evil. *p.*

بديا *bidyá*, f. science, knowledge. *s.*

بر *bar*, f. bosom; produce; (prep.) upon. *p.*

برا *burá*, bad, wicked. *h.*

برابر *barábar*, equal, like, level. *p*

برابري *barábarí*, f. equality; competition. *p*

برباد کرنا *barbád k.* or *bar-bád d.* a. to cast upon the wind; to destroy or waste. *p s*

برپا کرنا *bar-pá k.* to excite. *p*

برتانت *británt*, m. affair, circumstance. *s*

برتن *bartan*, m. a dish, plate, vessel, utensil. *h*

برج *Braj*, name of a district, *h*

برخوردار *bar-khurdár*, happy; a term applied to a son (p. 22). *p*

برس *baras*, a year. *s.*

برسات *barsát*, rain, the rainy season. *s.*

برسنا *barasná*, n. to fall (as rain), to shower. *s.*

برن *baran*, m. colour, complexion. *s*

برهم *barham*, offended, confused, angry. *p*

بريان *biriyán*, f. time. *h*

بڑا *bará*, large, great, (adv.) very. *s*

بڑاي *bará,í*, greatness, *s.*

بڑهانا *barháná*, a. to increase, to promote. *s.*

بڑهنا *barhná*, n. to increase. *s.*

بس *bas*, enough, abundantly. *p.*

بستار *bistár*, m. extent, latitude. *s*

بستي *bastí*, f. an abode, a village. *s*

بسري كرنا *ba-sarí karná*, a. to pass, to spend (one's time). *p*

بسن پد *bisan-pad*, a song in praise of Vishnu. *s*

بسورنا *bisúrná*, n. to weep, to sob. *h*

بصارت *basárat*, f. sight, vision. *a*

بظاهر *ba-záhir*, ostensibly. *a*

بعد *ba'd*, after, afterwards, at the end. *a*

بعض *ba'z*, some, certain ones. *a*

بعضي *ba'ze* or *ba'zí*, some, certain. *a*

بعيد *ba'íd*, remote, far off. *a*

بغل *baghal*, s. f. the arm-pit. *p*

بغير *baghair*, ad. without, besides, except. *a*

بقال *bakkál*, m. a grain-merchant, a shopkeeper. *a*

بكرا *bakrá*, m. a he-goat. *s*

بكري *bakrí*, f. a goat, a female goat. *s*

بكهان *bakhán*, m. explanation. *s*

بگلا *baglá*, m. a crane, a heron. *s*

بل *bil*, m. a hole. *s*

بلا *balá*, f. calamity. *a*

بلا نا *buláná*, a. to call for, to summon. *billáná*, to cry. *h*

بلبل *bulbul*, f. a nightingale. *p*

بلكه *balki*, yea, on the contrary. *p*

بلند *buland*, high, lofty. *p*

بلي *billí*, f. a cat. *s*

بمدد *ba-madad*, with the help of, by means of. *p a*

بمرتبه *ba-martaba*, in a degree, considerably. *p a*

بموجب *ba-mújib*, by reason, on account of. *p a*

بن *bin*, without, not having. *s*

بنانا *banáná*, a. to make, to form. *h*

بنج *banaj*, m. trade, traffic. *s*

بند *band-k.* to shut up, to make fast. *p h*

بندگي *bandagí*, f. slavery, service, devotion. *p*

بندهوانا *bandhwáná*, a. to cause to be fastened. *h*

بننا *banná*, n. to be made. *h*

بنوانا *banwáná*, a. to cause to be made. *h*

بني *baní*, pl. sons, children; *baní Isrá'íl*, the Israelites. *a*

بنيا *banyá*, m. a shopkeeper, merchant. *s*

بو *bú* or *bo*, f. smell, fragrance. *p*

بوجه *bojh*, m. a load, weight. *h*

بوجه *bújh*, f. understanding, idea. s

بوجهنا *bújhná*, a. to understand, comprehend. *s*

بولنا *bolná*, to speak, say. *h*

بونا *boná*, a. to sow, plant. *s*

به *ba*, by, with, in; *ba-nisbat*, with regard to. *p*

بها *bahá*, m. price, value. *p*

بهاشا *bháshá*, see *bhákhá*. *s*

بهاشنا *bháshná*, to speak, say. *s*

بهاكها *bhákhá*, f. language, dialect. *h*

بهاگ *bhág*, m. good luck; destiny. *s*

بهاگنا *bhágná*, n. to flee, to run away; *bhág-j.* to run off. *h*

بهانت *bhánti*, m. manner, mode, way. *h*

بهانه *bahána*, m. pretence, evasion, contrivance. *p*

بهائي *bhá,í*, m. brother, friend. *s*

بهت *bahut*, much, many, very. *s*

بهتر *bihtar*, good, well, better. *p*

بهتيرا *bahuterá*, much. *s*.

بهجوانا *bhijwáná*, a. to cause to be sent. *h*

بهر *bhar*, full; *'umr-bhar*, during life; *din-bhar*, all day; *bhar-d.* a. to pay, to fill; *bhar-páná*, to be satisfied. *s*

بهرا *bahrá*, deaf; *bhará*, full. *h*

بهرمن *bhraman*, a walk. *s*

بهرنا *bharná*, a. to fill. *h*

بهروسا *bharosá*, m. hope, faith. *s*.

بهره *bahra*, m. portion, lot. *p*.

بهستي *bhisti*, *bhishti* or *bihishti*, m. a water-carrier. *p*

بهكانا *bahkáná*, a. to delude, to mislead. *h*

بهلا *bhalá*, good, worthy; *bhalá ádmí*, a gentleman. *s*

بهلائي *bhalá,í*, f. kindness, good deed. *h*

بهم *baham*, together, one with another, one against another. *p*

بهوكها *bhúkhá*, hungry. *s*

بهول *bhúl*, f. forgetfulness. *s*

بهولنا *bhúlná*, n. to forget, to mistake, to be deceived. *s*

بهونكنا *bhaunkná*, n. to bark. *s*

بهي *bhí*, even, also. *h*

بهيا *bhaiyá*, m. friend, brother. *s*

بهيت *bhít*, f. a wall. *s*

بهيتر *bhítar*, within, inside. *h*

بهيجنا *bhejná*, a. to send, convey. *h*

بهيد *bhed*, m. a secret, separation, secrecy. *s*

بهيڑ *bheṛ*, f. a sheep, an ewe. *s*

بهيڑي *bheṛí*, f. an ewe. *s*

بهيڑيا *bheṛiyá*, m. a wolf. *s*

بهيش *bhesh* or *bhes*, m. garb, habit. *s*

بهيگا *bhígá*, wet, moist (past part. of بهيگنا, to be wet).

بي *be* (also *abe*), an interjection of reproach, as: sirrah! you rascal! *h*

بي *be*, (prep.) without; much used in forming negative adjectives, as *be-adab*, unmannerly, and these again become substantives by adding *í*, as *be-adabí*, rudeness. *p*

بيان *bayán*, m. explanation, relation. *a*

بياه *byáh*, m. marriage. *s*

بي بس *be-bas*, helpless, destitute. *p*

بيبي *bíbí*, f. a lady; (vulgarly) a wife. *h*

بيت *bait*, f. a couplet, poetry. *a*

بيتاب *be-táb*, powerless, without endurance; *be-tábí*, helplessness. *p*

بي تعلقي *be-ta'allukí*, f. freedom from worldly ties, immediate communion with God. *p a*

بيٹا *beṭá*, m. a son, a child. *h*

بيٹهانا *baiṭhána*, a. to set down, to place. *h*

بيٹهنا *baiṭhná*, n. to sit, to be placed. *h*

بيج *bíj*, m. seed; principle. *s*

بيجا *be-já*, ill-timed, ill-placed, improper. *p*

بيجگر *be-jigar*, cowardly; *be-jigarí*, cowardliness, want of 'pluck.' *p*

بيچ *bích*, (prep.) among, between, during. *h*; the middle. *s*; *bích-bicháw*, mediation, intermediate means. *h*

بيچاره *bechára*, helpless. *p*

بيچنا *bechná*, a. to sell. *h*

بيشتر *beshtar*, generally, for the most part. *p*

بيدار *bedár*, awake, wakeful. *p*

بيربل *Bírbal*, name of one of Akbar's ministers. *h*

بيس *bís*, twenty. *h*

بيشمار *be-shumár*, incalculable. *p*.

بي قرار *be-karár*, uneasy, restless. *a p*

بيگانه *begána*, strange, undomestic, foreign. *p*

بيگم *begam*, (fem. of *beg*), a lady. *p*

بيل *bail*, m. a bullock. *h*

بيمار *bímár*, sick, a patient. *p*

بيماري *bímárí*, f. sickness. *p*

بينڈا *benḍá*, crooked; absurd. *h*

بيورا *byaurá*, m. account, history. *s*

بيوقوف *be-wukúf*, foolish, stupid. *p a*

پ

پاپوش *páposh*, f. a slipper. *p*

پاٹ *páṭ*, a mill-stone. *h*

پادشاه *pádsháh*, m. a king (same as *bádsháh*). *p*

پار *pár*, m. the opposite bank; (adv.) over, beyond; *pár sál*, last year. *s*.

پارسا *pársá*, devout, pious. *p*

پاس *pás*, near, before. *h*

پاسباني *pásbání*, f. keeping watch. *p*

پاكيزه *pákíza*, clean, fine, elegant. *p*

پال *pál*, m. a shade, shelter.

پالكي *pálkí*, f. a sedan-chair common in India. *h*

پانا, *páná*, a. to get, find, reach, accept. *s*

پانچ *pánch*, five. *s*.

پانڈا *pánḍá*, a master; priest. *s*

پانو *pánw*, m. leg, foot. *s*

پاني *pání*, m. water; lustre. *s*

پتا *patá*, m. token, indication, *h*

پتا *pattá*, m. a leaf. *s*

پتهر *patthar*, m. a stone, a rock. *s*

پتي *pattí*, f. a leaf; hemp. *s*

پٹكنا *paṭakná*, a. to dash, to beat. *h*

پچاس *pachás*, fifty. *h*.

پچهاڑي *pichhárí*, f. the rear; the hind-quarter of an animal. *s*

پچهلا *pichhlá*, latter, last, modern. *s*

پچيس *pachís*, twenty-five. *s*

پدر *padar*, m. (*pidar*, *h*), a father. *p*

پر *par*, (conj.) but; (postp.) on *or* upon, at. *h*

پر *par*, m. a wing. *p*

پرانا *puráná*, old, ancient. *s*

پرتهويناتهه *prithwi-náth*, Lord of earth, your majesty. *s*

پرتيت *pratít*, f. trust, confidence. *s*

پرده *parda*, m. a curtain, a screen. *p*

پرديشي *pardeshí* (or *pardesí*), a stranger. *s*

پرسرم *parisram*, m. care, labour. *s*

پرسن *prasanna*, pleased, content. *s*

پرسنسا *prasansá*, f. praise. *s*

پرش *purush*, man, a person. *s*.

پرکار *prakár*, m. mode, manner. *s*

پرگٹ *pragaṭ*, current, well-known. *s*

پرنده *paranda*, m. a bird. *p*

پرورش *parwarish*, f. breeding, nourishment. *p*

پرهيز *parhez*, m. temperance, continence, control of the passions. *p*

پري *parí*, f. a fairy. *p*

بريت *prít*, f. love, friendship. *s*

پريشان *pareshán*, scattered, ruined, distressed. *p*

پريشاني *pareshání*, f. destruction, distress. *p*

پڑنا *paṛná*, n. to fall, to happen. *h*

پڑوسي *paṛosí*, m. a neighbour. *s*

پڑهانا *paṛháná*, a. to teach to read, to instruct. *s*.

پڑهنا *paṛhná*, a. to read, to repeat, to say, to speak. *s*

پس *pas*, hence, therefore. *p*

پسند *pasand*, f. choice, approbation. *p*

پشم *pashm*, f. wool, fur. *p*

پشو *pashu* (or *pasu*), m. an animal, beast. *s*

پکارنا *pukárná*, a. to call aloud, to bawl, to cry out. *h*

پکڑنا *pakaṛná*, a. to catch or seize. *h*

پکهال *pakhál*, f. a leathern bag for carrying water. *s*

پلانا *piláná*, a. to give to drink. *s*

پنجرا *pinjrá*, m. a cage. *s*

پنڈت *panḍit*, a learned brahman. *s*

پوچهنا *púchhná*, a. to ask, inquire. *s*

پور *paur*, f. a door, gate. *s*

پورا *púrá*, full; accomplished. *s*

پوري *purí*, f. a kind of cake. *s*

پوست *post*, m. poppy; *postí*, one who intoxicates himself with infusion of poppy. *p*

پوشاک *poshák*, f. vestments, dress, habits, garments. *p*

پهاڑ *paháṛ*, m. a mountain. *h*

پهاڑنا *pháṛná*, a. to rend, to tear. *s*

پهٹا *phaṭá*, rent, torn (from *phaṭná*, n. to be rent). *s*

پهچاننا *pahchánná*, a. to know, to recognize. *s*

پهر *pahar*, a space of about three hours, a watch (of the day or night). *p*

پهر *phir*, again, back. *h*

پهرنا *phirná*, n. to turn back, return. *h*

پهل *phal*, m. fruit; effect; advantage; progeny. *s*

پهلا *pahlá* or *pahilá*, first, before; rather; *pahle*, at first, previous to. *h*

پهلنا *phalná*, n. to bear fruit, to be produced. *s*

پهنچانا *pahuncháná*, a. to convey; *ba-ham pahuncháná*, to get together, to store up. *h*

پهنچنا *pahunchná*, n. to arrive. *h*

پهنسنا *phansná*, n. to be caught in a noose, to be strangled. *h*

پهننا *pahanná*, a. to put on, to wear. *h*

پهولنا *phúlná*, n. to blossom, to bloom. *s*

پهيا *pahiyá*, m. a wheel (of a chariot, etc.) *h*

پهير *pher*, back, again. *h*

پهيرنا *pherná* or *pher-dená*, a. to turn, to circulate, to give back. *h*

پهيلنا *phailná*, n. to spread, to be divulged. *h*

پياده *piyáda*, m. a pedestrian, an attendant on foot; *piyáda-pá*, on foot, as a pedestrian. *p*

پيار *pyár*, m. affection. *s*

پيارا *piyárá*, dear, beloved. *s*

پياسا *piyásá*, thirsty. *s*

پياله *piyála*, m. a cup, goblet. *p*

پيٹ *peṭ*, m. the belly, stomach, womb. *s*

پيٹهه *píṭh*, f. the back. *s*

پيٹهنا *paiṭhná*, n. to rush in, to enter. *s*

پيچها *pichhá*, m. pursuit, following. *h*

پيچهاڑي *pichháṛí*, f. the hinder part. *h*

پيچهے *pichhe*, after, in the rear, in pursuit of. *h*

پيدا کرنا *paidá-k.*, a. to produce, to procure; *paidá-h.*, to be born; to be found. *h p*

پير مرشد *pír murshid*, your highness, sire, your worship. *p a*

پيراک *pairák*, m. a swimmer. *h*

پيرنا *pairná*, n. to swim. *h*

پيسا *paisá*, m. a copper coin, money, cash. *h*

پيسنا *písná*, a. to grind, triturate. *s*

پيشه *pesha*, m. trade, profession. *p*

پيغام *paighám*, m. a message. *p*

پيمان *paimán*, m. a promise, an oath, a compact. *p*

پينا *píná*, a. to drink. *s*

ت

تاب *táb*, power, endurance. *p*

تابع *tábi'*, m. a subject; (adj.) submissive. *a*

تاپنا *tápná*, a. to warm one's self before a fire. *s*

تاثير *ta,sír*, f. impression. *a*

تازه *táza*, fresh, new, green, young; fat; happy. *p*

تازي *tází*, Arab, Arabian. *a*

تاکنا *tákná*, a. to look, stare at. *s*

تا که *tá-ki*, so that, to the end that. *p*

تامل *ta,ammul*, m. meditation, reflection, purpose. *a*

تانسين *Tán-sen*, name of a musician. *s*

تب *tab*, then, at that time, afterwards; *tabhí se*, from that very time. *s*

تباه *tabáh*, ruined, lost; *tabáh-h.* to be in misery. *p*

تجارت *tijárat*, f. trading, traffic. *a*

تجهه *tujh*, inflection of *tú*, thou. *h*

تحصيل *tahsíl*, f. acquisition. *a*

تخت *takht*, m. a throne. *p*

تد *tad*, conj. or adv. then. *h*

تدبير *tadbír*, f. deliberation, counsel; management. *a*

تدرو *tadarv*, a pheasant. *p*

تر *tar*, moist; تربتر *tar ba tar*, all wet or weltering. *p*

تراشنا *taráshná*, a. to cut or clip, to shave, to shape out. *p h*

تربيت *tarbiyat*, f. education. *a*

ترك *tark*, abandoning, leaving. *a*

تركش *tarkash*, a quiver. *p*

تركي *Turkí*, of or belonging to Turkomania. *p*

تڑپهنا *taraphná*, n. to tremble, quiver. *h*

تس *tis* (inflect. of *so*), which; *tis-par*, whereupon. *h*

تسلي *tasallí*, f. consolation, soothing. *a*

تشنگي *tishnagí*, f. thirst. *p*

تصديع *tasdí'*, f. trouble, privation. *a*

تصديق *tasdík*, f. verifying, attesting. *a*

تصرف *tasarruf*, possession, use. *a*

تصوير *taswír*, f. a picture, an image. *a*

تضحيك *tazhík*, f. ridicule, sport. *a*

تعجب *ta'ajjub*, wondering, astonishment. *a*

تعريف *ta'ríf*, f. praise, description. *a*

تعظيم *ta'zím*, f. reverence, honouring. *a*

تفاوت *tafáwut*, m. distance, distinction, difference. *a*

تفنن *tafannun*, m. recreating, refreshing. *a*

تقاضا *takázá*, m. demanding, exacting; urgency. *a*

تقدير *takdír*, f. predestination. *a*

تقصير *taksír*, f. fault, crime, blame. *a*

تك *tak*, postp. up to, as far as. *h*

تكلف *takalluf*, m. ceremony, pomp. *a*

تكليف *taklíf*, f. trouble, annoyance. *a*

تلاش *talásh*, f. search, seeking. *a*

تلخ *talkh*, bitter. *p*

تلك *talak*, up to (same as *tak*). *h*

تلوار *talwár*, f. a sword. *s*

تلونمزاجي *talawwun-mizájí*, f. fickleness of disposition. *a*

تم *tum*, you (*tumh* and *tumhoṅ* in the inflection). *h*

تماشا *tamáshá*, m. an entertainment, show, spectacle, sight; *tamáshá'í*, a spectator. *a*

تماش بين *tamásh-bín*, a spectator. *p*

تمام *tamám*, entire, perfect, complete. *a*

تمبورا *tambúrá*, m. a kind of drum. *a*

تمهيد *tamhíd*, f. subterfuge, shift. *a*

تنخواه *tan-khwáh*, f. wages, salary. *p*

تنگ *tang*, narrow, strait; *tang áná*, to be disquieted, annoyed. *p*

تنگ دستي *tang-dastí*, f. distress, poverty. *p*

تو *to* or *tau*, adv. then; *tú*, pron. thou. *h*

توڑا *torá*, m. a purse containing 1000 rupees. *h.*

توڑنا *torná*, a. to break, to change (as coin) *s*

توفيق *taufík*, f. divine direction. *a*

تولنا *tolná*, a. to weigh. *s*

تون *toṅ* or *tauṅ*, then, in that manner. *h*

تها *thá*, was (verb auxil.). *h*

تهن *than*, m. breast. *s*

تهوڑا *thorá*, little, scarce, seldom, less, few. *h*

تهيلي *thailí*, f. a purse tied round the waist, a bag. *h*

تيار *taiyár*, ready, prepared, finished, complete. *a*

تياري *taiyárí*, f. preparation. *p*

تيتري *titrí*, f. a butterfly. *h*

تير *tír*, m. the bank of a river. *s*

تير *tír*, m. an arrow. *p*

تيز *tez*, sharp. *p*

تيس *tís*, thirty. *s.*

تيسرا *tísrá* (f. *tísrí*), the third. *s*

تين *tín*, three; *taiṅ*, thou; *teṅ*, from.

ٹ

ٹالي *ṭálí*, f. a sort of musical instrument. *h.*

ٹانگ *ṭáng*, f. the leg, foot. *h*

ٹپکنا *ṭapakná*, n. to drip. *h*

ٹٹ پونجيا *ṭaṭ-púnjiyá*, bankrupt. *h*

ٹٹولنا *ṭaṭolná*, a. to feel, to handle. *h*

ٹکڑا *ṭukṛá*, m. a piece, a bit, a morsel. *s*

ٹوٹنا *ṭúṭná*, n. to break. *h*

ٹوڑلمل *ṭoral-mal*, a man's name. *h*

ٹهٹها *ṭhaṭhá*, m. a joke, a jest. *h*

ٹهٹهول *ṭhaṭhol*, m. a jester, a buffoon. *h*

ٹهٹهولي *ṭhaṭholí*, f. fun, humour, sport, joking. *h*

ٹهہرنا *ṭhaharná*, n. to stay, to rest, to be settled. *h*

ٹهہرانا *ṭhahrána*, a. to determine, to deem. *h*

ٹهسا *ṭhassá*, m. vanity, ostentation. *h*

ٹهنڈا *ṭhandá*, cold. *h*

ٹهور *ṭhaur*, f. place, spot. *h*

ٹيپ *ṭíp*, m. a note of hand. *h*

ث

ثاني *sání*, second, equal. *a*

ثقه *siḳa*, trusty, confidential. *a*

ثمره *samra*, m. fruit; result. *a*

ثواب *sawáb*, m. the future reward of virtue. *a*

ج

جاڑا *jáṛá*, m. cold, winter. *s*

جاگنا *jágná*, n. to awake, to be awake. *s*

جال *jál*, m. net. *s*

جامه *jáma*, m. a garment, robe, vest. *p*

جان *ján*, f. m. life, soul, spirit, dear, beloved; *ján pahchán*, an intimate friend. *p*

جانا *jáná*, n. to go; to be; to pass; to reach; to continue. *játá-rahná*, to vanish. *s*

جانچنا *jánchná*, a. to test, to try, prove. *s*

جاندار *ján-dár*, a living being. *p*

جاننا *jánná*, a. to know, to understand, to consider. *s*

جانور *jánwar*, m. an animal, a bird. *p*

جاهل *jáhil*, m. a fool; (adj.) barbarous, brutal. *a*

جب *jab*, when, at the time when; *jab-na-tab*, now and then. *s*

جبا *jubá*, young, youthful. *s*

جب تک *jabtak* or *jab-talak*, so long as, till when. *s h*

جتا *jittá*, as much (as), whatever much. *h*

جتانا *jatáná*, a. to point out, to teach. *s*

جتنا *jitná*, as many (as), how many soever. *h*

جدا *judá*, separate, apart. *p*

جس *jis*, the inflection of the relat. *jo*, who, which. *h*

جست *jast*, f. a leap. *p*

جفاكار *jafá-kár*, m. a tormentor, oppressor. *a p*

جگانا *jagáná*, a. to waken, to rouse up. *s*

جگہہ *jagah*, f. place, quarter, room, vacancy, stead. *h*

جلاد *jallád*, m. an executioner; (adj.) cruel, hard-hearted. *a*

جلد *jald*, expeditious, quick, quickly. *p*

جلدي *jaldí*, f. quickness, rashness. *p*

جلنا *jalná*, n. to burn, to be kindled; to get into a passion. *s*

جلوه *jalwa*, m. light; *jalwa-gar*, brilliant, beautiful. *a*

جليو *jalev*, f. retinue, attendance. *h*

جمع *jam'*, f. a congregation, collection; sum total, number; *jam'-k.* or *-rakhná* or *-kar-rakhná*, to collect; *-hond*, to be collected. *a*

جن *jan*, m. person, individual. *s*

جنس *jins*, f. genus; goods, commodity. *a*

جنگل *jangal*, m. a forest, a wood. *s*

جننا *janná*, a. to bear, to bring forth. *s*

جو *jo*, (rel. pron.) he who; *jo-ko,í*, whosoever; *jo-kuchh*, whatsoever. *h*

جو *jau*, m. barley; *jó*, if, when; *jú*, searching. *p s*

جوا *jú,á*, m. a yoke; dice, gambling. *s*

جواب *jawáb*, m. an answer. *a*

جوان *jawán*, young, a young person; *jawán-mardí*, valour, *p*

جواني *jawání*, f. youth or rather that period of life to which the Romans applied the term *juventus*. *p.*

جواهر *jawáhir*, f. (plur. of جوهر), gems, jewels; *jawáhir-khána*, a jewel-house or treasury. *a*

جوهري *jauharí*, m. a jeweller. *a*

جوتا *jútá*, m. a shoe, a pair of shoes. *h*

جوتک *jotik*, m. astrology. *s*

جوتکی *jotikí*, an astrologer. *s*

جوتي *jútí*, a slipper, a small shoe. *h*

جوتنا *jotná*, to yoke. *h*

جوڑنا *joṛná*, a. to join, clasp. *h*

جون *jon* or *jaun*, when, as; *jon-hín*, or *jaun-hín*, the instant when. *h*

جونپور *Jaunpúr*, name of a city. *s*

جھاڑ *jháṛ*, m. bushes; continued rain. *h*

جھاڑ جھوڑ *jháṛ-jhúṛ*, f. a thicket. *h*

جهاز *jaház*, m. a ship. *a*

جهالت *jahálat*, f. ignorance. *a*

جهالر *jhálar*, f. a fringe; *jhálar-dár*, possessed of a fringe, fringed.

جهان *jahán*, m. the world; *jahání*, of or belonging to the world, mankind. *p*

جهان *jahán*, where, in whatever place. *h*

جهان پناه *jahán panáh*, m. refuge of the world; your majesty! *p*

جهانجھ *jhánchh*, f. a cymbal. *s*

جهانکنا *jhánkná*, a. to peep, to spy. *h*

جهٹ *jhaṭ*, quickly. *h*

جهرنا *jharná*, n. to ooze, to flow. *h*

جهروکها *jharokhá*, m. a lattice, a window. *s*

جهگڑا *jhagṛá*, m. wrangling, quarrelling. *h*

جهگڑنا *jhagaṛná*, n. to quarrel. *h*

جهمجهماتا *jhamjhamátá*, glittering. *h*

جهمکڑا *jhamakṛá*, m. splendour, beauty. *h*

جهن *jhan*, m. a clashing sound of metals, etc. *h*

جهوٹھ *jhúṭh*, false; a lie. *s*

جهوٹها *jhúṭhá*, a liar; false. *s*

جي *jí*, m. life, soul, mind: (added to names, professions, etc., it signifies sir, master). *s*

جيب *jeb*, f. a pocket. *p*

جيتا *jítá*, alive, living. *s*

جيتنا *jítná*, a. to win (at play), to conquer. *s*

جينا *jíná*, n. to live, to be alive. *s*

جيسا *jaisá*, in the manner which, as, such as. *s*

چ

چابک *chábuk*, m. a horsewhip. *p*

چابنا *chábná*, a. to gnaw. *h*

چاشني *cháshní*, f. taste. *p*

چال *chál*, f. way, practice. *s*

چالاک *chálák*, active, fleet. *p*

چاندني *chándní*, f. a kind of cloth; moonlight. *s*

چاهنا *cháhná*, a. to love, to like, to desire, to choose; *cháhiye* (in Braj. *cháhiyatu*), it is fit, proper, necessary, etc. *s*

چبانا *chabáná*, a. to gnaw. *h*

چبلا *chibillá*, stupid, impudent. *h*

چپ *chup*, } silent, speechless. *h*
چپکا *chupká*, }

چتر *chatur*, clever; *chaturá,í*, expertness. *s*

چٹکانا *chaṭkáná*, a. to rend, split. *h*

چٹھي *chiṭhí*, f. a letter, an epistle. *h*

چراغ *chirágh*, m. a lamp, a light. *p*

چراگاه *charágáh*, f. a pasture, a meadow. *p*

چرانا *charáná*, to graze; *churáná*, a. to steal; *ánkhen churáná*, to withdraw the eyes. *s*

چڑهنا *charhná*, n. to ascend, to come up. *h*

چڑهانا *charháná*, a. to raise up. *h*

چڑیا *chiriyá*, f. a bird. *h*

چڑیمار *chirímár*, a bird-catcher, a fowler. *h*

چشم *chashm*, the eye. *p*

چشمه *chashma*, m. a spring, a well, a fountain. *p*

چغلي *chughlí*, slandering, backbiting. *p*

چکت *chakit*, astonished. *s*

چکنا *chukná*, n. to have done, to have completed. *h* (Vide Gram. p. 65).

چکي *chakkí*, f. a mill, a mill-stone. *s*

چلانا *chilláná*, n. to scream out. *h*

چلنا *chalná*, n. to move, to go, proceed, go off, pass (as coin), to be discharged (as a gun); *chalá-j.* to go; *chalá-áná*, to come. *s*

چمک *chamak*, f. brilliancy, glitter, beauty. *h*

چمن *chaman*, m. a lawn, a meadow. *p*

چنانچه *chunánchi*, thus, accordingly. *p*

چنتا *chintá*, f. care, anxiety. *s*

چنگل *changul*, m. a claw; *changul márná*, to grasp with the claw. *p*

چوپ *chop*, f. desire, selfishness. *h*

چوپایه *chaupáya*, four-footed, a quadruped. *s*

چوتها *chauthá*, the fourth. *s*

چور *chor*, m. a thief, a robber. *s*

چورانا *choráná*, a. to steal. *s*

چوري *chorí*, f. theft, robbery. *s.*

چوک *chúk*, f. defect, error; *chauk*, an open place in a city. *h*

چوکس *chaukas*, expert, alert. *s*

چوگنا *chauguná*, a. fourfold. *s*

چونچ *chonch*, f. beak, bill. *s*

چونڈول *chaundol*, m. a kind of sedan or pálkí. *s*

چونري *chaunrí*, f. a whisk, a fly-flapper. *h*

چوها *chúhá*, m. a mouse; *chúhe-már*, a kind of hawk which feeds on mice. *h*

چه *chha*, six. *h*

چهاتي *chhátí*, f. the breast; *chhátí se lagáná*, to embrace. *h*

چهپنا *chhipná*, n. to be concealed, hidden, absent. *h*

چهتري *chhatrí*, f. a covering or hood; *chhatrí-dár*, covered, hooded. *s*

چهٹاپا *chhutápá*, m. smallness. *h*

چهچهه *chahchaha*, m. warbling. *h*

چهره *chihra*, m. the face. *p*

چهوٹا *chhotá*, little, small. *h*

چهوٹنا *chhútná*, n. to escape. *h*

چهور *chhor*, m. end, extremity. *h*

چهوڑنا *chhorná*, a. to release, leave, let go. *h*

چهوکرا *chhokará*, m. a boy, *h*

چهيد *chhed*, m. a hole, an opening. *s*

چيتا *chítá*, m. a leopard. *s*

چيز *chíz*, f. a thing. *p*

چينا *chainá*, m. a kind of corn. *s*. *chená*, millet. *h*

ح

حاجب *ḥájib*, m. an usher. *a*

حاجت *ḥájat*, need, want. *a*

حاصل *ḥáṣil*, m. produce, result, purport, profit, revenue; *ḥáṣil-i-kalám*, in fine, in short; *ḥáṣil-h.*, to be obtained; *ḥáṣil-k.*, to obtain. *a*

حاضر *ḥáẓir*, a. present, willing; *ḥáẓir-jawábí*, ready wit. *a*

حاكم *ḥákim*, m. a ruler. *a*

حال *ḥál*, m. state, condition, business, affair; present time. *a*

حالت *ḥálat*, f. state, condition. *a*

حبشي *ḥabshí*, m. Abyssinian, Caffre. *a*

حجتي *ḥujjatí*, cavilling, arguing the point. *a*

حد *ḥadd*, extreme, extremely. *a*

حرص *ḥirṣ*, avidity, greediness. *a*

حركت *ḥarakat*, f. proceeding, conduct. *a*

حريف *ḥaríf*, an opponent (in play), a rival, an associate. *a*

حسب الحكم *ḥasbu-l-ḥukm*, according to command. *a*

حسد *ḥasad*, f. envy, malice; emulation, ambition. *a*

حصه *ḥiṣṣa*, m. share, lot, portion, division. *a*

حضر *ḥaẓr*, m. rest, repose. *a*

حضرت *ḥaẓrat*, your *or* his majesty, your *or* his excellency, etc. *a*

حضور *ḥuẓúr*, m. presence, appearance; a regal court; his majesty. *a*

حق *ḥaḳḳ*, just, true; the Deity; right, justice; lot. *ḥaḳḳ-bíní*, perception of right. *a*

حقارت *ḥiḳárat*, f. contempt, disgrace, baseness. *a*

حقيقت *ḥaḳíḳat*, f. truth, a true statement, an account.

حكايت *ḥikáyat*, f. a history, tale, narration. *a*

حكم *ḥukm*, m. order, decree. *a*

حكمت *ḥikmat*, f. wisdom, knowledge, skill, contrivance. *a*

حكومت *ḥukúmat*, f. reign, rule. *a*

حكيم *ḥakím*, m. a sage, a philosopher, a physician. *a*

حلوائي *ḥalwá,í*, m. a confectioner. *a*

حواس *ḥawáss*, (pl.), senses. *a*

حوالي *ḥawále-k.* to give in charge, to consign. *a*

حيات *ḥayát*, life. *a*

حيران *ḥairán*, confounded, perplexed. *a*

حيرت *ḥairat*, f. confusion. *a*

حيف *ḥaif*, (interj.) ah! alas! m. iniquity, a pity; *ḥaif-k.* or *-kháná*, to sigh, to express one's sorrow. *a*

حيله *ḥíla*, m. artifice, ruse. *a*

حيوان *ḥaiwán*, m. animal. *a*

دريافت کرنا *daryáft-k.*, a. to conceive, understand. *h p*

دش *das* (or *dash*), ten. *s*

دست *dast*, m. the hand; *dast-bardár-h.*, to forbear, to desist. *p*

دسترخوان *dastar-khwán*, m. the cloth on which orientals eat. *p*

دشمن *dushman*, m. an enemy. *p*

دشمني *dushmaní*, f. enmity. *p*

دشنام *dushnám*, f. abuse. *s p*

دعا *du'á*, f. benediction, prayer, wish. *a*

دعوت *da'wat*, f. entertainment, banquet. *a*

دکھ *dukh*, m. pain, labour; *dukhí*, grieved, afflicted. *s*

دکهانا *dikháná* and *dikhláná*, a. to shew, to point out. *s*

دل *dil*, m. heart, mind, soul; *dil-pasand*, pleasing, agreeable. *p*

دلانا *diláná*, a. to cause to give. *s*

دلتي *du-lattí*, f. a kick with the two hind legs. *h*

دل جمعي *dil-jam'-í*, f. ease of mind. *p*

دليل *dalíl*, f. argument, proof. *a*

دم *dam*, m. breath, life. *p*

دم *dum*, f. tail, end. *p*

دن *din*, m. a day, *s*

دنيا *dunyá*, f. the world; people. *a*

دو *do*, a. two. *p*

دوا *dawá*, f. medicine; a remedy. *a*

دوار *dwár*, m. a door, a gate. *s*

دودھ *dúdh*, m. milk. *s*

دور *dúr*, f. distance; distant; *dúr-andesh*, far-sighted, wise; *dúr-andeshí*, prudence, foresight.

دوڑانا *dauṛáná*, a. to cause to run, to drive. *s*

دوڑنا *dauṛná*, n. to run. *s*

دوست *dost*, m. a friend, lover; *dost-rakhná*, to hold dear, to love. *p*

دوستي *dostí*, f. affection, friendship. *p*

دوسرا *dúsrá*, the second, other, next. *s*

دوش *dosh*, m. fault, defect. *s*

دوکان *dúkán*, f. a shop. *p*

دولت *daulat*, f. riches, fortune, empire; *daulat-mand*, a. wealthy. *a*

دون *dún*, low, vile, abject; *dún-himmatí*, low-mindedness. *a*

دونو or دونوں *dono* or *donoṅ*, the two, both. *h*

دهرم *dharm*, m. virtue; *dharm-avatár*, incarnation or personification of virtue; sire, your majesty. *s*

دهرنا *dharná*, a. to place, to lay. *s*

دهکا *dhakká*, m. a push, jolt. *h*

دهن *dhan*, m. wealth; *dhaní*, wealthy. *s.*

دهندهلپنا *dhandhalpaná*, m. fraud, trickery. *h*

دهؤان *dhú,áṅ*, m. smoke. *s*

دهوبي *dhobí*, a washerman; *dhobin*, a washerwoman. *h*

دهوم *dhúm*, f. noise, tumult. *h*

دهونا *dhona*, a. to wash; *dho-dháná*, to wash thoroughly. *s*

دهيان *dhyán*, m. mind, thought. *s*

ديانت *diyánat*, f. conscience, honesty, piety; *diyánat-dár*, honest, just. *a*

ديبي *daibí*, f. fate, by chance. *s*

ديدار *didár*, viewing, seeing. *p*

ديده *dída*, m. the eye. *p*

دير *der*, f. a long time, late. *p*

ديس *des*, m. country, region. s

ديكهنا *dekhná*, a. to see, experience. *s*

دينا *dená*, a. to give, grant. *s*

دينار *dinár*, m. the name of a coin, a ducat. *a*

ديندار *dindár*, faithful, true. *p*

ديوار *diwár*, f. a wall. *p*

ديوان *diwán*, m. a hall of audience. *p*

ڈ

ڈاڑہ *ḍáṛh*, f. a tooth. *h*

ڈاڑهي *ḍáṛhí*, f. the beard. *s*

ڈالنا *ḍálná*, a. to throw down, to pour out, to rush forth; *ḍál-d.*, a. to throw away. *h.*

ڈانڈ *ḍánḍ*, m. retaliation; an oar; a stick; *ḍánḍ-l.*, to take revenge. *s*

ڈبانا *ḍubáná*, a. to cause to sink. *h*

ڈبكي *ḍubkí*, f. a dip, dive; *ḍubkí-márná*, to bathe. *h.*

ڈر *ḍar*, m. fear. *s*

ڈرنا *ḍarná*, n. to fear. *s*

ڈريا لينا *ḍuṛiyá-l.*, to lead by the bridle. *h*

ڈلوانا *ḍalwáná*, a. to cause to be thrown, placed. *h*

ڈوبنا *ḍúbná*, to sink, to be drowned. *h*

ڈولي *ḍolí*, a plain kind of litter or sedan. *h*

ڈونڈي *ḍonḍí*, f. a proclamation. *h*

ڈهانپنا *ḍhámpná*, a. to cover up, conceal. *h*

ڈهانچا *ḍhánchá*, m. a frame, framework. *h*

ڈهب *ḍhab*, m. mode, manner. *h*

ڈهول *ḍhol*, m. a drum; *ḍholak*, a little drum. *h*

ڈهونڈهنا *ḍhúnḍhná*, a. to seek, to search for. *s*

ڈهير *ḍher*, m. a heap. *h*

ڈيرا *ḍerá*, m. a dwelling, a tent; (adj.) squint-eyed. *h*

ڈيل *ḍíl*, m. stature; *ḍíl-ḍaul*, size and shape; *ḍel*, a clod. *h*

ذ

ذره *z̤arra*, m. an atom, a little; the least bit. *a*

ذكر *z̤ikr*, m. remembrance; *z̤ikr-k.*, to mention, to praise. *a*

ر

رات *rát*, f. night. *s*

راجا *rájá* or راجه *rája*, a king. *s*

راجمندر *ráj-mandir*, m. a palace. *s*

راز *ráz*, m. a secret, a mystery. *p*

راست *rást*, right, true; *rást-go,í*, speaking truth, veracity. *p*

راكهنا *rákhná*, to keep, stop. *s*

رم چيرا *rám-cherá*, a name frequently given to slaves. *s*

راحت *ráhat*, f. quiet, ease. *a*

راه *ráh*, f. road, way. *p*

راي *rá,e*, f. sense, opinion. *a*

رتبه *rutba*, m. rank, dignity. *a*

رتهه *rath*, m. f. a chariot (four-wheeled). *s*

رتي *rati*, f. a weight of about eight barley-corns. *s*

رخصت *rukhsat*, f. leave, discharge, *rukhsat-h.*, to depart. *a*

رخنا *rakhná*, m. rent, hole. *p*

رسا *rassá*, m. a rope. *h*

رسانا *risáná*, n. to be enraged. *h*

رسته *rasta*, m. a road, way, mode. *p*

رسوا *ruswá*, exposed, disgraced. *p*

رسوائي *ruswá,í*, f. ignominy, disgrace. *p*

رسي *rassí*, f. a string, cord. *p*

رشک *rashk*, m. envy, jealousy *p*

رضا *rizá*, f. favour. *a*

رعيا *ra'íyyat*, f. subjects, people. *a*

رغبت *raghbat*, f. desire, liking. *a*

رفيق *rafík*, m. a friend, ally. *a*

رقعه *ruk'a*, m. a letter, note. *a*

رکابدار *rikáb-dár*, m. a stirrup-holder, groom. *a p*

رکهنا *rakhná*, a. to place, possess, save; *rakh-d.*, to put down, to place; *rakh-l.*, to establish. *s*

رکهوانا *rakhwáná*, a. to cause to be placed, or put. *s*

رنج *ranj*, pain, grief. *p*

رنجيده *ranjída*, annoyed, vexed. *p*

رنڈي *randí*, a woman. *h*

رنگ *rang*, m. colour; pleasure. *p*

رنگين *rangín*, coloured, gaudy. *p*

رو *rú*, m. face, surface. *p*

روبرو *rú-ba-rú*, in the presence of; face to face, before. *p*

روپا *rúpá*, m. silver. *s*

روپيه *rúpiya*, m. a rupee. *s*

روٹي *rotí*, f. bread, a loaf. *s*

روح *rúh*, f. soul, spirit. *a*

روز *roz*, m. a day. *p*

روس *ros*, m. anger; *ros-k.*, to feel wroth. *s*

روشن *roshan*, clear, illumined. *p*

روشني *roshní*, light, brightness. *p*

رونا *roná*, n. to weep; m. lamentation, grief. *s*

رهزني *rahzaní*, f. robbery, plunder. *p*

رهس *rahas*, m. witticism. *s*

رهنا *rahná*, n. to stay, be, live, continue; *rahne-wálá*, an inhabitant. *h*

رهوار *rahwár*, swift; (lit., fit for the road.) *p*

ريت *ret*, f. sand, filings; *rít*, custom. *h*

ريتي *ríti*, f. custom, habit. *s*

ريجهنا *ríjhná*, n. to be pleased, satisfied. *s*

ز

زاده *záda*, m. a son, child; (used in composition, as *sháh-záda*, a king's son, a prince.) *p*

زبان *zabán*, f. the tongue, language, dialect; *zabán-i rekhta*, the Urdú or mixed Hindústání. *p*

زبردستي *zabar-dasti*, f. tyranny, oppression. *p*

زر *zar*, m. gold, wealth, money. *p*

زمين *zamín*, ground, a field. *p*

زناني *zanáni*, belonging to women. *p*

زنبور *zambúr*, m. a bee. *p*

زندگي *zindagi*, زندگاني *zindagáni* } f. life, existence *p*

زنگ *zang*, m. a small bell. *p*

زور *zor*, m. force, strength. *p*

زورآور *zoráwar*, powerful, strong. *p*

زهر *zahr*, m. venom, *p*

زياده *ziyáda*, m. addition, additional; (adv.) more; *ziyáda-k.* to increase. *a*

زيان *ziyán*, m. loss, damage. *p*

زير *zer*, under, beneath. *p*

زيست *zist*, life. *p*

س

سا *sá* (*se, si*), a termination added to substantives or adjectives to denote similitude or intensiveness. *h*

سابق *sábik*, formerly. *a*

ساتهه *sáth*, (prep.) with. *s*

ساتهي *sáthi*, m. a companion. *s*

ساده *sáda*, plain, unadorned. *p*

سارا *sárá*, all, the whole. *s*

ساڑها *sáṛhá*, with a half added. *s*

ساز *sáz*, m. furniture, harness, etc. *p*

ساس *sás*, f. a mother-in-law. *s*

ساق *sák*, f. the leg, thigh.

سال *sál*, m. a year. *p*

سامهني *sámhne*, (prep.) in front of. *s*

ساونگي *sá,úngi*, f. a support for the pole of a chariot. *h*

ساهوكار *sáhúkár*, m. a great merchant. *s*

سايس *sá,is* m. a groom. *p*

سايه *sáya*, m. shadow, protection. *p*

سب *sab*, all, every, the whole. *s*

سبب *sabab*, m. cause, reason, motive; (prep.) on account of. *a*

سبق *sabak*, m. a task, lesson. *a*

سبک *subuk*, light, not heavy; *subuk-bár*, lightly burdened. *p*

سبهاو *subháv*, m. nature, disposition. *s*

سپرد كرنا *supurd-k.* a- to give in charge, to consign. *p*

ستري *stri*, a woman. *s*

سجوانا *sajwáná*, a. to cause to be fitted, prepared. *s*

سچ *sach* or سچا *sachchá*, m. truth, true. *s*

سخت *sakht*, hard, severe; very. *p*

سخي *sakhi*, generous. liberal. *a*

سدا *sadá*, always, *s*

سڈول *sudaul*, well-shaped, graceful. *h*

سر *sar*, head; *sar-anjám*, m. livelihood, success; *sar-anjám-h.* to succeed. *p*

سر *sir*, m. the head, the top. *s*

سراهنا *saráhná*, a. to praise, extol. *h*

سراي *saráe*, f. a caravansary, house. *p*

سردار *sardár*, m. chief, ruler. *p*

سردي *sardí*, f. coldness, cold weather. *p*
سرزمين *sar-zamín*, f. empire, region. *p*
سركار *sarkár*, f. court, mansion. *p*
سرور *surúr*, f. joy. *a*
سزا *sazá*, f. punishment. *p*
سست *sust*, lazy, idle. *p*
سستي *sustí*, f. laziness, dilatoriness. *p*
سعادت *sa'ádat*, f. felicity; *sa'ádat-mandí*, gratitude, felicity. *a*
سفر *safar*, a journey, voyage. *p*
سفيد *sufed*, *sufaid*, white. *p*
سكنا *sakná*, n. to be able. *s*
سكندر *Sikandar*, m. Alexander. *p*
سكها *sikhá* (*sikshá*), a lecture. *s*
سكهانا *sikháná*, سكهلانا *sikhláná*, } a. to teach. s.
سكهپال *sukh-pál*, m. a kind of sedan. *s*
سكهك *sikhak* (*sikshak*), a teacher, preacher. *s*
سلام *salám*, salutation; hail! *a*
سلامت *salámat*, f. safety, safely. *a*
سلطان *sulṭán*, m. a sovereign; Ar. pl. *saláṭín*, sovereigns. *a*
سلوك *sulúk*, f. behaviour, treatment. *a*
سليقه *salíka*, m. skill, taste. *a*
سليمان *Sulaimán*, Solomon. *a*
سم *samm*, m. poison. *a*
سماچار *samáchár*, m. news, tidings. *s*
سمان *samán*, like, similar. *s*
سمت *samt* or *simt*, f. a way, path; point of the compass. *a*
سمجه *samajh*, f. comprehension. *s*
سمجهنا *samajhná*, a. to comprehend, understand. *s*
سمرن *smaran*, m. remembrance, recollection. *h*
سمندر *samundar*, m. the sea, the wide ocean. *s*
سمي *samay*, m. time, season. *s*
سنانا *sunáná*, a. to cause to hear. *s*
سنپت *sampat*, f. wealth. *s*
سنديسا *sandesá*, m. a message. *s*
سنسار *sansár*, the world. *s*
سنگوتي *singauṭí*, f. an ornament of gold, etc., on the horn of a bullock. *s*
سننا *sunná*, a. to hear. *s*
سو *so*, correlat. pron. that very, that same; *sau*, a hundred. *h*
سوا *siwá*, except, besides. *a*
سوار *sawár*, a rider, one mounted or riding; embarked. *p*
سواري *sawárí*, f. riding; equipage. *p*
سوال *sawál*, m. request, begging, petition. *a*
سوامي *swámí*, m. master, husband. *a*
سواي *siwáe*, same as *siwá*. *a*
سوچ *soch*, thought. *s*
سوچنا *sochná*, to consider, reflect. *s*
سودا *saudá*, m. a bargain, purchase. *p*
سوداگر *saudágar*, m. a merchant. *p*
سوداگري *saudágarí*, f. merchandize, trade. *p*
سوڈول *sú-ḍaul*, elegant, well-shaped. *s*
سوراخ *súrá<u>kh</u>*, m. a hole, cavity. *p*
سورج *súraj*, m. the sun. *s*
سورداس *Súrdás*, name of a poet. *h*

سومپنا *saumpná*, a. to deliver over, consign. Also سونپنا *saunpná*. *s*

سونا *soná*, m. gold; *súná*, void, empty. *s*

سونا *soná*, n. to sleep, to die. *s*

سونٹا *sonṭá*, m. a pestle. *h*

سونهين *sonhín*, in front. *h*

سهارا *sahárá*, m. aid, assistance. *s*

سهج *sahaj*, ease, facility. *s*

سهسر *sahasra*, a thousand. *s*

سهي *sahí*, sure, certain. *s*

سياست *siyásat*, f. punishment. *a*

سيانا *siyáná*, wise, intelligent. *s*

سياه *siyáh*, black; unfortunate. *p*

سيدها *sídhá*, straight, opposite. *s*

سير *sair*, f. a walk, perambulation. *a*

سير *ser*, a certain weight, nearly two pounds. *h*

سيکڑون *saikṛon*, hundred, *h*.

سيکهنا *síkhná*, a. to learn. *s*

سينکنا *senkná*, a. to parch, to warm one's self. *h*

سينگ *sing*, m. a horn. *s*

ش

شاخ *shá<u>kh</u>*, a branch; horn. *p*

شادماني *shádmání*, f. joy, gladness, *p*

شامت *shámat*, f. spot, blemish. *a*

شامل *shámil*, comprehensive; extending to. *a*

شاه *sháh*, m. a king, prince; *sháh-záda*, a royal son, a prince. *p*

شاهجهان *sháhjahán*, name of one of the Emperors of Delhí.

شايد *sháyad*, possibly, probably, perhaps. *p*

شبد *shabd*, m. a voice, sound. *s*

شبيه *shabíh*, f. a picture, likeness. *a*

شتابي *shitábí*, f. quickness, haste; quickly. *p*

شتر *shutur*, m. a camel. *p*

شجاعت *shujá'at*, f. bravery. *a*

شخص *sha<u>kh</u>s*, m. a person, individual. *a*

شدت *shiddat*, f. violence, force; adversity, affliction. *a*

شراب *sharáb*, f. wine. *a*

شرط *sharṭ*, f. condition, stipulation, wager. *a*

شرم *sharm*, f. bashfulness, modesty, shame; *sharm-áná*, n. to feel ashamed. *p*

شرمندگي *sharmandagí*, f. bashfulness, shame. *p*

شرمنده *sharmanda* or *sharminda* ashamed, abashed. *p*

شروع *shurú'*, f. beginning, commencement. *a*

شرير *sharír*, vicious, wicked. *a*

شفقت *shafaḳat*, f. kindness, affection. *a*

شکار *shikár*, m. hunting, prey; *shikár-gáh*, f. hunting-field. *p*

شکاري *shikárí*, relating to hunting; m. a fowler, hunter. *p*

شکر *shukr*, m. thanks, gratitude. *a*

شکل *shakl*, f. shape, figure. *a*

شکم *shikam*, m. the belly; *shikam-parwar*, a pamperer of his belly. *p*

شور *shor*, m. cry, noise, disturbance. *p*

شوق *shauk*, m. desire, love. *a*

شوقين *shaukín*, desirous; amateur fanciers. *a*

شهد *shahd*, m. honey. *p*

شهر *shahr*, m. a city. *p*

شهزاده *shahzáda*, a prince; *shahzádí*, a princess. *p*

شير *sher*, m. a tiger, a lion. *p*

شيرني *sherní*, f. a tigress. *p*

شيريني *shíríní*, f. sweetness; eloquence. *p*

شيگر *shígra*, quickly. *s*

ص

صاحب *ṣáḥib*, m. a lord, master; companion; possessed of, as, *ṣáḥib-khána*, the master of the house; *ṣáḥib-i 'iṣmat*, possessed of chastity. *a*

صاف *ṣáf*, clean, clear, candid. *a*

صبح *ṣubḥ*, f. morning, dawn. *a*

صبر *ṣabr*, f. patience, endurance. *a*

صحبت *ṣuḥbat*, f. society. *a*

صراف *ṣarráf*, m. a banker, a money-changer. *a*

صرف *ṣarf*, expenditure; *ṣarf-k.*, to spend. *a*

صرف *ṣirf*, merely, only. *a*

صفاي *ṣafá,í*, purity, beauty. *a*

صفت *ṣifat*, f. praise, quality. *a*

صفحه *ṣafḥa*, face, surface. *a*

صلاح *ṣaláḥ*, f. counsel, advice. *a*

صلاحًا *ṣaláḥan*, peaceably, advisably, by way of advice. *a*

صندوق *ṣandúk*, m. f. a box, a trunk. *a*

صواب *ṣawáb*, m, rectitude, a virtuous action; success. *a*

صورت *ṣúrat*, f. form, face. *a*

صياد *ṣaiyád*, a hunter. *a*

صيد *ṣaid*, f. game, hunting, chase. *a*

ض

ضرور *ẓarúr* or *ẓurúr*, necessary, expedient. *a*

ضعيف *ẓa'íf*, frail, bedridden. *a*

ضيافت *ẓiyáfat*, f. entertainment. *a*

ط

طاق *ṭák*, m. a shelf, a recess. *a*

طاقت *ṭákat*, f, power, endurance. *a*

طالع *ṭáli'*, fortune; star. *a*

طبع *ṭab'*, m. constitution, nature. *a*

طبيب *ṭabíb*, m. a physician, doctor. *a*

طرح *ṭaraḥ*, f. manner, mode. *a*

طرز *ṭarz*, m. make, shape. *a*

طرف *ṭaraf*, f. side, direction; extremity. *a*

طريق *ṭarík*, f. way, path. *a*

طريقه *ṭaríka*, m. way, rule of life. *a*

طشت *ṭasht*, m. a basin. *p*

طعام *ṭa'ám*, m. food, victuals. *a*

طعمه *ṭu'ma*, m. food, bait.

طفلي *ṭiflí*, f. infancy. *a*

طلب *ṭalab*, f. search; demand, summoning; pay; *ṭalab-k.*, to seek for, to send for. *a*

طمع *ṭam'*, f. avarice, greediness. *a*

طور *taur*, m. mode, manner. *a*

طوطي *túti*, f. a parrot. *p*

طوفان *túfán*, m. a storm of wind and rain. *a*

طول *túl*, m. length. *a*

طويله *tawíla*, m. a tether, footband; *tawela*, a stable, stall. *a*

ظ

ظاهر كرنا *záhir-k.*, a. to manifest, display. *a h*

ظالم *zálim*, an oppressor, a tyrant. *a*

ظلم *zulm*, m. injustice, violence; *zulm-gudáz*, a melter of injustice, a crusher of oppression. *a*

ع

عاجز *'ájiz*, weak, helpless. *a*

عاجزي *'ájizí*, f. weakness, helplessness. *a*

عاقل *'ákil*, wise, a sage. *a*

عالم *'álam*, m. the world, universe; *'álam-panáh*, the asylum of the universe, his majesty. *a*

عالم *'álim*, a. learned, knowing. *a*

عبارت *'ibárat*, f. term, expression. *a*

عجائب *'ajá,ib*, m. wonders, curiosities. *a*

عجب *'ajab*, m. wonder, admiration; a. wonderful. rare. *a*

عجوبه *'ajúba*, a. wonderful, a strange thing. *a*

عدالت *'adálat*, f. justice. *a*

عدم *'adam*, non-existence. *a*

عذر *'uzr*, m. excuse. *a*

عرض *'arz*, f. representation; a petition, request. *a*

عزيز *'azíz*, precious, eminent, dear; (used substantively, like 'mon cher,' 'my dear friend.') *a*

عشرت *'ishrat*, enjoyment. *a*

عشق *'ishk*, m. love. *a*

عصا *'asá*, m. a stick. *a*

عطار *'attár*, m. a perfumer, druggist. *a*

عقل *'akl*, f. wisdom, opinion. *a*

عقلمند *'aklmand*, a. wise. *a*

علاج *'iláj*, m. cure, remedy. *a*

علاقه *'aláka* (or *'iláka*), m. connection. *a*

علاوه *'aláwa*, moreover, *a*

علم *'ilm*, m. science, knowledge; *'ilm-i-nujúm*, astrology.

علي *'alá*, upon, after; *'aláház-al kiyás*, in like manner. *a*

عليحده *'alaihida*, distinct, peculiar. *a*

عمده *'umda*, noble, fine. *a*

عمر *'umr*, f. age, life, lifetime. *a*

عمل *'amal*, m. action, practice, conduct. *a*

عنايت *'ináyat*, f. favour, gift. *a*

عوام الناس *'awám-unnás*, m. the common people. *a*

عورت *'aurat*, f. a woman, a wife; (Arab. plur.) *'aurát*. *a*

عوض *'iwaz*, m. return, substitute. *a*

عيادت *'iyádat*, f. visiting the sick. *a*

عيار *'aiyár*, cunning; a knave. *a*

عيش *'aish*, m. pleasure, delight. *a*

عين *'ain*, m. the eye, essence, the very (thing, etc.). *a*

غ

غار *ghár*, m. a pit, cavern, hole. *a*

غافل *gháfil*, careless, negligent. *a*

غائب *ghá,ib*, missing. *a*

غرا *gharra*, impudence. *a*

غرض *gharaz*, f. design, view; (ad.) in short, in fine. *a*

غريب *gharíb*, poor; a stranger. *a*

غربا *ghurabá*, the poor; pl. of *gharíb*. *a*

غزنوي *ghaznavi*, a. residing at Ghazna. *p*

غفلت *ghaflat*, f. carelessness; moral torpor. *a*

غلاف *ghiláf*, m. a covering. *p*

غلام *ghulám*, m. slave. *a*

غم *gham*, m. grief, sorrow. *a*

غيب *ghaib*, the invisible world. *a*

غير *ghair*, other, different. *a*

غيرت *ghairat*, f. jealousy. *a*

ف

فائده *fá,ida*, m. profit, gain; *fá,ida-mand-h.*, to benefit. *a*

فائق *fá,ik*, superior, excelling. *a*

فجر *fajr*, f. morning, dawn of day; early. *a*

فدوي *fidwi*, devoted, loyal subject or slave. *a*

فراغت *farághat*, f. comfort, leisure. *a*

فراموش كرنا *farámosh-k.* to forget. *p h*

فرزند *farzand*, m. a son, boy. *p*

فرصت *fursat*, f. opportunity. *a*

فرض *farz-k.* to grant, assume. *a*

فرمانا *farmáná*, a. to order, say, speak. *p*

فرياد *faryád*, f. complaint. *p*

فريادي *faryádi*, a. complainant, plaintiff. *p*

فريب *fareb*, fraud, a trick. *p*

فساد *fasád*, m. depravity, violence. *a*

فصل *fasl*, f. time, season, harvest. *a*

فضل *fazl*, bounty, munificence. *a*

فقط *fakat*, merely, only, no more. *a*

فقير *fakír*, m. a beggar, dervise; poor, indigent. *a*

فكر *fikr*, m. f. thought, reflection. *a*

فلانا *fuláná* or *fulána*, a certain one. *a*

فوج *fauj*, f. army, a multitude. *a*

فوراً *fauran*, quickly, instantly. *a*

في *fí*, in (used in Ar. phrases, as, *fi,l-wákí*, in truth; *fi,l-faur*, instantly; *fi,l-hakíkat*, of a verity). *a*

ق

قابل *kábil*, fit, worthy. *a*

قاضي *kázi*, m. a judge. *a*

قامت *kámat*, f. bulk, height, size. *a*

قانع *káni'*, contented, frugal. *a*

قبضه *kabza*, m. grasp, possession. *a*

قبول *kabúl*, m. consent; *kabúl-k.*, to agree, accept. *a*

قتل *katl*, m. slaughter, killing. *a*

قد *kadd*, m. stature, size. *a*

قدر *kadr*, f. worth, price. *a*

قدم *ḳadam*, m. foot, footstep. *a*

قديم *ḳadím*, ancient, old. *a*

قرار *ḳarár*, confirmation, rest. *a*

قرض *ḳarẓ*, m. a loan; *ḳarẓ dená*, to lend. *a*

قسم *ḳasam*, f. an oath; *ḳism*, kind, species. *a*

قصور *ḳuṣúr*, m. want, fault. *a*

قصه *ḳiṣṣa*, m. a story. *a*

قضا *ḳaẓá*, m. decree. *a*

قضاق *ḳaẓẓáḳ*, m. a robber; (hence Cossack).

قضاکار *ḳaẓákár*, by chance. *a p*

قضيه *ḳaẓiya*, m. a quarrel. *a*

قطره *ḳaṭra*, m. a drop. *a*

قلعه *ḳil'a*, m. a fort, palace. *a*

قناعت *ḳiná'at*, f. contentment. *a*

قول *ḳaul*, m. a statement, a word. *a*

قيامت *ḳiyámat*, f. the general resurrection; calamity. *a*

قيد *ḳaid*, f. fetter, imprisonment. *a*

قيمت *ḳímat*, f. price, value. *a*

ك

کاتب *kátib*, m. a writer. *a*

کاٹنا *káṭná*, a. to cut. *s*

کار *kár*, m. use, business, service, work, deed. *p*

کار چوبي *kár-chobí*, embroidered cloth. *p*

کاريگر *kárígar*, skilful; a cunning workman.

کاغذ *kághaẓ*, m. paper, a scrap of paper. *p*

کافر *káfir*, m. infidel. *a*

کال *kál*, m. time. *s*

کام *kám*, m. business, action, use; desire; *kám áná*, to be useful, of service. *s p*

کامراني *kámrání*, f. happiness. *p*

کان *kán*, m. the ear. *s*

کانپنا *kámpná*, m. to tremble, to shiver. *s*

کاندها *kándhá*, m. the shoulder. *s*

کانکه *kánkh*, the armpit. *h*

کانهکوبج *kánhkúbja*, the city of Kanoj. *s*

کايته *káyath*, m. name of a caste of Hindús; a scribe, a copyist. *s*

کب *kab*, when? *s*

کبي *kabí*, m. a poet. *s*

کبهو *kabhú*, ever, some time or other; *kabhú-kabhú*, occasionally; کبهي *kabhí*, same as *kabhú*. *s*

کپڑا *kapṛá*, m. cloth, clothes. *s*

کپوت *kapút*, unfilial. *s*

کتا *kuttá*, m. a dog. *s*

کتاب *kitáb*, f. a book, writing. *a*

کتنا *kitná*, how much? how many? *s*

کتوال *kutwál*, an officer of police. *s*

کٹوري *kaṭorí*, f. a small metal cup. *h*

کچه *kuchh*, any, some, something, a little; *kachhu*, any, the least. *h*

کچهوا *kachchhú'á*, m. a tortoise. *s*

کراي لينا *kiráe lena* or *kiráe mangwáná*, to get on hire, to borrow. *h*

کرشن *Krishn*, the god Krishna. *s*

کرنا *karná*, a. to do, to place. *s*

کروده *krodh*, angry, wroth. *s*

كس *kis*, inflection of *kaun*, who? frequently joined to the following word, as *kis-ṯarah*, how? *kis-wáste* or *-liye*, why? *h*

كسان *kisán*, m. a peasant, farmer. *h*

كسبي *kasbí*, a prostitute, courtesan. *a*

كسنا *kasná*, a. to draw, cover. *h*

كسي or كسو *kisí* or *kisú*, inflection of *ko,í* or *kuchh*, some, certain, any. *h*

كشت *kisht*, m. f. a sown field. *p*

كشتي *kishtí*, f. a boat, ship. *p*

كل *kal*, to morrow, yesterday. *s*

كلام *kalám*, m. a word, speech. *a*

كلاونت *kaláwant*, m. a minstrel, musician. *h*

كليجه *kaleja*, m. the liver; courage. *h*

كم *kam*, deficient, less, little, rarely; (used in composition: as *kam-bakht*, ill-starred; a rascal). *p*

كمال *kamál*, m. perfection, excellence; (used adjectively, as: extreme, the utmost, etc.) *a*

كمانا *kamáná*, a. to earn one's living. *h*

كمرا *kamará* (camera), m. a room, chamber. (Port.)

كمينه *kamína*, base, mean fellow. *p*

كناره *kinára*, m. shore, side, limit. *p*

كنجي *kunjí*, f. a key. *s*

كنڈ *kunḍ*, m. a cistern, basin. *s*

كنگال *kangál*, poor, wretched. *h.*

كني *kane*, near, beside. *h*

كوا *kauwá*, m. a crow; *kú,á*, a well, a draw-well, a pit. *s*

كوتاه *kotáh*, short; *kotáh-k.* to hold back, to refrain. *p*

كوتاهي *kotáhí*, smallness, deficiency. *p*

كوتوال *kotwál*, m. the chief officer of police.

كوٹهري *koṭhrí*, f. a room. *s*

كوچ *kúch*, departure. *p*

كوچه *kúcha*, m. a lane, a street. *p*

كوڑا *koṛá*, m. a whip, a lash; *kúṛá*, rubbish. *h*

كومل *komal*, soft, weak. *s*

كون *kaun*, who? which? what? *h*

كونا *koná*, m. a corner. *s*

كونڈي *kúnḍí*, f. a mortar. *h*

كونسا *kaunsá*, what-like? of what sort? *h*

كوه *koh*, a mountain. *p*

كوئي *ko,í*, any, some one; (artic.) a or an, a certain (person, etc.). *s*

كه *ki*, that, thus, as follows: (sometimes a relative, who? which?) *p*

كها *kahá*, m. bidding, order; *kahá-suní*, f. altercation. *s*

كهال *khál*, f. skin, hide. *s*

كهاں *kaháṅ*, where? whither? *h*

كهانا *kháná*, a. to eat, suffer; m. food, dinner. *s*

كهاوت *kaháwat*, f. a byword, a saying. *s*

كهجلانا *khujláná*, a. to tickle, to rub. *s*

كهرها *kharahá*, m. a hare. *s*

كهڑا *khaṛá*, erect, standing. *h*

كهڑكي *khiṛkí*, f. a window. *h*

کهلنا *khulná*, n. to be opened, to be revealed; to clear up after rain. *s*

کهلانا *khiláná*, a. to give to eat, to feed. *s*

کهل کهلانا *khil-khiláná*, n. to laugh. *h.*

کهلنا *khilná*, n. to blow (a flower). *h*

کهنا *kahná*, a. to tell, say, bid, call, affirm. *s*

کهودنا *khodná*, a. to dig. *h*

کهولنا *kholná*, a. to open, untie, let loose. *s*

کهونا *khoná*, a. to lose, to waste. *s*

کهيت *khet*, m. a field. *s*

کهيتي *khetí*, f. husbandry, crop. *s*

کهيل *khel*, m. play, game, sport. *s*

کهيلنا *khelná*, n. to play, to sport. *s*

کهين *kahín*, somewhere, anywhere, somewhat. *s*

کهينچنا *khenchná* or *khainchná*, a. to delineate, draw. *h*

کئي *ka,í* or *ka,e*, some, a few. *h*

کيا *kyá*, (pro.) what? how? why? whether (or not); *kyá khúb*, how glorious! what fun! *s*

کيا *kiyá*, done, a deed; (past part. of *karná*, to do, make.) *s*

کيسا *kaisá*, how? in what manner? of what sort? what like? *h*

کيفيت *kaifiyat*, f. nature, state, condition, pleasure. *a*

کيون *kyún, kyaun*, why? how? well? what? *kyún ki*, because; *kyún-kar*, how? *h*

گ

گاڙي *gáṛí*, f. a chariot, cart. *h*

گالي *gálí*, f. abuse. *s*

گانا *gáná*, a. to sing. *s*

گانٹهه *gánṭh*, a knot; *gánṭh-ká púrá*, very rich. *h*

گانو *gánw*, m. a village. *s*

گاو *gáw*, f. a cow. *p*

گپ شپ *gap shap*, chit-chat, conversation. *h*

گجراتي *gujarátí*, belonging to Gujerat. *h*

گدها *gadhá*, m. an ass, (metaph.) a fool. *s*

گدڙيا *gudaṛyá*, a shepherd. *h*

گذارا *guzárá*, m. passing. *p*

گذرانا *guzaráná*, a. to forward. *p*

گذرنا *guzarná*, n. to pass; *dar-guzarná*, to refrain, to forbear. *p*

گر *gur*, m. a preceptor. *s*

گرد *gard*, f. dust (Scotticè, 'stour.') *p*

گرد *gird*, (prep.) around. *p*

گرداب *girdáb*, m. a gulph, whirlpool. *p*

گردن *gardan*, f. the neck. *p*

گرفتار *giriftár*, captive. *p*

گرانا *giráná*, a. to cause to fall, to throw down. *h*

گرم *garm*, hot; *garmí*, f. heat, hot season. *p*

گرنا *girná*, n. to fall, to drop down. *h*

گروه *guroh*, m. a troop, a class. *p*

گڙنا *gaṛná*, n. to be buried. *s*

گڑه *gaṛh*, m. a fortress, palace. *h*
گفتگو *guftgú*, conversation. *p*
گل *gul*, m. a rose; *gul-karná*, to extinguish. *p*
گلا *galá*, m. a flock of sheep, a herd of cattle. *p*. the neck. *h*
گلاب *guláb*, m. a rose. *p*
گله *galla*, m. a flock. *p*
گلي *galí*, f. a lane. *h*
گم *gum*, lost. *p*
گمان کرنا *gumán karná*, a. to imagine, fancy, opine. *p h*
گن *gun*, m. skill; *guní*, skilful. *s*
گناه *gunáh*, m. fault, crime, sin. *p*
گنتهوانا *gunthwáná*, a. to cause to be fixed (as a string). *s*
گنوار *ganwár*, m. a villager, a peasant. *h*
گواه *gawáh*, a witness; *gawáhí*, evidence, testimony. *p*
گوپال *Gopál*, one of the names of Krishna. *s*
گور *gor*, m. the grave, tomb. *p*
گوشت *gosht*, m. flesh. *p*
گوشه *gosha*, m. a corner. *p*
گوکه *gokh*, m. a portico. *h*
گول *gol*, or *golsá*, round. *s*
گونگا *gúngá*, mute, dumb. *h*
گويا *goyá*, as if, as one would say. *p*
گهات *ghát*, an ambush. *h*
گهاٹ *gháṭ*, m. a landing-place. *s*
گهبرانا *ghabráná*, n. to be confused, perplexed. *h*
گهٹا ٹوپ *ghaṭá-ṭop*, m. a canopy, covering. *h*
گهر *ghar*, m. house, dwelling. *s*
گهرانه *gharána*, m. house, family. *s*
گهڑا *ghaṛá*, m. a jar, pitcher. *s*
گهڑي *ghaṛí*, f. an hour; a watch. *s*
گهسنا *ghisná*, n. to be worn; *ghusná*, to enter. *h*
گهنٹالي *ghanṭálí*, f. a small bell. *s*
گهنگرو *ghungrú*, m. a small bell. *s*
گهوڑا *ghoṛá*, m. a horse. *s*
گهولنا *gholná*, a. to dissolve, to pound. *s*
گهي *ghí*, m. clarified butter. *s*
گيا *gayá*, gone (past part. of *jáná*). *h*
گيل *gail*, f. a road. *h*
گينا *gainá*, m. a small bullock. *h*
گيني *gainí*, f. a small chariot. *h*
گيهون *gehún*, m. wheat. *s*

ل

لات *lát*, f. a kick. *h*
لاٹ *láṭ*, f. trunk of a tree. *h*
لاثاني *lá-sání*, unequalled, unrivalled. *a*
لاج *láj*, m. shame. *s*
لاجواب *lá-jawáb*, silent, silenced. *a*
لاچار *lá-chár*, helpless, destitute. *p.*
لاحاصل *lá-ḥáṣil*, useless, without result. *a*
لادنا *ládná*, a. to load, to embark. *h*
لاڑ کپور *Láṛ Kapúr*, two celebrated minstrels at the court of Akbar. *h*
لازم *lázim*, necessary, urgent. *a*
لاکه *lákh*, one hundred thousand. *h*
لالا *lálá*, m. master, sir. *h*
لالچ *lálach*, m. avarice, desire. *s*

لالچي *lálchí*, covetous, greedy. *s*

لانا *láná*, a. to bring; to breed, produce, make. *s*

لائق *lá,ik*, worthy, befitting, perfect. *a*

لپٹنا *lipatná*, n. to cling, to stick to. *h*

لپیٹنا *lapetná*, a. to wrap up. *h*

لٹکانا *latkáná*, a. to suspend. *h*

لجانا *lajáná*, n. to be ashamed. *s*

لجت *lajjit*, ashamed. *s*

لدنا *ladná*, n. to be loaded, to ride. *h*

لذيذ *laziz*, delicate, delicious. a

لڑائي *lará,i*, f. battle, quarrel, war. *h*

لڑکا *larká*, m. a boy, child, babe. *s*

لڑنا *larná*, n. to fight, to quarrel. s

لڑھانا *lurháná*, a. to spill, upset. *s*

لڑھکنا *lurhakná*, n. to be spilt, upset. *s*

لشکر *lashkar*, m. an army. *p*

لطف *lutf*, m. pleasure, enjoyment. *a*

لعنت *la'nat*, a curse. *a*

لقب *lakab*, m. a surname. *a*

لقمان *Lukmán*, name of a famous Eastern fabulist. *a*

لقما *lukmá*, m. a morsel, mouthful. *a*

لکڑي *lakrí*, f. wood, a staff, stick. *h*

لکھنا *likhná*, a. to write. *s*

لکھوانا *likhwáná*, a. to cause to be written. *s*

لگام *lagám*, bridle, bit. *s*

لگانا *lagáná*, a. to attach, to apply. *s*

لگنا *lagná*, n. to touch; to begin; to reach or come up to. *s*

لگوانا *lagwáná*, a. to cause to be applied. *s*

لنبا *lambá*, long, tall. *s*

لنگڑا *langrá*, lame. *p h*

لوٹنا *lútná*, a. to rob, plunder; *lotná*, to roll on the ground. *s*

لوکا *lúká*, m. spark, flame. *s*

لوگ *log*, m. people. *s*

لومڑي *lomrí*, f. a fox. *s*

لونڈي *laundí*, f. a slave. *h*

لوهو *lohú*, blood.

لوها *lohá*, m. iron. *s*

لیٹنا *letná*, n. to repose, to lie down. *h*

لیجانا *lejáná*, a. to take away, to carry off. *s*

لیکن *lekin*, (conj.) but, yet, however. *a*

لیکھا *lekhá*, m. account, reckoning. *s*

لیکھک *lekhak*, m. a writer, one who is writing. *s*

لیلا پیلا *lílá-pílá*, blue and yellow; (applied to the appearance of the eyes of a person enraged). *s*

لینا *lená*, to take, accept; set; buy. *s*

لیي *liye*, for the sake of. *h*

م

ما *má*, f. a mother; *má-báp*, parents. *s*

ماجرا *májará*, m. state, circumstance, incident. *a*

مارڈالنا *már-dálná*, a. to smite, to kill. *s*

مارگ *márg*, m. a road, path. *s*

مارنا *márná*, a. to smite, strike. *s*

ماري *máre*, by reason of, in consequence of. *s*

مال *mál*, m. property, wealth, goods. *a*

5

مآل *ma,ál*, end, issue. *a*

مالك *málik*, m. master, lord, possessor. *a* [tressed, *p*

مانده *mánda*, left behind, tired, dis-

مانگنا *mángná*, a. to ask for, to beg. *s*

ماننا *mánná*, a. to believe, obey, agree to. *s*

مای *má,í*, f. mother. *s*

مبارك *mubárak*, good, auspicious; *mubárak-bádí*, congratulation. *a*

مت and متا *mat* and *matá*, f. mind, judgment. *s*

مت *mat*, don't (used with imperat.) *h*

متاع *matá'*, m. goods, property. *a*

متر *mitr*, a friend. *s*

متصدي *mutaṣaddí*, an accountant. *a*

متعجب *muta'ajjib*, astonished. *a*

متهرا *Mathurá*, name of a province and town near Agra. *s*

متهاس *miṭhás*, sweetness. *h*

متائي *miṭhá,í*, f. sweetness, sweets. *h*

متهي *muṭhí*, f. the fist, a handful. *s*

متي *miṭṭí*, f. earth, dust. *s*

مثل *maṣal*, f. a fable, simile, proverb. *a*

مجلس *majlis*, f. an assembly, convention. *a*

مچانا *macháná*, a. to make, stir up, commit. *h*

محاوره *muḥáwara*, m. idiom, usage. *a*

محتاج *muḥtáj*, necessitous, needy. *a*

محرم راز *maḥram-i ráz*, privy to secrets, a confidant. *a p*

محروم *maḥrúm*, disappointed, excluded. *a*

محمود *Maḥmúd*, a man's name. *a*

محنت *miḥnat*, f. labour, misfortune. *a* [ous. *a*

مختلفه *mukhtalifa*, different, vari-

مخفي *makhfí*, hidden. *a*

مخلصي *makhlisí*, f. escape, deliverance. *a*

مدت *muddat*, f. a space of time, a long time. *a*

مدد *madad*, f. aid, help; *madad-gár*, a helper, auxiliary. *a*

مدعا *mudd'á*, m. desire, wish. *a*

مدعي *mudda'í*, m. a plaintiff, claimant. *a* [grees. *a*

مراتب *marátib*, m. (pl.) steps, de-

مراد *murád*, f. desire, meaning, inference. *a*

مرتبه *martaba*, m. a step, degree, dignity, office, time; *ek martaba*, once upon a time. *a*

مرحوم *marḥúm*, deceased, the late. *a*

مرد *mard*, m. a male, a man, a hero; *mardána-wár*, like a man. *p*

مردار *murdár*, a dead body. *p*

مرده *murda*, dead, a dead body. *p*

مرضي *marẓí*, f. wish, inclination. *p*

مرغ *murgh*, m. a fowl, bird. *p*

مرنا *marná*, n. to die, to expire; *mar-jáná*, to die, expire. *s*

مروت *murawwat*, generosity.

مزاج *mizáj*, m. temperament, disposition. *a*

مسافر *musáfir*, m. a traveller. *a*

مستغرق *mustaghrik*, immersed, absorbed. *a*

مستول *mastúl*, m. a mast. *a*
مستي *masti*, f. intoxication. *p*
مسجد *masjid*, f. a mosque. *a*
مسخره *maskhara*, a jester. *a*
مسكرانا *muskuráná*, n. to smile. *h*
مسلمان *Musalmán*, a Muhammadan, a follower of Muhammad. *a*
مشك *mashk*, f. a leathern bag for water. *p*
مشورت *mashwarat*, f. consultation. *a*
مشهور *mash,húr*, noted, well-known. *a*
مصاحب *musahib*, m. a companion, friend, aide-de-camp. *a*
مصور *musauwir*, m. a painter. *a*
مصيبت *musíbat*, f. calamity, affliction. *a*
مضبوطي *mazbúti*, f. solidity, firmness. *a*
مطابق *mutábik* (prep.) conformable to. *a*
مطلب *matlab*, m. a question, purpose, meaning. *a*
مطلع *muttali'*, acquainted, informed. *a*
مطلق *mutlak*, in the least, at all.
مظفر خان *Muzaffir-khán*, a man's name. *a*.
مظلوم *mazlúm*, injured, oppressed; *mazlúm-nawáz*, a cherisher of the oppressed. *a p*
معًا *ma'an*, together. *a*
معاف *mu'áf*, absolved, forgiven, excused; *mu'áf-karná*, to forgive. *a*
معذور *ma'zúr*, excused, excusable. *a*
معطر *mu'attar*, scented, perfumed. *a*

معلم *mu'allim*, m a teacher, doctor. *a*
معلوم *ma'lúm*, known, apparent; *ma'lúm-h.* to seem, to appear. *a*
معما *mu'ammá*, m. an enigma, an acrostic.
معيوب *ma'yúb*, blameable, disreputable. *a*
مغرور *maghrúr*, proud, fastidious. *a*
مغز *maghz*, m. brain. *p*
مفت *muft*, free, gratis. *p*
مفلس *muflis*, poor, wretched. *a*
مفلسي *muflisi*, f. poverty. *a*
مفيد *mufíd*, profitable, useful. *a*
مقابل *mukábil*, opposite. *a*
مقام *makám*, m. place, occasion. *a*
مقرر *mukarrar*, assuredly. *a*
مكان *makán*, m. a place, dwelling. *a*
مكهه *mukh*, m. mouth. *s*
مكهي *makkhi*, a fly. *h*
مگر *magar*, but, except. *s*
ملازم *mulázim*, an attendant. *a*
ملاقات *mulákát*, f. meeting, interview. *a*
ملك *mulk*, m. a country, kingdom; *malik*, a king; (pl. Ar.) *mulúk*, kings. *a*
ملنا *malná*, a. to rub, to tread on, to anoint. *h*
ملنا *milná*, a. to be found, to meet. *s*
ممكن *mumkin*, possible. *a*
من *man*, m. the mind, soul. *s*; name of a certain weight, a maund. *p*
منادي *manádi*, f. proclamation. *a*

منتخبات *muntakhabát*, selections, extracts. *a*

منڈا *munḍá*, open, exposed. *h*

منجھولي *manjholí*, f. a small chariot. *h*

منش *manish*, f. dignity, rank. *p*

منش *manush*, a person. *s*.

منطق *mantik*, m. logic. *a*

منطقي *mantiki*, m. logician. *a*

منع *man'*, m. prohibition. *a*

منگوانا *mangwáná*, a. to cause to be brought. *h*

منہ *muṅh*, m. the mouth, face; *muṅh-zor*, headstrong, obstinate. *s*

مو *mú*, a hair. *p*

موا *mú,á*, dead, (past part. of *marná*). *s*

موافق *muwáfik*, conformable to. *a*

موت *maut*, death. *a*

موتي *motí*, m. a pearl. *s*

موٹا *moṭá*, gross, coarse. *h*

موجب *mújib*, cause, means. *a*

موچي *mochí*, m. a cobbler; saddler. *h*

موڑھ *múṛh*, m. a fool. *s*

موسم *mausim* or *mausam*, m. time, season. *a*

موش گیر *músh-gír*, a kind of hawk which feeds on mice. *p*

موقوف *maukúf*, depending on; *maukúf-k.*, to conclude, to stop. *a*

مول *mol*, m. price; *mol-lená*, to buy. *h*

موم *mom*, wax; *mom-jáma*, cloth covered with wax, oil-cloth.

موم‌دل *mom-dil*, soft-hearted. *p*

مونڈھا *múnḍhá*, m. a footstool. *h*

مہابلي *mahábalí*, powerful. *s*

مہاجن *mahájan*, a rich merchant. *s*

مہاڈول *mahádol*, a large sedan. *h*

مہاراج *mahárráj*, great king! sir! sire! *s*

مہارت *mahárat*, f. proficiency, skill. *a*

مہرہ *muhra*, m. the thigh bone. *p*

مہنگا *mahngá*, dear, high-priced.

مہنگي *mahngí* or *mahnagí*, f. dearth, scarcity.

مہینہ *mahína*, m. a month. *p*

میان *miyán*, a master, gentleman. *p*

میانہ *miyána*, m. a pálkí. *p*

میر *mír*, m. a chief, a leader. *p*

میرا *mírá*, lord, heir. *p*

میر بخشي *mír bakhshí*, m. the pay-master-general. *p*

میرزا *mírzá*, a noble, grandee. *p*

میز *mez*, f. a table. *p*

میسر *muyassar*, a. attained, attainable. *a*

میلا *mailá*, a. dirty, defiled; *melá*, a fair; *melá ṭhelá*, m. a crowd of people. *s*

مینہ *meṅh*, m. rain, rainy season. *s*

ن

ناچیز *ná-chíz*, worthless, useless. *p*

ناخوش *ná-khush*, displeased. *p*

ناخوشي *ná-khushí*, f. displeasure. *p*

نادان *ná-dán*, a. ignorant, simple. *p*

ناداني *ná-dání*, f. ignorance. *p*

ناکا *náká*, m. a lane, avenue. *h*

ناگورا *nágaurá*, m. a kind of bullock (of the country Nagaur). *h*

ناگہان *ná-gahán*, suddenly, unexpectedly. *p*

نالان *nálán*, complaining, lamenting. *p*

نالش *nálish*, f. complaint, lamentation. *p*

نالشي *nálishí*, complaining, a complainant. *p*

نالكي *nálkí*, f. a sort of sedan for princes, etc. *h*

ناله *nála*, m. weeping, lamentation. *p*

نام *nám*, m. name, fame, reputation. *s*

نامحرم *ná-mahram*, unprivileged, applied to such males as are not entitled to visit the harem. *a*

نامرد *ná-mard*, unmanly, a coward. *p*

نامردي *ná-mardí*, f. unmanliness. *p*

ناممكن *ná-mumkin*, impossible. *p a*

ناموس *námús*, m. f. honour, dignity, the female part of a family. *a*

نانو *náṅw*, m. name. *s*

ناو *náw*, f. a ship. *p*

نايب *ná,ib*, m. a deputy. *a*

نبيدن *nibedan*, m. representation, statement. *s*

نپٹ *nipaṭ*, very, exceedingly. *h*

نجوم *najúm* or *nujúm*, astrology, (lit., stars). *a*

نجيب *najíb*, noble; *najíb-záda*, noble-born, a gentleman; *najíb-zádí*, daughter of a noble. *a*

ندامت *nadámat*, f. repentance, contrition, regret. *a*

ندان *nidán*, at length, at last. *s*

ندي *nadí* or *naddí*, f. a river. *s*

نراس *nirás*, hopeless, despair. *s*

نرالا *nirálá*, apart, aside. *s*

نرتر *nir-uttar*, without an answer. *s*

نزديك *nazdík*, (prep.) near; used idiomatically like the Latin *apud*, as *dáná,oṅ-ke nazdík*, 'apud sapientes,' 'in the opinion of the wise.' *p*

نشا *nashá*, f. intoxication. *a*

نصفا نصفي *nisfá-nisfí*, by halves; with *karná*, to divide into two equal shares. *p*

نصيحت *nasíhat*, f. advice, admonition; *nasíhat-d.* or *-k.*, to counsel, instruct, reprove. *a*

نظارا *nazárá*, m. sight, looking. *a*

نظر *nazar*, f. sight; *nazar-áná* or *-pahuṅchná*, to come in sight. *a*

نعمت *ni'mat*, f. favour, benefit, delight, affluence. *ni'mat-khwár*, a devourer of delights, a man of pleasure, a 'bon vivant.' *a*

نفيس *nafís*, precious, delicate, exquisite. *a*

نفرين *nafrín*, f. regret, detestation. *p*

نقاشي *nakkáshí*, f. painting; *nakkáshí-dár*, painted, having paintings. *a*

نقد *nakd*, m. ready money. *a*

نقش *naksh*, m. painting, picture, map, portrait; *naksh-i díwár*, a painting on a wall. *a*

نقص *naks*, m. defect, failure. *a*

نقصان *nuksán*, m. loss, defect, detriment. *a*

نقل *nakl*, f. a history, tale. *a*

نكالنا *nikálná*, a. to extract, to take out. *s*

نكلنا *nikalná*, n. to issue, to result. *s*

نكٹ *nikaṭ*, near, before. *h*

نکما *nikammá*, useless, worthless. *s*

نگاهباني *nigáhbání*, f. watching over, protecting. *p*

نگر *nagar*, m. a city, a town.

نلج *nilajj*, shameless. *s*

نماز *namáz*, f. prayer. *p*

نمودار *namúdár*, apparent. *p*

نندولا *nandolá*, m. a trough, an earthen vessel. *s*

ننگا *nangá*, naked, bare. *h*

نو *nau*, new, fresh; *nau-jawán*, quite young. *p*

نواب *nauwáb*, a viceroy. *h*

نوبت *naubat*, f. time, occasion. *a*

نور *núr*, light. *a*

نوكر *naukar*, m. servant, attendant. *p*

نوم توم *naum-taum*, sing-song, stuff. *h*

نويوبنا *nava-yaubaná*, quite young. *s*

نه *na*, no, not. *s*

نهال *nihál*, a young plant, a shoot, *p*. pleased, exalted. *h*

نهايت *nihàyat*, f. the extremity; (ad.) very, much, excessive. *a*

نهين *nahín*, no, not, nay. *s*

نيابت *niyábat*, f. deputyship. *a*

نيچي *niche*, beneath, close under. *h*

نيش *nesh*, m. sting (of a bee, etc.) *p*

نيك *nek*, good, virtuous; *nek-bakht*. of good disposition; *nek-andeshí*, good intention. *p*

نيكي *nekí*, f. goodness, kindness. *p*

نيه *neh*, love, affection. *s*

و

و *wa* or *o* (conj.), and, but. *a p*

واپس دينا -كرنا *wápas- d.* or *k.*, a. to return, give back. *h p*

واجب *wájib*, right, proper. *a*

وارد *wárid*, arrived; *wárid-h.*, to arrive. *a*

واسطي *wásṭe*, (prep.) on account of, for the sake of; because. *a*

واعظ *wá,iẓ*, m. a preacher. *a*

واقعي *wáḳi'í*, verily, in truth. *a*

واقف *wáḳif*, aware, acquainted. *a*

والا *wálá*, a termination added to the inflected infinitive denotes the agent; added to nouns it denotes the owner, wearer, etc. *h*

وزير *wazír*, a minister, counsellor; *wazír-zádí*, the daughter of a *wazír*. *a*

وسيله *wasíla*, m. means. *a*

وعظ *wa'ẓ*, m. a discourse, sermon. *a*

وغيره *wa-ghaira*, et cetera, and so forth. *a*

وصف *wasf*, m. praise, encomium, virtue, worth. *a*

وطن *waṭan*, m. native country, home, abode. *a*

وعده *wa'da*, m. a promise. *a*
وفا *wafá*, f. performing a promise, sincerity, fidelity. *a*
وقت *wakt*, m. time, season, opportunity. *a*
ون *win*, inflec. plur. of *wuh*, he, she, etc. *h*
ونہين *wonhin*, that instant. *h*
وه *wuh*, (pro.) he, she, that, it. *h*
وهان *wahán*, there, thither, yonder. *h*
وهي *wahí* or *wuhí*, (pro.) he himself, that very (person or thing). *h*
وهين *wuhín*, immediately *h*
وي *we*, they, those; pl. of *wuh*. *h*
ويسا *waisá*, in that manner, so, like that, such as that. *h*.

ه

هاته *háth*, m. the hand, a cubit. *s*
هاتهي *háthí*, m. an elephant. *s*
هاٹ *háṭ*, f. a market. *h*
هارمان *hár-mán*, despairing, helpless.
هان *hán*, yes, even so. *h*
هانڈي *hánḍí*, f. a pot.
هاي *há,e*, alas! *há,e-k.*, to groan, sigh. *h*
هانکنا *hánkná*, to drive away. *h*
هتو *hitú*, m. a friend. *s*
هتهيار *hathyár*, m. a weapon, offensive armour. *s*
هچکولا *hachkolá*, m. jolt, jolting. *h*
هڈي *haḍḍí*, f. a bone. *s*
هر *har*, each, every. *p*
هرا *hará*, a. green, fresh, verdant. *s*
هرايک *harek*, (pro.) every one. *p h*
هرچند *harchand*, how much soever, howsoever, although. *p*
هر روز *har-roz* (ad.) every day. *p*
هرگز *hargiz*, (ad.) ever.
هرن *hiran*, m. a stag, a deer. *s*
هزار *hazár*, a thousand. *p*
هزل *hazl*, m. jest, joke. *a*
هشيار *hushyár* (same as *hoshyár*), careful. *p*
هشياري *hushyárí*, f. wakefulness, vigilance. *p*
هفت هزاري *haft-hazárí*, a commander of seven thousand. *p*
هلاکت *halákat*, f. ruin, destruction. *p*
هلانا *hiláná*, a. to move, set in motion. *h*
هلنا *hilná*, n. to move *or* be moved. *h*
هلکا *halká*, light, not heavy. *h*
هم *ham*, we; plu. of *main*. *s*.
همت *himmat*, f. mind, ardour, energy. *a*
هم *ham*, a particle denoting 'together,' used in composition, as,
هم جولي *ham-jolí*, a companion. *p*
همدم *ham-dam*, m. a friend, companion. *p*
همراهي *ham-ráhí*, m. a companion, fellow-traveller. *p*
همسايه *ham-sáya*, m. neighbour, nighbourhood. *p*
هم عمر *ham-'umr*, a companion, one of the same age. *p*

هم مكتب *ham-maktab*, class-fellow. *p*

هميشه *hamesha*, always, ever, perpetually. *p*

هند *Hind*, India. *p*

هندو *Hindú*, a Hindú, one who follows the faith of Brahmá. *p*

هندوستان *Hindústán*, m. India. *a p*

هنر *hunar*, m. art, skill, virtue; *hunar-mand*, skilful. *p*

هنسنا *hańsná*, n. to smile. *s*

هنگامه *hangáma*, m. an assembly, tumult, assault. *p*

هوا *hawá*, f. wind, air. *a*

هوجانا *ho-jáná*, n. to become. *h*

هوش *hosh*, m. sense, consciousness, perception. *p*

هوشيار *hoshyár*, intelligent, attentive, cautious. *p*

هونا *honá*, n. to be, become, grow. *s*

هي *hí*, (an emphatic particle) even, indeed, very. *h*

هين *híń*, even, indeed. *h*

هين *hín*, void of, without. *s*

هيا *hiyá*, m. mind, sense. *h*

ي

يا *yá*, (conj.) or, either. *s*

ياد *yád*, f. memory, recollection. *p*

يار *yár*, m. a friend, lover. *p*

يقين *yakín*, m. certainty, certain, true. *a*

ياور *yáwar*, propitious. *p*

يک *yak*, one, a, an. *p*

يگانه *yagána*, kindred, single, incomparable. *p*

يون *yúń* or *yoń*, thus, in this manner. *h*

يونهين *yúńhíń*, thus, even so. *h*

يه *yih*, this; he, she, etc. *h*

يهان *yahán*, here, used with the genitive (inflec.) to denote possession, etc., as *mere yahán*, in my possession; 'apud me.' *h*

يهي *yihí*, this same. *h*

يهين *yahíń*, here, in this very place. *h*

يي *ye*, they, these. *h*

HINTS TO THE LEARNER.

1.—EXTRACTS IN THE PERSIAN CHARACTER.

EXTRACT 1ST.

Sustí-se ziyán hai. Jaldí-ká phal nadámat hai.
Idleness-from loss is. Haste-of (the) fruit regret is.

Ḳiná'at árám-kí kunjí hai. Miḥnat-se baṛá,í hai.
Contentment ease-of (the) key is. Labour-from greatness is.

Parhez achchhí dawá hai. 'Áḳil-ko ishára bas hai.
Abstinence good medicine is. (The) wise-to (a) hint enough is.

K͟hudá-ká k͟hauf dánish-kí aṣl hai. Gúngí zabán bihtar hai
God-of (the) fear wisdom-of the root is. Mute tongue better is

jhúṭhí zabán se. 'Ilm-kí áfat bhúl hai.
lying tongue than. Knowledge-of (the) calamity forgetfulness is.

Inṣáf-se k͟halḳ-ko árám hai.
Justice-from (the) people-to ease is.

In the same way as the above, let the student endeavour to transcribe neatly into the Roman character the first two or three pages of the Extracts. Let him be careful to write every letter with its appropriate mark; and, in the course of a week or two, let him restore the same into the Persian character. This is one of the best and speediest methods of making himself familiar with the elements of the language. Let me not be misunderstood here, as if I recommended the bare-faced quack system of the so-called "Hamiltonians." No, what I recommend is, that "every man should be his own Hamiltonian," in which case he will be the gainer. It is utterly absurd to expect that a language can be learned without labour and thought on the part of the student. The Hamiltonians would persuade us that it can; but their system is a mere deception, which flatters the vanity of the student with a show of progress utterly unreal, and which admirably conceals the ignorance and incapacity of the teacher; hence its popularity.

NOTES, ETC., ON THE FIRST FIFTY STORIES IN THE PERSIAN CHARACTER.

THE following few notes and observations are intended to illustrate such parts of the Reading Lessons as may appear least obvious to a beginner. The figures refer to the particular page and paragraph in the Grammar, in which the subject is fully explained.

N.B. In this work, the final *nún* ن when it has the nasal sound (vide page 6), is marked with an extra dot over it, as in the words مَیں *maiṅ*, and تَیں *taiṅ*. This should have been stated in its proper place, but the author was not aware at the time those sheets were sent to press that the printer had the ں in his fount.

Extract 1.—*Jaldí-ká phal,* 'the fruit of rashness;' the genitive placed first, 95. 64. It will be observed that these sentences are arranged according to the rule, 93. 62, each sentence finishing with the verb *hai,* 'is.'—*Gúngí zabán,* etc., 'a speechless tongue is better than a lying tongue:' in this sentence there are two clauses; the verb *hai* is expressed at the end of the first clause, and is consequently unnecessary at the end of the second. 135. *a.*

Ex. 2.—*Thoṛá khháná,* 'little eating;' the infinitive used substantively, 129. *a.*—*ṭalab kar 'ilm-ko,* 'seek for knowledge': *ṭalab karná,* a nominal verb, 65, last line; here the verb, contrary to the general usage, comes first. There are in this Extract a few more exceptions to the general rule as to arrangement, agreeably to what we have stated. 93. *a.*

Ex. 3.—*Jalne lagá,* 'began to burn'—*senkne lagá,* 'began to warm himself,' 131. *c.*—*ṭhaṭhol-ne kahá,* 'a jester said,' or, 'by a jester was said.'—*jale,* 'burns,' *tápe,* 'warms himself,' the aorist for the present, 122. *b.*

Ex. 4.—The sentences in this extract follow the general rule as to arrangement, which is, to commence with the nominative or agent, and end with the verb, the remainder or complement of the sentence being between these.—*bar-pá,* literally, 'on foot.'—*ziyáda kharáb haiṅ,* 'are more wicked,' the comparative degree, 71. *b.*

Ex. 5.—*Bahut kám*, 'many uses;' the nominative plural of masculine nouns of the second class (29), can be distinguished from the singular only by the context, such as a plural verb, etc.—*bajá,e*, 'in place of,' preposition requiring the genitive in *ke*, 98.—*kám áte haiṅ*, 'become useful.'—*bandyá játá hai*, passive voice of *banáná*, 57, 42.—Vide p. 47, note to 'Extracts from the Árá,ish-i Maḥfil.'

Ex. 6.—*Ek úṅṭ aur gadhe-se*, 'between a camel and an ass.'—*safar dar pesh hú,á*, lit. 'a journey came in front,' i.e., 'they both had occasion to travel;'—*ma'lúm hotá hai*, 'it appears;'—*ḍúb-já,úngá*, 'I shall be drowned,' intens. verb, 64.

Ex. 7.—*Jo dáná*, etc. 116. *a.*—*be kahe*, 'without being told,' 132.—*ḍál-rakhtá hai*, 'tosses away,' intensive verb;—*ki jis-ke wáṣte*, 'on whose account,' 117. *c.*

Ex. 8.—*Ek kamíne aur bhale ádmí-se*, 'between a base man and a gentleman.'—*hote-hí*, 'on becoming,' adverbial particip. 134. *e.*

Ex. 9.—*Ek shakhṣ-ne*, etc., 'by a certain person it was asked of Plato;' respecting the use of the proposition *ne*, read carefully, 102, etc.—*bahut barsoṅ*, 'many years,' 106. *b.*—*kyá kyá 'ajá,ib*, 'what various wonders,' 114. *a.*—*dekhe*, 'were seen' (*tú-ne*, 'by thee,' understood).—*yihí 'ajúba*, 'this wonder merely.'

Ex. 10.—*Kyá kám átá hai*, 'what quality is most useful?'—*ho-jáwe*, 'should become.'

Ex. 11.—*Chashme-pás* 'to (or near) a fountain' (*ke* understood), 99. *d.*—*chaṛh na saká*, 'he was not able to descend.'—*utarne-se pahle*, 'previous to descending.'—*dekh na liyá*, 'you did not thoroughly look at,' intensive verb.

Ex. 12.—*Sher-se kahá*, 'said to the tiger;' the verbs 'to say or speak' and 'to ask,' construed with the ablative, 102. *b.*—*agar sher muṣawwir hotá*, 'if a tiger had been the painter,' 81. *a.*

Ex. 13.—*Kuchh sawál kiyá*, 'asked something in charity.'—*ek bát merí*, 'one request of mine.'—*mat máng*, 'ask not,' the negative particle *mat*, 'don't,' used with the imperat., 123. *d.*—*uske siwá*, 'with the exception of that.'

Ex. 14.—*Ek-ne un-men-se*, 'one of them.'—*já,iye* and *baiṭhiye*, respectful forms of the imperative, 123. *d.*

Ex. 15.—*Apní angúṭhí*, 'thine own ring,' 112.—*yád karná* (*tujh ko* understood), the infinitive used imperatively, like the Latin gerund, 129. a.

Ex. 16.—*Billí á,í thí*, pluperfect tense, 127. *d.*—*bujhá de*, 'extinguish,' intensive verb.—*paṛá paṛá*, etc., 'all the time lying down, he continued giving answers.'

Ex. 17.—*Agar maiṅ bází na jítúṅ*, 'if I do not win the game.'—*ser bhar gosht*, 'an exact pound of flesh;' the *ser* is nearly two English pounds.—*tarásh-le*, 'cut off.'—*us-ne na-máná*, 'he did not (or would not) agree.'—*ḳáẓí-pás* (for *ḳáẓí-ke pás*), 'near the judge.'—*ek ser-se ek ratí ziyáda*, 'a single grain more than one *ser*.

Ex. 18.—*'Ain ḳil'e-ke níche*, 'close under the very palace.'—*lúṭá gayá*, 'was plundered,' passive voice.—*khidmat-meṅ*, 'in the presence.'—*'arẓ kí*, 'made representation,' *kí*, fem. of *kiyá*, agrees with *'arẓ*, but *'arẓ kiyá* is also used as a nominal verb.—*chirágh*, etc., 'under the lamp is darkness,' a proverb analogous to our own saying, 'the nearer the church, the farther from God.'

Ex. 19.—*Anján hokar*, 'as a stranger.'—*kyá mujhe*, etc., 'do you not recognize me?' *kyá*, here used as a sign of interrogation, 93. *b.*

Ex. 20.—*Us-ke*; *yaháṅ* is here understood; *mar-gayá* and *bánṭ-lí* and *uṛá-dí*, all intensive verbs, 65. 44. 1.

Ex. 21.—*Ádmiyoṅ-ko iṣṭabal-meṅ jáne detá*, 'he allowed the people to go into the stable,' 131. *c.*—*phirtá* and *kartá*, continuative past tenses, 124. *b.*—*apná kám kar-liyá*, 'gained his own object.'

Ex. 22.—*Aṣnáe ráh-meṅ*, 'in the midst of the way.'—*chirágh ghar-ká*, etc., 'I did not put out the lamp of the house before I came away,' literally, 'I have not come (after) having put out,' etc.—*á,e ga,e*, 'you have come and gone.'—*jútá na ghisá hogá*, 'must not your shoes have been worn?'

Ex. 23.—*Is waḳt*, 'at present;' *ko*, understood, 100. *a.*—*honge* and *na-den*, etc., the plural used out of respect, 118. 78.—*jo unhoṅ-ne*, etc., 'even should his worship have given the medicine.'—*bándhá-karegá*, frequentative verb, 66. III. 1.—*marná bar ḥaḳḳ hai*, 'death is certain.'

Ex. 24.—*Tabáh hokar*, 'being in distress.'—*paṛháne*, 'to make read,' 'to teach;' casual form of *paṛhná*, 62. 43.—*leṭe leṭe hí*, 'even when lying down;' the repetition of the conjunctive participle denotes a continuation of the state, or repetition of the action, denoted by the verb.—*be háth páṅw-ke hilde*, 'without the moving of his hands and feet.'—*hiláyá*, the preterite participle, used as a substantive.

Ex. 25.—*Sab-ke ḥawále ki* 'he gave into the charge of each.' *kát-ḍálí,* 'cut off;' the intensive of *káṭná.*

Ex. 26.—*Donoṅ ḳáẓí-ke pás ga,íṅ, aur inṣáf cháhá,* 104. *d.*—*ek ek* 'one to each,' 106, *c.*—*laṛke-ko use supurd kiyá,* 101, *c.*

Ex. 27.—*Chha roṭí-se,* 'with six loaves;' the termination *oṅ* denoting the plural omitted, 107. 70.—*wuh ḍál-dene-meṅ dák͟hil hai,* 'that amounts to throwing it away.'

Ex. 28.—*'Arẓ kiyá,* (a nominal verb), 'he represented;' *'arẓ kí* is also used in the same sense, vide Ex. 19.—*dar-k͟hwást karná,* 'to make request.'—*do sawál bejá* (properly *do sawál-i-bejá*), 'two improper requests.'

Ex. 29.—*Likhní thíṅ,* 'were to be written,' 83.—*dam khá rahá,* an idiomatic expression, denoting, 'he remained quite silent,' lit., 'continued devouring his breath.'

Ex. 30.—*Dekhne-wále,* 'the spectators,' 66.—*dúsre-ke ghar* (*ko* understood), 'to the house of the other.'—*samjhá,* etc., 'he perceived that it was not a screen.'—*fareb kháyá,* 'were deceived,' lit., 'experienced deception.'

Ex. 31.—*Síkhne-ká,* etc., 'why then mention the learning of it?'—*itne-meṅ,* 'in the meantime.'—*bar bád kí,* 'have cast away,' lit., 'placed upon the wind.'

Ex. 32.—*Dushnám dí thí,* pluperfect tense, 127. *d.*—*áṭh áṭh áne,* etc., 'you share between you, each eight *ánás*;' observe that sixteen *ánás* make a *rupí.*

Ex. 33.—*Gardan márná,* 'to decapitate.'—*mere rú-ba-rú,* 'in my presence.'—*mardána-wár,* 'like a man or hero.'—*terá baṛá kalíja hai,* 'thou hast great courage.'—*jawán-mardí,* 'heroism' or 'courage.'—*dar-guzrá,* 'he passed over (or passed by) his fault.'

Ex. 34.—*Ek baṛá sak͟hí,* 'a very generous man,' 107. *b.*

Ex. 35. *K͟habar karná,* the infinitive used as an imperative.

Ex. 36. *Karte húe,* vide 131, 84.—*wájib-tar,* Persian comparative, by adding *tar* to the positive.

Ex. 37. *Báiṭhá diyá,* intensive of *baiṭháná.*—*baṛa,* in the last line means 'greater,' 'more important.'

Ex. 38.—*Baṛá mom-dil,* 'very soft-hearted.'—*in miyán-kí,* 'of this reverend gentleman;' plural used out of respect.—*apná* is here used for *merá,* 113. *e.*

Ex. 39.—*Kuchh gol gol sá,* 'something quite round.'

Ex. 40.—*Ṣubḥ hote hí,* 'immediately it was dawn of day.'—*kauṅ si jins,* 'what sort of commodity.'—*itní dáná,í par,* 'notwithstanding so much wisdom.—*yihí faḳaṯ,* 'this only and no more.—*maiṅ báz áyá,* etc., 'I will have nothing to do with such wisdom;' past used for the future, 126, *a.*

Ex. 41.—*Jo wuh beṛ mile,* 'if that (lost) sheep should be found.'—*khudá-kí ráh-par,* 'in charity,' 'pour l'amour de Dieu.'—*khudá-kí ḳasam* (*khátá húṅ*) 'I swear by God.'

Ex. 42.—*Ádmí-ke,* etc., 'taller than a man's stature.'—*khaṯṯ pahunchne tak,* etc., 'by (the time of) the letter's arrival, the (wheat) season had expired.'—*i'tibár kí jáwe,* 'can be credited.'

Ex. 43.—*Maḥmúd of Ghazní* died, A.D. 1030. *Ayyáz* was one of his favourite slaves. Maḥmúd is famous both for his patronage of learned men, and for his success as a warrior. He made several incursions into India, in the last of which, A.D. 1026, he is supposed to have carried away in triumph the gates of Somnáth, of which we heard so much some years ago.—*Jauhar-kháne meṅ,* 'into the jewel-house or treasury.'

Ex. 44.—*Jude jude makánoṅ-meṅ,* 'in places quite apart,' or 'each in a separate place.—*salámat,* 'in safety.'

Ex. 45.—*Súḍaul,* 'well-shaped,' 'elegant.'—*bad kho-wále-ke,* 'of the man of a bad disposition.'—*jo jaisá,* etc., 'whatever sort (of seed) a man may sow, the same will he reap.'

Ex. 46.—*Ḳasam khá,í,* 'swore an oath.'—*ímándár,* 'faithful' or honest.'—*rutba,e a'lá,* 'very high rank.'—*is baháne-se,* 'by this pretext.'

Ex. 47.—*Nau-jawán,* 'quite young:' the same phrase occurs in the Devanágarí Extracts under the Sanskrit form, *nava-yauvaná.*—*der kar,* 'though late.'

Ex. 48.—*Likhá húá,* 'written:' the participle with *húá,* agreeably to 131.—*likhá hai*; here the agent *kisí-ne* is understood.

Ex. 49.—*Ṣaláḥan,* 'by way of advice.'—*bát kahte hí,* 'immediately.'—*us-ke kahne ba-mújib,* 'in conformity with what he said.'

Ex. 50.—*Diyánat-dár,* 'conscientious.'—*jis waḳt,* 'when,' or 'at the time when.—*ḥáṣil-i-kalám,* 'in short.'

2.—EXTRACTS FROM THE 'KHIRAD AFROZ.'
(From page ۲۵ to page ۲۷).

These Extracts are selected as a specimen of genuine Urdú, the dialect spoken by the educated classes of the Musalmán population throughout India. The style is exceedingly easy and elegant, and presents no difficulty to those who have acquired an elementary knowledge of Persian. Before the student commences with these, he is requested to read with care from page 88 to page 100 of the Grammar, which portion treats of Persian compounds, etc. I may here add (what I am afraid has been omitted in its proper place in the Grammar) viz., that "in phrases from the Persian, the adjective follows the substantive, and the substantive is in that case marked with the *iẓáfat*, as if it governed another substantive in the genitive." Thus *mard-i pársá*, 'a pious man;' *mard-i nek*, 'a good man.' The reader will see in page 90, *b.* of the Grammar that when, in a Persian phrase, the adjective comes *before* the substantive, the two together form a compound epithet, as, *tang-dil*, 'distressed in heart:' whereas 'a distressed heart' would be written '*dil-i tang.*'

3.—EXTRACTS FROM THE 'ÁRÁ,ISH-I MAḤFIL.'
(Page ۲۷).

This extract from the 'Ára,ish-i Maḥfil' was for the first time correctly printed in the first edition of this work. In the Calcutta edition, the printers misplaced the letter-press of two pages, so that, while the paging appeared perfect, the text made nonsense. Several years ago I discovered this when endeavouring to make sense of the passage as it has all along stood in Mr. Shakespear's 'Selections,' vol. i. p. 105. Mr. S. has endeavoured to *cement* the matter by throwing in a few connecting words of his own, which are certainly no improvement. A conscientious critic would have stated the fact of such an *amendment*, so that the original author might not incur blame for the sins of the Bengal printers, or of the English editor. I am glad to find that Mr. Shakespear in his more recent edition has adopted *my amendment* (without any acknowledgment, however), as preferable to his own.

The subject of the extract is a description of a kind of chariot drawn by bullocks common in the province of Gujerat, more especially in the city of Ahmadábád. An account of the same, accompanied by a beautiful engraving, will be found in the travels of Albert Mandelslo, who visited the spot in the reign of Sháh Jahán. The edition of his travels to which I allude is the folio, printed at Leyden, 1719, page 74. In pages 21 and 22, of the same work there is an engraving of the Great Indian Fig-tree, commonly called the Banyán Tree, alluded to in our 5th Extract, page ۲ It is the same as that mentioned by Quintus Curtius, Lib. ix. cap. i. "Having thus vanquished Porus and crossed the river (Acesines), he marched further into the country. There he found forests of vast extent, in which were shady trees of prodigious height. Most of their branches (or arms) equalled in size the trunks of ordinary trees; for, bending down into the earth, they grew up again in the same place, and appeared rather like separate trees, than boughs springing from another stem."

4.—EXTRACTS IN THE DEVANÁGARÍ CHARACTER.

The first seven anecdotes in the Devanágarí character correspond respectively with stories 3, 8, 10, 6, 18, 16, and 23, in the Persian character. They are the same word for word, and, consequently, require no further notice here. Nos. 8, 9, and 10, in the Devanágarí, correspond respectively with Nos. 29, 38, and 39, in the Persian character; with this difference, however, that in the Devanágarí text, Arabic and Persian words are carefully excluded, and their places supplied with words purely Indian: and this exclusion of Arabic and Persian words, constitutes the main difference between the dialect of the Hindús, commonly called '*Hindí*,' or '*Kharí Bolí*,' and that of the Musalmáns, generally called '*Hindústání*,' '*Urdú*,' or '*Zabán-i Rekhta*.' The style throughout is exceedingly easy, and there is only one peculiarity in the orthography to which it may be requisite to draw the student's attention in this place, viz., that in the Devanágarí character the letter य (y) is sounded like the vowel ए (e) when following any of the long vowels आ *á*, or ओ *o*: thus जाय *já,e*, रिसाय *risá,e*, होय *ho,e*, etc., instead of जाए etc. I may mention, in conclusion, that in the last seven pages or so of these extracts, the symbol called the *viráma* is purposely discontinued, as the *jazm* is in the selections from the 'Khirad Afroz.' The student should always bear in mind that he must ultimately qualify himself to read correctly books and manuscripts utterly void of vowel-points and all other orthographical symbols, such as the *jazm*, the *tashdíd*, the *viráma*, etc.

APPENDIX.

It has been suggested to me that a more detailed explanation of the following fourteen engraved plates in the Ta'lîḳ character would be very desirable for beginners. I have discussed the subject rather briefly in page 143, etc.; and now, at the risk of a few repetitions, I deem it advisable to enter upon it again more fully, by giving a literal transcript of each plate in the Roman character, together with a few additional explanatory notes and observations.

PLATE I.

TRANSCRIPT INTO THE ROMAN CHARACTER.

Div. 1.—*a, b, j, d, ẕ, r, z, s, sh, ṣ, t, ع, f, ḳ, k, k, l, m, n, w, h,*
hhhδ, lá, y, y.

„ 2.—*bá, bt, bḥ, bd, br, bs, bsh, bṣ, bt̤, bع, bf, bḳ, bk, bl, bm,*
bn, bw, bδ, bhδ, blá, by, by.

„ 3.—*já, jt, jḥ, jd, ḥr, hr, js, jsh, ḥẓ, ḥṭ, ḥع, jf, jḳ, jk, jl, ḥm, ḥn,*
ḥw, jδ, jhδ, jlá, ḥy, jy.

Division 1.—The first division of this Plate shows the mere elements of the *ta'lîḳ* alphabet; the small cross mark indicates the spot where the pen starts from in the formation of the letter, and a double cross denotes an additional formation. The first elementary form on the right hand is the *alif*, which differs very little from the printed character. The second form is the letter *be* (*b*), which by a mere change of its dots may become *p, t, ṡ*. The third form, now a *jím* (*j*), becomes, in the same manner, *ch, kh, ḥ*. The fourth makes two letters, *d* and *ẕ*. The fifth, *r*, *z*, *zh*, and *ṛ*. The sixth is represented as consisting of two forms—one an indented, the other a protracted line, and either may be used as *sín* and *shín* (*s* and *sh*), as the only distinction between them is, that the *sín* (*s*) wants, and the *shín* (*sh*) has, three dots superscribed, whether short or protracted. The seventh form, *ṣád* and *ẓád*. The eighth, *ṯ*, *ẕ*. The ninth, *'ain* and *ghain*. The next letters are *f*, *ḳ*, *k*, *l*, *m*, *n*, *w*, and *h*, which are nearly the same as the printed type. Then follow the initial, medial, and final forms of the *he* linked together; then the *lá* and *hamza*; and lastly, the letter *ye* under two varieties of form, the latter of which is now conventionally used by the natives to denote the *yá,e majhúl*.

a. The *dál* may at first sight appear to resemble the *w*; the distinction consists in this, that the *dál* has an angular top, whereas the *w* has it round.

b. As the letters *'ain* and the imperceptible *he* have no exact representatives in the Roman character, they have been allowed to stand in the transcript of the plates in their proper form.

c. The *fe* and last form of *yá* are written above the line to show the mode they adopt where there are more words than the line will contain.

d. The bottom of the *káf* may be protracted, as in the second example, to fill up the line, a liberty frequently taken with letters by the Oriental penman. This letter is formed by two sweeps of the pen, the first commencing from the top of the vertical line at the angle—(marked in the plate with a single cross); the slanting top is put on afterwards. In old *Naskhí* MSS. the slanting top is never used, but instead thereof the mark ى is written over the letter.

e. The *yá* (*y*) has two forms in the Plate. The former was appropriated by Dr. Gilchrist for the sound *í*, the latter for the *e* (or *yá,e majhúl*), a distinction still observed by the natives of India in writing Hindústání.

Division 2 exhibits the second elementary form, viz., that of *b, p, t, s̤, n,* and *y,* as they appear initially, when combined with each of the others following them. Here are given all the combinations of the letter *be,* with each of the elementary forms of division first. It will be seen that many of the *nuktas,* or dots, are omitted; as, for example, those necessary to form *bs, bt̤, bع, bf, bm, bn, bh, by,* and without them the linear portion of the *be,* in these compounds, has no meaning. It may, of course, become *b, p, t, s̤, n,* or *y,* ad libitum, by the addition (above or below it) of one, two, or three dots.

Division 3 shows the initial form of the *j, ch, ḥ,* and *kh,* prefixed to each of the elements in their order. Here a similar irregularity of punctuation occurs, but as the form ح constitutes a perfect letter in itself, without any dots, it is transcribed into the Roman character by *ḥ.* It may be observed once for all, that the object of these Plates is to exhibit the combinations of all letters of a certain form, independent of the adventitious dots which each form may necessarily require.

PLATE II.

Div. 4.—*sá, st, sj, shd, sr, ss, shs, sz, st̤, sع, sf, s, skk, sl, sm, sn, shw, sẓ, s,hẓ, slá, sy, sy.*

„ 5.—*ṣá, ṣt, ṣj, ṣd, ṣr, ṣs, ṣsh, ṣz, ṣt̤, ṣع, ṣf, ṣḳ, ṣk, ẓl, ṣm, ṣn, ẓw, ẓ, ẓẓ, ẓlá, ṣy, ṣy.*

„ 6.—*t̤á, t̤t, t̤j, t̤d, t̤r, t̤s, t̤sh, t̤z, t̤t, t̤ع, t̤f, t̤ḳ, t̤k, ẓl, t̤m, ẓn, t̤w, t̤ẓ, ẓẓ, t̤lá, t̤y, t̤y.*

Division 4 represents the *sin* or *shin* in combination with the rest of the letters. It is needless to observe that the letters *alif, dál, re,* and *waw,* never join to the left—consequently they have no distinct initial form.

Divisions 5 and 6 show the *ṣád* and *t̤o,e* followed by each of the elementary forms.

PLATE III.

Div. 7.—*عd, عt, عj, عd, عr, عs, عsh, عẓ, عt̤, عع, عf, عḳ. عk, عl, عm, عn, عw, عs, عhs, علá, عy, عy.*

,, 8.—*fá, ft, fj, fd, fr, fr, fs, fsh, fṣ, ft̤, fع, ff, fḳ, fk, fl, fm, fn, fw, fs, fhs, flá, fy, fy.*

,, 9.—*ká, kt, kj, kd, kr, ks, ksh, kẓ, kt̤, kع, kf, kḳ, kk, kl, km, kn, kw, ks, khs, klá, ky, ky.*

Plate III. shows the letters *'ain, fe,* and *káf* in combination with all the rest; and, with the exception of *lá*, the initial form of the *lám* is found by omitting the bent top stroke of the letter *káf.*

Division 8.—The dots of the *fe* are again omitted in *fá, fd, fr* (2nd), *fs, fẓ, ft̤, fع*, etc., leaving the letter imperfect. It may become *ḳáf*, by superscribing two dots.

Division 9.—The formation of the *ká* (made by two sweeps of the pen) commences from where the four lines meet; the pen stops at the top of the *alif*, made upwards, and then forms the slanting top. *Klá* is made by three strokes of the pen, the *alif*, made downwards, being the second, the slanting top of the *káf* the third.

PLATE IV.

Div. 10.—*má, mt, mj, md, mr, ms, msh, mẓ, mt̤, mع, mf, mḳ, mk, ml, mm, mn, mw, mh, mhs, mlá, my, my.*

,, 11.—*há, ht, hj, hd, hr, hr, hs, hsh, hẓ, ht̤, hع, hf, hḳ, hk, hl, hm, hn, hw, hh, hhhhhs, hlá, hy, hy.*

,, 12.—*abjd, hwz, ḥt̤y, klmn, sعfṣ, ḳrsht, s̤ḵẖẕ, ẓẕg͟h, lá.*
alعbd, almẕnb, alfḳyr, عbyd, allh ḥsyny shyryn rḳm g͟hfr ẕnwbh.

Division 11.—The tail of the *he* is given only in *há, hd, hk, hl,* and *hlá*, but omitted in all the rest, according to the practice of Oriental writers. Hence the initial form of this letter is often too apt to be mistaken for the *mím* (*m*).

Division 12 contains the combination of the characters as arranged in alphabetical notation, noticed in p. 20 of the Grammar, forming the fanciful words, *'Abjad, hawaz, ḥuṭṭi, kaliman, sa'faṣ, ḳarashat, ṣakhaẓ, ẓaẓagh*; and the last line may be read thus, indicating the name of the chirographer: *Al' abd ul muẕnib, al faḳir 'ubaidu-l-láhi ḥusaini shirin raḳm ghaffara ẕunúbahu.*

PLATE V.

Consists of words beginning with letters of the *be* class; i.e., *b, p, t, s̤,* in which might be included *n* and *y*.

L. 1. *bkht, bhjt, bhsht, pnj, blkh, blnd.*
2. *bʿyd, bstr, pyghmbr, blghys, bkhshsh, bghẓ.*
3. *byẕ, bsyṭ, byʿ, bḳbk, plnk, bkhyl.*
4. *blghm, bykm, bṭn, byn, bychw, byẕs, bnkls, byshky.*
5. *tʿjb, tsbyḥ, tḳlyd, tlmyẕ, tḳsyr, tksyr.*
6. *tfyr, tjss, tftysh, tkhsyṣ, tkhlys̤, tslṭ.*
7. *tjmʿ, tṣnyf, tkhfyf, tḥḳyḳ, tmsk, tʿjyl.*
8. *tfṣl, tḳsym, tmkyn, tlḳyn, tnbw, tḥnt, tḳy.*

Plate V.—Coming now to complete words of more than two consonants; we may premise, as a general remark, that when these contain any of the letters *b, p, t, s̤, n, y,* consisting of a horizontal or sloping line, with one or more dots, for each letter there should be an incurvation in the continued running line, and at least two bends for the short indented *sin* or *shin*. When several such letters come together, for the sake of distinction it is usual to give the middle one a bold dash upwards, terminating in a sharp point vertically.

L. 1.—The *n* of *blnd* is protracted to fill up the line, according to custom. The *plnk* of line 9, *bykm* of line 4, with a dash on *káf*, here wanting, are intended for *palang*, 'a tiger,' and *begam*, 'a princess,' this being a very usual omission, especially where the word cannot be mistaken. In some works, indeed, the *káf* is never distinguished from the *gáf*, neither is *b* from *p*, nor *jím* from *che*.

PLATE VI.

Contains a list of words commencing with letters of the third form, viz. *j, ch, ḥ* or *kh*

L. 1. *jnt, ḥshmt, ḥkmt, ḥkyḳt, khlḳt, khṣlt.*
2. *jlyj, jʿd, ḥmyd, ḥmd, khld, jʿfr, ḥkyr, ḥshr.*
3. *khmyr, khnjr, khnẓr, jlys, ḥbs, jhyẓ, jlṭ.*
4. *khlṭ, ḥfẓ, jmyʿ, jyf, khfyf, jkjk, khlḳ.*
5. *chychk, khshk, jlyl, jmyl, jnkl, ḥnẓl.*
6. *jhnm, ḥlym, ḥkm ḥkym, khshm, jbyn, jstn.*
7. *ḥsn, khftn, jlw, ḥẓw, chmchʾ, khlyfʾ, ḥlḳʾ.*
8. *ḥṣʾ, ḥḳnh, khymʾ, khṭnʾ, jbly, ḥkyky, khṣmy.*

PLATE VII.

Consisting of words beginning with *sin* or *shin*.

L. 1. *syb, slb, snj, slḥ sṭḥ sfyd.*
2. *sṭbr, slys, sybsh, sʿfṣ, skyṭ, smʿ.*
3. *skf, syf, sbḳ, slk, sjnjl.*
4. *smsm, shm, shkyn, shw, sfynʾ, ssty.*
5. *shkst, fhfḳt, shykh, shhyd, shyr, shmshyr, shms.*
6. *shsh, shkhṣ, shmyṭ, shmʿ, shnyʿ, shʿẓf, shfyḳ.*
7. *shlk, shkyl, shkl, shlghm, shkm, shbnm, shkstn.*
8. *shstn, shfw, shknjʾ, shyshʾ, shḳykʾ, shky, shkftgy.*

PLATE VIII.

Words beginning with *ṣád, ẓád, ṭo,e* or *ẓo,e.*

L. 1. *ṣʿb, ṣlyb, ṣhbt, ṣḥyḥ, ṣlḥ, ṣyd.*
2. *ṣmd, ṣghyr, ṣfyr, ṣmgh, ṣʿyf, ṣkyḳ.*
3. *ṣmkyk, ṣyḳl, ṣmym, ṣḥn, ṣʿw, ṣhyfʾ, ṣylby.*
4. *ṭlb, ṭbyb, ṭbyʿt, ṭykh, ṭpyd.*
5. *ṭyr, ṭnz, ṭshysh, ṭmʿ, ṭbʿ, ṭfyf.*
6. *ṭbḳ, ṭlyḳ, ṭnk, ṭfl, ṭlyl, ṭlsm.*
7. *ṭhw, ṭbkchʾ, ṭnṭnʾ, ṭʿnʾ, ṭbṭy, ṭbṭy.*

PLATE IX.

Words beginning with *'ain, ghain, fe* or *ḳáf.*

L. 1. *ʿjyb, ʿjlt, ʿṣmt, ʿjyj, ʿhd, ʿyd, ʿṭr.*
2. *ʿnbr, ʿss, ʿks, ʿshʿsh, ʿtsh, ʿṣyṣ, ʿmlṭ.*
3. *ʿlf, ʿkyḳ, ʿmḳ, ʿlyk, ʿshḳ, ʿynk, ʿlyl, ʿḳl.*
4. *ʿll, ʿml, ʿlm, ʿẓym, ʿjyn, ʿfw, ʿjlś, ʿjmy.*
5. *fẓyḥt, fẓylt, fṣyḥ, ftḥ, fṣd, fjr.*
6. *fkr, fls, fysh, fyẓ, fṭyʿ, fyf.*
7. *ftḳ, flk, fyṣl, fyl, fʿl.*
8. *fhm, ftn, ftw, fshfw, ftylś, flsfy.*

PLATE X.

Words beginning with *káf, gáf* or *lám.*

L. 1. *ksb, klb, ksht, kyfyt, knj, klknd, knbẕ, kmtr.*
2. *kshnyz, khms, kshf, ksyṣ, ksht, kʿkʿ, kṣyf, ktf.*
3. *klk, klnk, knk, kmk, khjshk, kḥl, klym.*
4. *kmyn, kfn, kshtn, kftn, kysw, kfchś, knjfś.*
5. *kysś, klmś, klktś, khtś, kshty, kmy, kyty, kyfy.*
6. *lḳb, lʿnt, ljlj, lkd, lnkr, lshkr.*
7. *lms, lfs, lykhsh, lḥyṣ, lghṭ.*
8. *lḳyṭ, lmʿ, lṭyf, lḳlk, lnk, lḥm.*
9. *lbn, lykn, lhw, lḥyś, lḳmś, lḥy, lyly.*

PLATE XI.

Words beginning with *mím.*

L. 1. *msbb, mṯlb, mnṣf, mktb, mḥtsb.*
2. *mtʿjb, mṭyb, mṣlḥt, mhlt, msht.*
3. *mmlkt, mkhnṣ, mṣlṣ, mbthj, mtḥ, mykh.*
4. *mlkh, mṭbkh, mḥmd, msjd, mʿtḳd, mʿtmd.*
5. *mnjmd, mfsd, mstʿd, mtfkr, mʿṭr, mẓfr.*
6. *mntshr, mkhtṣr, mʿskr, mnzr, mʿtbr.*
7. *mʿṣfr, mʿjr, mnjẕ, mks, mjls.*
8. *mfls, mnsh, mkhls, mshkhṣ, mnghẕ.*

PLATE XII.

Words beginning with *mīm*—continued.

L. 1. *mnḳbẓ, mḥyṭ, mmtnع, mṭyع, mjmع, mṭlع.*

2. *meg͟h, mblg͟h, mk͟htlf, mṣnf, mtfḳ.*

3. *mtعlḳ, mnjnyḳ, mshḳ, mlk, mmsk.*

4. *mshk, mhml, mfṣl, myl, msht͟ghl.*

5. *mk͟hml, mعtl, mtعlm, mtklm, mnjm, mḳym.*

6. *msṭḥkm, mslm, mtmkn, msmn, mtعyn.*

7. *mtẓmn, mmkn, mḥw, mḥkmة, mntkة, mshعlchy*

8. *mṣṭky, mfty, mnshy, mg͟hny, mk͟hfy, mtḳy.*

PLATE XIII.

Words beginning with *nūn.*

L. 1. *nṣb. nṣyb, njyb, nshyb, nḳb.*

2. *nعmt, nṣyḥt, nkht, nyst, nsj.*

3. *nḥj, nḳd, nshr, nyshkr, nẓr.*

4. *nk͟hs, nfys, nfs, nysh, nعsh.*

5. *nḳsh, ng͟hẓ, nmṭ, nfع, nṣf, nṭḳ.*

6. *nhnk, nعl, nḳl, nsym, nylm, nkyn.*

7. *nmkyn, nhftn, nshstn, nḥw, nfkة, nعmة.*

8. *nhftة, nfẓ, nfshة, nfy, nhy, nysty.*

PLATE XIV.

Words beginning with *he* and *ye.*

L. 1. *hmt, hybt, hft, hsht, hnkft.*

2. *hych, hnd, hjr, hmnfs, hshysh, hbṭ.*

3. *hmyع, hlf, hyḳ, hshnk, hkhk, hykl.*

4. *hmm, hftm, hmsn, hjw, hlylة, hsty.*

5. *ylعb, yftḥ, yعṭd, ysyr, yksr.*

6. *yknfs, ytfẓ, ylmع, ylḳ, ylk.*

7. *yعml, yshm, yḳyn, ymyn, ymn.*

8. *yksw, yk͟hchة, ymnة, yky, ykjhty*

Pl. I.

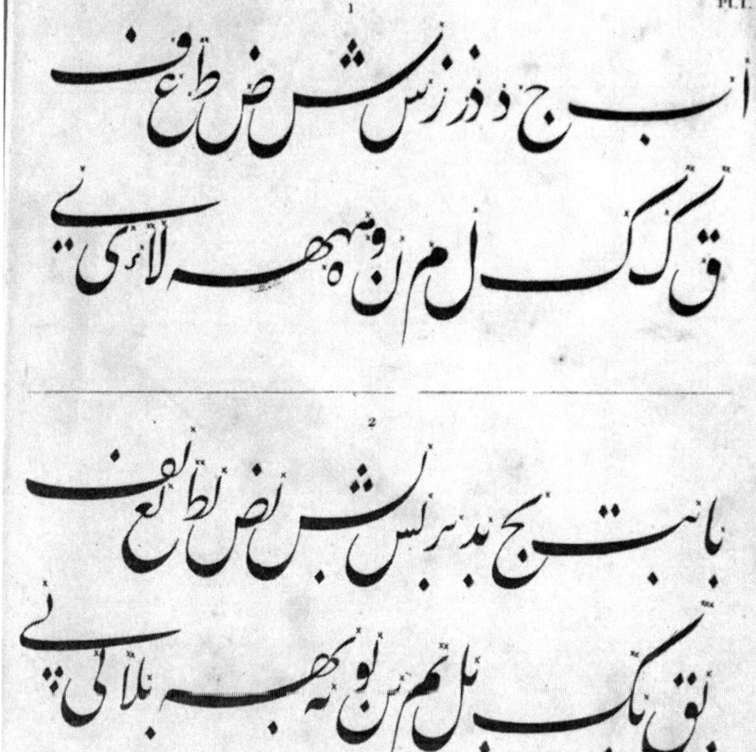

W. H. Allen & Co. London.

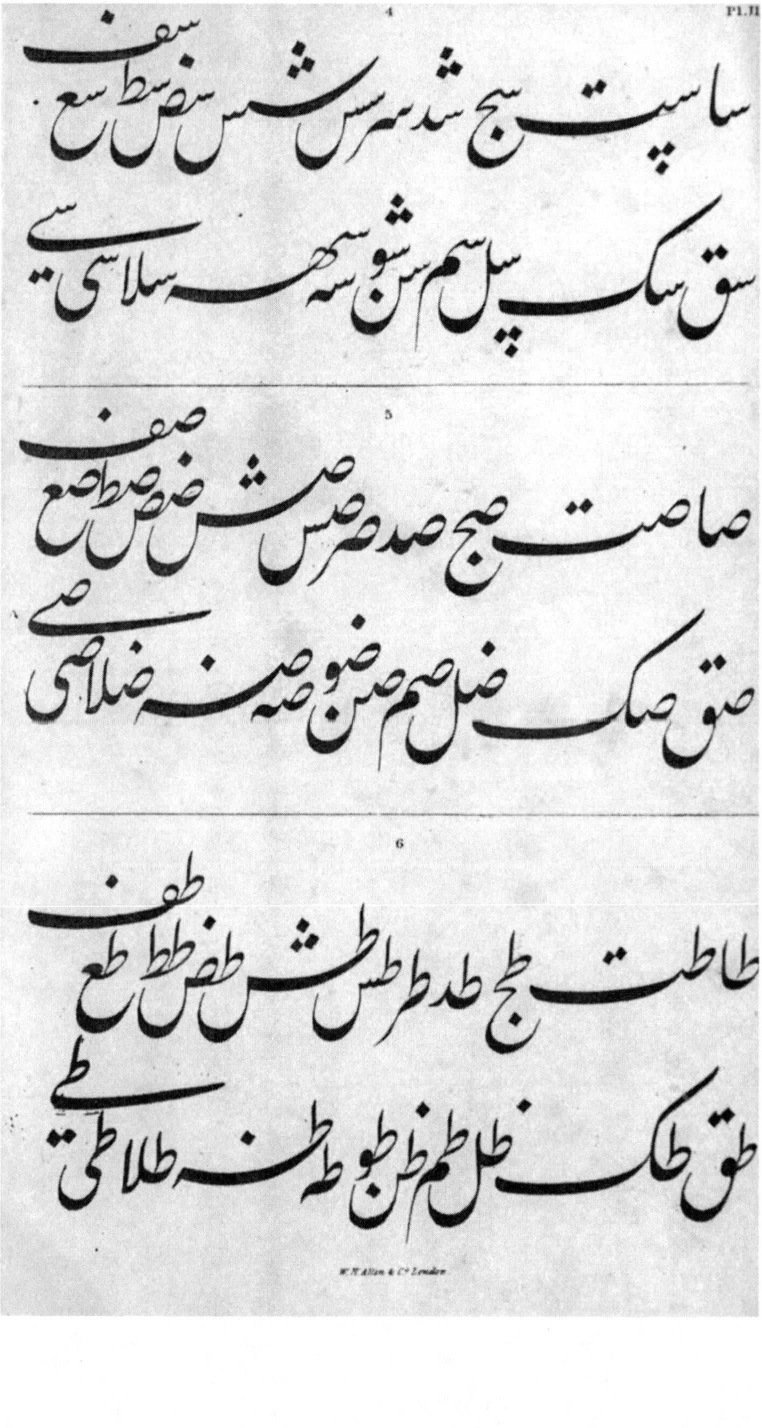
Pl. II
4
سا سپ سج سد سر سس سش سص سط سع سف
سق سک سل سم سن سو سه سهـ سلا سی سے
5
صا صت صج صد صر صس صش صص صط صع صف
صق صک صل صم صن صو صه ضلا صی صے
6
طا طت طج طد طر طس طش طص طط طع طف
طق طک طل طم طن طو طه طلا طی طے
W. H. Allen & Cº London

عا عت عج عد عر عس عش عص عط عع عف

عق عک عل عم عن عو عه علا عی

8

فا فت فج فد فر فس فش فص فط فع فف

فق فک فل فم فن فو فه فلا فی

9

کا کت کج کد کر کس کش کص کط کع کف

کق کک کل کم کن کو که کلا کی

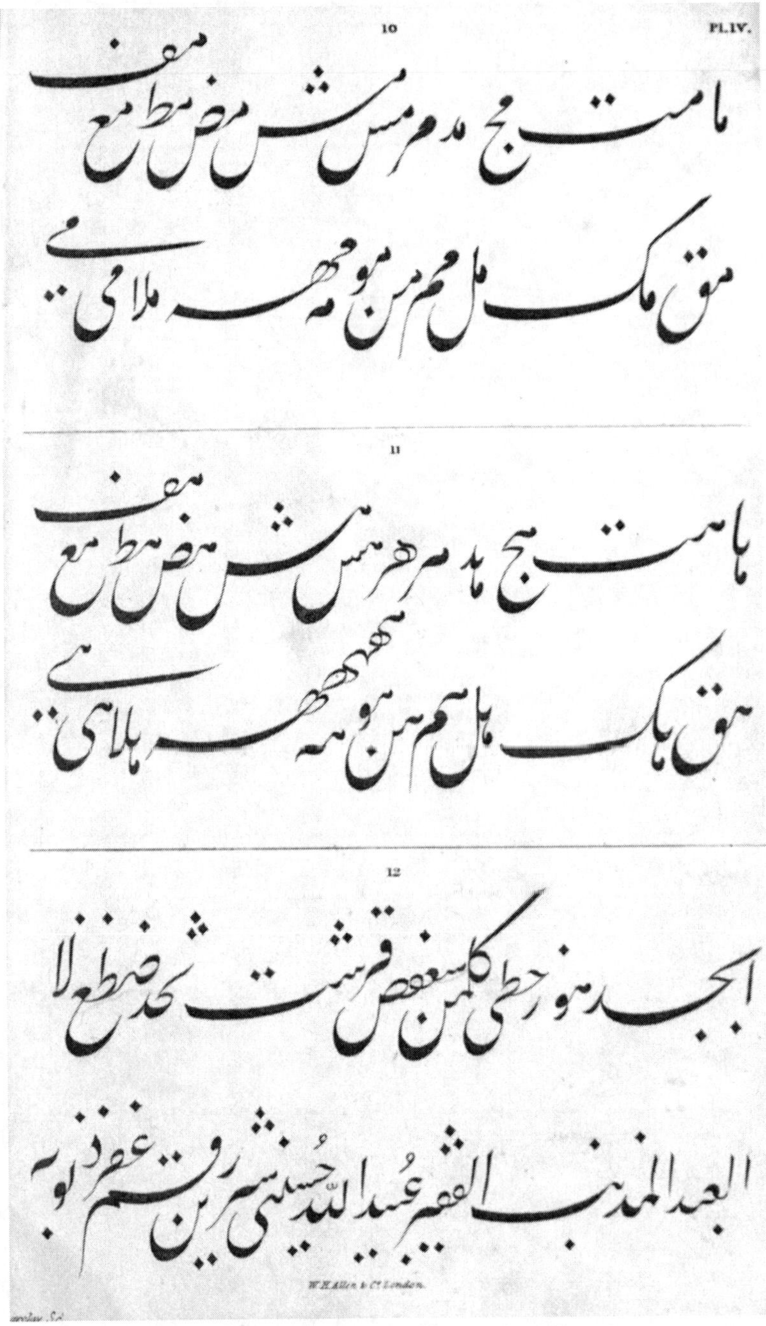

Pl. IV.
10
11
12
W. H. Allen & Cº London.

Pl. V

بخت بهجت بهشت پنج بلخ بلند

بعید بستر پیغمبر بلغیس بخشش بغض

بیض بسیط بیع بقبق پلنگ بخیل

بلغم بیکم بطن بین بیچو بیضه بنکله بنشکی

تعب تتبع تقلید تلمیذ تقصیر تعبیر

تفسیر تجسس تفتیش تخصیص تخلیص تسلط

تجمع تصنیف تخفیف تحقیق تمسک تعجیل

تفضل تقسیم تمکین تلقین تنبو تحنه تقی

W. H. Allen & Co. London.

جنت حشمت حکمت حقیقت خلقت خصلت

جلج جعد حمید حمد خلد جعفر حقیر حشر

خمیر خنجر خضر جلیس جبس جهیض جلط

خلط حفظ جمیع جیف خفیف ججقیق خلق

چیچک خشک جلیل جمیل جنگل حنظل

جهنم حلیم حکم حکیم خشم جبین جستن

حسن خفتن جلو حضو چمچه جلیفه حلقه

حصه حقنه خیمه خنته جبلی حقیقی خصمی

W. H. Allen & Co London.

سیب سلب سنج سلح سطح سفید

سطبر سلبیس سپیش سعفص سقیط سمع

سقف سیف سبق سلک سبنجل

سستی سفینه سهو سهمگین سهم سمسم

شکست شفقت شیخ شهید شمشیر شمس

ششس شخص شمیط شمع شنیع شغظف شفیق

شلک شکیل شکل شلغم شکم شبنم شکستن

شستن شو شکنجه شیشه شقیقه شقی شگفتگی

W.H.Allen & Co. London.

G.Barclay Sc.

صعب صلیب صحبت صحیح صلح صید

صمد صغیر صفیر صمغ صیف صقیق

صمکیک صیقل صمیم صحن صعو صحیفه صیلبی

طلب طبیب طبیعت طبیخ طپید

طیر طنز طشیش طمع طبع طفیف

طبق طابق طنبک طفل طلیل طلسم

طحو طبقچه طنطنه طعنه طبتی طبتی

G. Barclay Sc. W. H. Allen & Co. London.

عجيب عجلت عصمت عجيج عهد عيد عطر

عنبر عسس عكس عشعش عطش عصيص عملط

علف عقيق عمق عليق عشق عينک عليل عقل

علل عمل علم عظيم عجين عفو عجله عجمي

فضيحت فضيلت فصيح فتح فصد فجر

فكر فلس فيش فيض فطيع فيف

فتق فلک فيصل فيل فعل

فهم فتن فتو فشفو فتيله فلسفي

W. H. Allen & Co. London.

کسب کلب کشت کیفیت کنج کلقند کنبد کمتر

کشنیز کهس کشش کصیص کشط کعکع کثیف کتف

کلک کلنک کنک کمک کنجشک کحل کلیم

کمین کفن کشتن کفتن کیسو کفچه کنجفه

کیسه کلمه کلکته کهته کشتی کمی کیتی کیفی

لقب لعنت لجلج لکد لنکر لشکر

لمس لفس لیخش لبحیص لغط

لقیط لمع لطیف لقلق لنک لحم

لبن لیکن لهو لحیه لقمه لحی لیلی

W.H. Allen & Co. London

مسبب مطلب منصب مکتب محتسب

متعجب مطیب مصلحت مهلت مشت

مملکت مخنث مثلث مبتنج مطح میخ

ملخ مطبخ محمّد مسجد معتقد معتمد

منجمد مفسد مستد متفکر معطر مظفر

منتشر مختصر معسکر منتظر معتبر

مصفر معجر منجز مگس مجلس

مفلس منش مخلص مشخص منغض

G. Barclay, Sc. W. H. Allen & Co. London.

منقبض محيط ممتنع مطيع مجمع مطلع

مبيع مبلغ مختلف مصنف متفق

متعلق منجنيق مشتق ملك ممسك

مشك مهمل مفصل ميل مشتغل

مخمل معطل متعلم متكلم منجم مقيم

مستحكم مسلم متمكن مسمن مبين

متضمن ممكن محو محكمه منطقه مشعلچي

مصطكي مفتي منشي مغني مخفي متقي

G. Barclay, Sc. W. H. Allen & Co London.

نسب نصیب نجیب نشیب نقب

نعمت نصیحت نکهت نبیت نسج

نهج نقد نشتر نیشکر نظر

نخس نفیس نفس نیش نعش

نقش نقض نمط نفع نصف نطق

نهنگ نعل نقل نسیم نیلم نگین

نگین نهفتن نشستن نحو نفقه نعمه

نهفته نقطه نفشه نفی نهی نیستی

arclay, Sc. W. H. Allen & Co. London.

Pl. XIV

همت هیبت هفت هشت هنگفت

هیچ هند هجر همنفس هشیش هبط

همیع هلف هیق هشنگ هکهک هیکل

همم هفتم همسن هجو هلیله هستی

یلعب یفتح یعطر یسیر یکسر

یکنفس یتنفض یلمع یلق یلک

یعمل یشم یقین یمیس یمن

یکسو یخچه یمنه یکی یکجهتی

W. H. Allen & Co. London.